Emotions and
Violence

Lexington Books Series on Social Theory

George Ritzer, editor

Metatheorizing in Sociology
George Ritzer

**Emotions and Violence: Shame And
Rage in Destructive Conflicts**
Thomas J. Scheff and Suzanne M. Retzinger

Emotions and Violence

Shame and Rage in Destructive Conflicts

By

Thomas J. Scheff
and
Suzanne M. Retzinger
University of California, Santa Barbara

Lexington Books
D.C. Heath and Company/Lexington, Massachusetts/Toronto

Library of Congress Cataloging-in-Publication Data

Scheff, Thomas J.
    Emotions and violence : shame and rage in destructive conflicts /
by Thomas J. Scheff and Suzanne M. Retzinger.
        p.   cm.
    Includes bibliographical references and index.
    ISBN 0-669-27626-X (alk. paper)
    1. Violence.   2. Shame.   3. Alienation (Social psychology)
4. Violence—Case studies.   I. Retzinger, Suzanne M.   II. Title.
    [DNLM: 1. Aggression.   2. Rage.   3. Shame.   4. Stress,
Psychological.   5. Violence.   BF 575.A3 S316e]
BF575.A3S26   1991
303.6—dc20
DNLM/DLC
for Library of Congress   90-13716
                                                            CIP

Published simultaneously in Canada
Printed in the United States of America
International Standard Book Number: 0–669–27626–X
Library of Congress Catalog Card Number: 90–13716

The paper used in this publication meets the minimum requirements of
American National Standard for Information Sciences—Permanence of
Paper for Printed Library Materials, ANSI Z39.48–1984. ∞™

Year and number of this printing:

91 92 93 94 95 8 7 6 5 4 3 2 1

Contents

List of Figures and Tables

Figures

Tables

Foreword

John Braithwaite

The ideas in this book are extraordinarily innovative. Scheff and Retzinger are unlike any other scholars in the freshness of the way they shift from the explanation of violence to exploring the way we understand our own emotions, the way we speak and understand each other, and the way we grow from emphathizing with literature. The book is a mine full of treasures for the willing prospector. The style is dazzling; it shifts focus from grand theory to epistemology to literature to analyses of discourse.

This book is a major theoretical contribution to social science as well as an important empirical one. The empirical material ranges from understanding psychotherapeutic encounters to behavior on television game shows, marital discourse and disputes, Goethe's fiction, the causes of crime and of World War II. To comprehend how such threads are part of the same cloth, it helps to have some preliminary insight into the authors' methodological position, as outlined in Scheff's *Microsociology* (1990) and Retzinger's *Violent Emotions* (1991).

In this work, there is an intimate connection between their theory of human action and their methodological framework. Actors in the everyday business of talking with spouses, reading novels and causing wars face a similar task to that of the scientist—the interpretation of ambiguous signs. Competent everyday actors and scientists both approach this task by processes of "abduction," cycling rapidly between observation and imagination, testing what has been imagined against further observation. This is how people converse. As we observe an utterance or a facial expression of another, we put ourselves in the role of the other, imagining what emotion and meaning the expression conveys. Often we will then further imagine what signs would be visible if our inference were correct. We test the inference by looking for these signs. Just as abduction is the way conversation works (when it does work), so shuttling back and forth between observation and imagination, between induction and deduction, is the way science works (when it does work).

Scheff and Retzinger's commitment to abduction involves a shuttling between micro-worlds and macrostructures, between parts and wholes. The imaginings of meaning that occur in microencounters are informed by macrostructures of power and deference, by knowledge of the whole history of a society. Similarly, if the social scientist wants revelatory understanding, she must observe small parts and imagine their meaning in terms of large wholes, moving back and forth between understanding wholes in terms of parts and parts in terms of wholes. This methodological commitment of Scheff and Retzinger astonishes the reader by repeatedly shifting the explanatory focus from the causes of shame in an encounter that takes a micro-second, to the causes of war in encounters that take generations.

The result is a work of extraordinary ambition, accomplishment, richness, complexity, intricacy, and scope. It is also a work with a sharp political edge. The authors are critical of micro analysis which is disconnected from macrostructure, for failing to inform programs for political change. They are equally critical of abstract understandings of macrostructures for fuelling political impotence among those disempowered by such structures. Faced with such analysis, the individual may despair about the futility of taking on large structures of domination by patriarchy, capitalism, or monopolies of professional expertise. An analysis which is a micro-macro synthesis, in contrast, holds out the prospect of informing individuals in both how to make a break with daily practices that reproduce structures of oppression, and how to join with others to struggle for transformative political programs. While many of us in the social sciences espouse an interest in micro-macro synthesis, it is hard to think of any scholar who has driven micro-macro synthesis to the scale of accomplishment delivered in this book.

The main theme of the work is an explanation relevant to all forms of destructive aggression. Shame leads to anger which leads to aggression. At the same time, there are forms of shame which prevent violence. Shame is both the major cause of violence and the emotion most implicated in preventing violence. The crucial question is how we distinguish forms of shame which cause aggression and forms which prevent it. Scheff and Retzinger argue that shame causes aggression when it is *unacknowledged*.

Figure 4–1 in chapter 4 (p. 68) summarizes the argument with elegant clarity. To those readers who are dipping into the book for ten minutes before deciding whether to read more, I would advise turning to this figure. It traces three sequences in interactions—an approval sequence, a disapproval sequence when shame is acknowledged, and a disapproval sequence when shame is not acknowledged.

1. Approval. When a sign from one actor is interpreted as approving toward another, this cements the social bond between them. The other feels pride in themselves and in the connectedness shared with the first actor. Showing respect builds cooperation and prevents aggression.

2. Disapproval—acknowledged shame. To show disapproval, in contrast, threatens the social bond. The disapproved actor may experience shame. If she acknowledges this shame, respects the other's reasons for expressing the disapproval, and the other reciprocates this respect so that they enter a dialogue about the problem, shame will have been a cause of constructive conflict. And constructive conflict can actually strengthen bonds between individuals. Here there may be a recursive relationship (not represented) between constructive conflict and intact bonds. One of the reasons I value and nurture a strong social bond with my spouse is that she will tell me when I get drunk and make an ass of myself at a dinner party (when no one else will tell me). Conversely, because I have a strong social bond with my spouse, it is easier for disapproval to be expressed than it is with others who have weak bonds with me. And it is easier for disapproval to be expressed constructively. If a person who I meet for the first time at the dinner party tells me that I am being a drunken ass, I am more likely to respond to this aggressively than I am when it comes from my wife whom I know loves and cares for me. When disapproval results in the acknowledgment of shame, shame can persuade actors against what they come to recognise as wrongdoing (such as violence).

3. Disapproval—unacknowledged shame. When the shame evoked by disapproval is repressed rather than confronted, however, people get angry. Actor A gets angry at B for disapproving of her instead of examining the (correct or incorrect) reasons for the disapproval. The anger of A toward B is typically expressed disrespectfully, causing B to experience shame, to become angry, to feed back more disrespect and shame toward A, and so on in a vicious circle, damaging the social bond. Unconfronted shame, disrespect and anger can ultimately get out of hand, unraveling in violence.

When actors have positive self-concepts and are what Scheff and Retzinger call "*attuned*" in their relationships with others, they have the internal and external strength to acknowledge shame. They know how to laugh openly at doing something stupid; how to apologize for doing something wrong; how to defend doing something they believe is right without showing disrespect for the differing opinions of others. But insecure individuals with insecure social bonds are more likely to deny their shame, to be ashamed of being ashamed. Then there is the risk of what Scheff and Retzinger call triple shame-rage spirals. Shame becomes triply recursive and self-perpetuating. Within each individual there is a series of loops of shame (as being ashamed of being ashamed causes further shame). Between the individuals there is a downward spiral into disrespect and interminable anger as the failure to confront escalating shame erects a wall separating them.

Others before Scheff and Retzinger have identified the shame-anger complexes which are the focus of their theory; Scheff and Retzinger generously acknowledge throughout their book the contributions of these other scholars. Where Scheff and Retzinger have moved beyond those contributions, however, is in contextualizing these shame-anger complexes within a dynamic structure/process model, a contribution of inestimable importance. An understanding of the sources of violence in our civilization is accomplished through an integration of theory, method, and concrete case studies involving sequences of interactions and context.

There are two keys to the way Scheff and Retzinger distinguish productive from counterproductive shame sequences. Shame provokes violence when it is (a) unacknowledged, and (b) communicated disrespectfully. Shame prevents violence when it is acknowledged and when it is communicated respectfully. The crucial feature of respectful shaming is that it shames a deed which is perceived as wrong while refraining from rejecting the wrongdoer as a person. So the loving mother chides her child for a naughty deed while leaving the child in no doubt that she enjoys love for the person she is. The child is shamed for deeds within a continuum of respect, indeed love, for her person.

In this way, respectful shaming can solve another of the pathologies of shame—the "inferiority complex", as formulated by Adler (1956) (see p. 13). Inferiority complexes are likely when parents shame children as bad or stupid children rather than as good, intellectually growing children who commit bad or stupid deeds. Inferiority complexes are likely when socialization practices neglect pride as an emotion to be cultivated in the nurturing of responsible citizens. In this regard, Scheff and Retzinger's criticism of my own work, as well as that of Goffman and Lewis, for giving insufficient emphasis to pride in our analysis of social control, is absolutely correct.

This understanding of the partitioning of shame into productive and counterproductive modalities is crucial to rebutting a possible criticism of acknowledged shame as a solution to violence. The criticism runs as follows: Strong cultural tendencies to shame wrongdoing may prevent acts of violence against others, but the internalizing of that shame will cause acts of aggression to be directed against the self, such as in suicide. Shame does not solve problems; it just displaces targets.

Scheff's (1990: 196) discussion of a study by Kobler and Stotland shows a flaw in this analysis. Kobler and Stotland concluded that two of the conditions for suicide were an attempt to gain reassurance from others and a response from others characterized by hopelessness and helplessness. Suicide, in other words, must be understood in part as arising from a failure of social bonds, from a lack of social integration, from a feeling of rejection when help is sought from others, or at least that others turn away when help is needed. When we shame in ways that nurture social bonds, that sustain social integration, that trigger dialogue in which help is offered, the implication of Scheff and Retzinger's theory is that we shame in a way that should prevent both externalized and internalized violence. Conversely, when we shame stigmatically—in a way that cuts the person off from others—external and internal aggression become more likely. When shame is unacknowledged, the downward spiral into escalating shame may produce a despair which becomes suicidal. Whether strong cultural tendencies to shame others will be associated with high suicide rates will depend, according to the theory, on whether that shame is associated with cultural tendencies to acknowledge it or repress it. And it will depend on the cultural context of pride as well as shame, as dramatised by the fact, peculiar in Western eyes, that some traditional Japanese occasionally enjoy pride rather than shame in an act of suicide.

No great distinction is made by Scheff and Retzinger between shame and guilt. Guilt is a shame-anger transformation where anger is directed at the self. Violence, hatred, and resentment are shame-anger transformations where anger is directed at others. The case study of Hitler's appeal to the German masses, bridling from the humiliation of Versailles, illustrates how the targeting of anger can be as bizzare as any twist that the writer of fiction could imagine.

The importance of secure social bonds in Scheff and Retzinger's formulation raises the question of just how socially integrated it is best for citizens to be in a social order designed to minimize violence. Through the case study of Albert Speer in the final chapter, they illuminate the risks of excessive social integration, "*engulfment*," and how this was implicated in the production of Nazi violence. According to Scheff and Retzinger, both societies in which the group is everything (the individual is *engulfed*) and societies of rampant individualism (the individual is *isolated*) risk endemic violence.

Engulfment entails individuals giving up parts of self in order to be accepted by others; it means fusion of individual needs with the needs of the group, as opposed to differentiation of individual needs from the needs of the group. One of the greatest intellectual challenges we confront is to work through the paradox of isloation and engulfment. Scheff and Retzinger show what it means to avoid both evils through case studies of emotional response. From these cases, we have no problem conceiving of what a family which isolates its children is like and what a family which engulfs its children is like. Interdependency, mutual respect, love, community are what are needed to avoid isolation in families. But paradoxically, interdependency and mutual respect are needed to avoid engulfment as well. In an engulfing family in which members have traditionally gone into the medical profession, a member who decides to be an artist might be ridiculed, labeled as a failure, or even as a traitor. The individuating family, in contrast, while communicating honest disappointment and disagreement with a choice of art over medicine, also communicates satisfaction that the children are their own persons capable of thinking for themselves, capable of breaking the mould set by their parents and siblings. The individuating family uses interdependency and mutual respect as resources to guarantee assurance of individuality; social bonds enable the constitution of a secure individual self that cannot be engulfed by the family or any other collectivity. The conquest of social isolation by immediate or intermediate groups constitutes a republic of individuated citizens who cannot be engulfed by a fascist or totalitarian state.

At the level of normative theory, this is one reason for rejecting a liberal conception of freedom (as the freedom which completely isolated individuals perfectly enjoy) in favor of a republican conception of freedom (as the freedom citizens enjoy in a social world where other citizens grant them social assurances of liberty). The normative theory of the inferiority of individualism compared with a republic of social bonds and social conventions which assure individuation has been well described. The meaning of individual isolation and engulfment in terms of emotional response is well mapped in this book. But what remains to be mapped is the exact cultural and structural patternings of assurances—rights, laws, and social conventions that restrain collective interference with the individual—that are required to create a social order free of engulfment while averting isolation.

While this challenge is still before us, the implications of Scheff and Retzinger's work are profound for those who seek a world wherein citizens enjoy freedom from the fear of violence, communion and respect from their fellow citizens, and individual horizons expanded by attunement with other citizens. At the micro end of the continuum, there are implications for the practice of psychotherapy. For example, the eloquent demonstration in chapter 4 of the importance of confronting not just what is said during marital conflicts, but *how* it is said, and the significance of that for the communication of respect, is of revolutionary importance for psychotherapy. At a more intermediate level, there are enormous implications for the way we practice child rearing, the way we conduct the criminal justice system, the way we avoid engulfment and isolation in the education system. At the most macro level, there are the implications for how we conduct world affairs in a way that averts the dangers of relations among and within nations that are either isolating or engulfing. Most critically, how do we avoid a world of bimodal alienation—where nations are engulfed within and isolated without (such as in Germany, USSR, or Japan in the 1930s when individuals were engulfed by the state while the state was isolated from other states)?

At each of these levels, this book has some very fundamental things to say about what kind of social order we should aspire to. We should seek a social order that offers public rewards for desirable acts that respect rights, that shames exploitative acts, that cultivates the virtue of forgiveness (reacceptance) after shaming, that cultivates the virtue of acknowledging shame and engaging in dialogue about it, that cultivates the art and virtue of shaming while nurturing respect for the other, that cultivates the art and virtue of acknowledging shame while sustaining one's self-respect. These may seem rather abstract matters. Yet the strength of this book is in making remarkable progress in bringing them to life in concrete cases.

The emphasis in the final chapter on the democratic struggle for the consciences of citizens gives some clues as to what those of us who share a community of scholarship with Scheff and Retzinger need to do to help build on their work. Citizens can feel shame or pride about things which are desirable or undesirable, variably according to their values. Violence is unproblematically undesirable to most people most of the time. So this is a book which does not get into deep trouble about the content of that which is approved and disapproved. It deals dextrously with some uncontroversially bad implications of managing shame in certain disastrous ways.

Ultimately, however, we need a normative theory about the content of the socializing institutions that mould our consciences. How can we construct a democratic theory of dialogue over the content of that which we find shameful, that which should give us pride? Certainly, what we cannot do in light of Scheff and Retzinger's arresting book is continue to manifest the liberal squeamishness whereby scholars avert their gaze from shame and pride as intellectual concerns. What we have in this work is a devastating case that the way we handle shame and pride are central problems for our civilization.

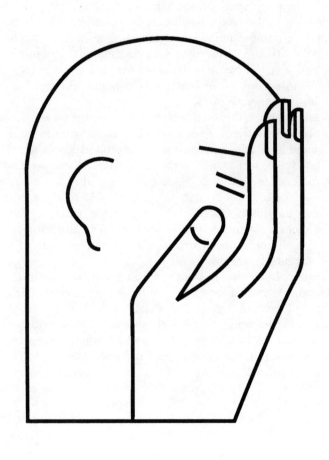

Introduction

The overall threat of violence is pervasive in our era, having reached what might be its highest level in human history. Domestic and street violence is an immediate fact of life in most societies. Collective violence between ethnic and racial groups and among nations brings about destruction on a catastrophic scale. The threat of this kind of violence is not new; indeed, some earlier societies may have faced even higher levels. What is new is that the threat is of almost unimaginable scope; virtually any outbreak could trigger vast cataclysms of high-tech destruction. Is there any hope of understanding the causes of violence?

To this point, theories of violence have not been much help in understanding its causes. One problem is the very number of competing approaches. Each discipline in the human sciences offers a variety of theories. Each contains schools of thought that approach the problem in different and often conflicting ways. Existing research does not seem to offer guidance; surveys of the research literature suggest that the findings provide minimal or contradictory support for the various theories. To be creditable in this welter of contending views, any new approach would need to build upon and integrate earlier discussions.

This book proposes a new theory of the sources of destructive violence in our civilization. Our approach integrates several approaches, particularly bridging the sociological, the psychological, the historical, and the political. Integration of this kind may overcome one of the key failings in existing views of violence—the question of agency. Like all formal accounts of human behavior, theories of the causes of violence lack a sense of agency, of how and why particular persons commit violent acts. (For a review of current discussions of the problem of agency, see Ritzer, 1991).

In examining journalistic and fictional depictions of violence, one of the first things we look for is agency: who is causing the violence, and why are they doing so. We want an immediate sense of the identities of perpetrator and victim and the motives underlying their actions.

When we come to scholarly and scientific accounts, however, the sense of human agency, of persons committing violent deeds, is usually missing. There seems to be a trade-off in this literature; the more "objective" it is, the less we can recognize the motives of the actors or even catch a glimpse of the actors themselves.

The basic thrust of this book is to develop an objective theory of violence without sacrificing a sense of agency. Such a project requires a radical break with the tradition in which social theory is kept completely separate from methods and empirical data. An understanding of violence that is both systematic and agentic would seem to require a new genre, a combination of approaches which have previously been separated; not theory alone, or method alone, or case study alone, or application alone, but theory-method-case-study-application. Such a combination may be needed to overcome hyperspecialization.

In each episode in this book, we provide at least some of the biographical background or the even denser verbatim information necessary to assess meaning in human actions. By seeing theory and method applied to actual episodes, the reader can assess their effectiveness in understanding the human causes of violence.

To preview the argument that will be presented; we develop an explanation of destructive conflict in terms of two interrelated concepts: *alienation* and *shame*. We argue that protracted violence occurs under two basic conditions. One, the parties to the conflict are alienated from each other and are in a state of shame; and two, their state of alienation and their shame go unacknowledged.

In our society, there is already some awareness of the role of shame in escalating disputes. The cycle of insult, humiliation, and revenge is a familiar one. In sports, a competent coach usually has a sense of the significance of this cycle and its relation to the social bond with the other coaches in the league. He or she knows that although the object is to win, one does not want to unnecessarily humiliate the other team; if one does, the other team may exact revenge in the next round. Unlike the players, coaches are relatively permanent; preserving relationships with other coaches is a real consideration.

In everyday disputes, however, and in large-scale disputes between groups, the shame component is usually carefully hidden. Shame is usually felt to be a weakness; the groups involved feel that it would introduce futher humiliation to reveal it.

Thus, in our theory, it is not alienation and shame per se that produce violence. These states can just as easily lead to the repair of damaged social relationships. Rather, alienation and shame lead to violence only when they are repressed or disguised—that is, when they are not acknowledged.

We argue that conflicts of interest do not necessarily lead to violence; objective conflicts can be negotiated. Violence occurs when the path toward negotiation is blocked by inadequate bonds and hidden cross-currents of emotion—that is, by unacknowledged alienation/ shame. We propose that *all* human violence is caused in this way.

This statement of the theory is necessarily stark and abstract in order to serve as a framework for the details that follow. In order to develop the theory, we have had to deviate from many traditional views of human conduct—traditions deeply held by laypersons and professionals alike. Perhaps the topic that has been most taboo is the role of emotion. As each of the chapters will suggest, we give emotion pride of place in the understanding of human affairs, even though we understand that it is only one force out of many. This imbalance in our discussion requires some preliminary justification.

As indicated above, our explanation of violent conflict involves not only shame but also alienation. We give exact parity to these two components since we consider them to be names for different facets of the same reality. That is to say, we treat shame as the individual aspect of social disconnection, and alienation as its social aspect. In our scheme, emotion and social relationships are conjugate pairs: pride is the emotional conjugate of social solidarity, and shame is the emotional conjugate of alienation.

Given our belief in parity, our book nonetheless gives much more attention to the emotion of shame than to its relational partner, alienation. We have done this for two reasons. First, there is already a rich vocabulary of cognates and suppositions that serves as a backdrop for the idea of alienation, but a very small and undeveloped endowment for the idea of shame. In order to understand the complex play of forces that leads to individual and collective violence, we have had to develop our own vocabulary of cognates and suppositions.

The second reason for the imbalance is the special place we assign to shame among the emotions: we consider it to be the *master emotion.* The major emotions—like shame, fear, grief, and anger—all have an instinctual basis; they are part of our genetic inheritance. In the absence of shame, we easily detect and express them. But shame may interfere with the effective management of these emotions; we are often ashamed of our emotions. As we will suggest, under some conditions shame can inhibit, and under other conditions amplify, emotion.

The effect of shame on the detection and expression of emotions may explain the enormous variation that we see in these processes both in persons and in cultures. Shame may be the key to understanding personal and cultural variation in emotions. Shame could be the basic engine of repression—the cause of complete inhibition, on the one hand, and the runaway fuel of massive conflagrations of physical and emotional violence, on the other.

A metaphor may help to convey our view of the centrality of shame to human conduct. Shame may be analogous to oxygen in the chemistry of the elements. Just as oxygen in combination with hydrogen and carbon forms the basis for living cells, so shame is a necessary part of personality and culture. But oxygen can also be destructive, since it is necessary for combustion. Shame, in combination with anger, can play a similar role in destroying relationships and societies. The chapters that follow will point out both the creative and destructive potentials of shame.

The new theory has five components. It involves an explanation of *causal sequences* in their richly detailed *context*. The explanation is based on precisely explicated *concepts*, applied to *concrete cases* using a clearly defined *method*. The integration of all five of these components (theory, method, cases involving sequences, and context) may be necessary for a systematic theory of violence that does not omit human agency.

Lack of agency is obvious in the highly abstract accounts offered by structural theories, such as those based on class conflict, on evolutionary and biological formulations, and on economic determinism. Not only have such macrotheories not been applied to the concrete acts of particular persons—they cannot be, at least not in their present forms. These theories lack definitions of their basic concepts that are sufficiently precise that they can be applied to actual episodes.

Durkheim's theory of suicide is a familiar example. Unlike most structural theories, Durkheim's is supported by empirical study. His data seem to show that suicide rates are consistently higher in Protestant populations than in Catholic ones. The differences, though consistent, are quite small—that is, there are many cases in his populations that do not support his theory (Catholics who commit suicide and Protestants who don't). Although Durkheim fashioned a plausible account of the causal link between religion and suicide rates, it is entirely speculative. Neither Durkheim nor anyone else has devised a theory-and-method-driven study of suicide. Such a study would require a precise definition of concepts and an application of these concepts to actual cases.

At first glance, it might seem that psychological theories would provide the sense of agency missing in structural explanations. But a close look at the field suggests that agency is also missing in psychological explanations.

In one field of psychology, the social psychology of violence and aggression, a sizable number of laboratory experiments have suggested causal agents, such as frustration or insult. These studies define the concepts precisely enough that they can be applied to concrete cases, and they use explicitly defined methods of collecting and analyzing data. But these studies have two major drawbacks. First, their data are static; they are not organized in a way that allows the investigation of causal sequences, moment by moment, in concrete episodes of behavior. Second, their experimental design requires the aggregation of data from many cases, so that all of the data are decontexualized. Even if such studies produced high levels of correlation between a cause and an effect, they would still lack a sense of agency.

At the other pole of psychology, psychoanalytic researchers have analyzed violence. The problem with these studies is not that the data are static and decontexualized but that they lack the discipline of precise definition of concepts and explicit methods for the analysis of data. As indicated in chapter 6, Freud's case histories are packed with human interest, but they are unsystematic and usually very brief.

The existing approaches to violence are highly specialized, to the point that they lack one or more of the five components necessary to afford a systematic, agentic explanation of violence. All the existing approaches emphasize some of the components at the expense of others. Structural explanations, for example, sacrifice concrete episodes and context; in psychoanalytic formulations, an explicit method of data collection and analysis is missing.

The specialization of viewpoint and method defeats our developing a sense of agency in the study of violence. Human intelligence is a general problem-solver, one that requires a rich backdrop of information providing context and the ability to shuttle back and forth between different perspectives. We can see this feature at work in our ability to understand ordinary language. Attempts to computerize translation from one ordinary language to another, for example, or even to successfully paraphrase in the same language, have failed because of the incredible scope, complexity, and resourcefulness of human intelligence.

To see the relevance to understanding motives in violence, it will be helpful to discuss the problem of understanding ordinary language. It turns out that the meaning of even a simple sentence—especially in spoken language—is quite ambiguous. Ordinary language is an open system—that is, it is composed of a very large number of elements, each of which is ambiguous. Most commonly used words have multiple meanings. We understand their specific meaning only in context.

Ordinary language in this aspect is starkly different than closed systems—that is, than games (like tic-tac-toe or chess), than mathematics, and than computer programs, in which there is no ambiguity whatever. Not only are words themselves ambiguous, but in spoken language there is an additional level of ambiguity because of the nonverbal elements of expression. We are able to understand ambiguous elements because of the vastness of human intelligence. What Steiner (1975) calls the "interpretive decipherment" of a single sentence requires understanding the complex relation of its elements to a vast matrix of other words and relationships, in the particular context in which it occurred. Human intelligence requires understanding the relationships between *parts* and *wholes* in the vast system of culture and practices of a society.

Understanding human motives involves a similar process, but it is even more complex and ambiguous. With language we at least have the assistance of dictionaries to guide us through the labyrinth of meanings. (Dictionaries furnish first approximations to the meaning of words in use.) But although motivations are partially conventional, there is no comparable Ariadne's thread. Cultures do not provide dictionaries of motivations—perhaps because motivations are much more complex than word meanings.

Ascertaining the human meaning of an action—its motivation—requires considerable biographical knowledge of the participants, a precise reading of the context in which the action occurs, and its relationship to a vast matrix of a culture's beliefs and practices. To the extent that specialized approaches to human behavior strip away context and verbatim sequences of events, they rob us of the ability to understand its meaning. Part/whole analysis implies the opposite of specialization, since it requires linking all parts and wholes at all levels of abstraction. "Common sense" makes sense because it involves part/whole analysis.

Structural analyses of behavior obviously leave out the identity of particular actors, context, and verbatim sequences of events. Psychological accounts, such as those in psychoanalytic formulations, usually provide elements of a general theory and information on identities and context, and occasionally sequences of events. But the concepts in psychoanalytic theory are defined casually, if at all, and the descriptions are usually quite impoverished compared with the event itself. Psychoanalytic concepts and case descriptions are, for the most part, abstract glosses on complex events.

Since most current approaches to violence provide neither the vast file of background information of biographies and novels, nor the dense cloud of gestures in mechanical event recordings, the reader is unable to check the inferences made by the analyst. Only the writer is free to make part/whole inferences; because of the absence of the requisite information, the reader is excluded. Nor is a sense of agency the only casualty of highly specialized approaches; the reader also loses the ability to make an immediate, if tentative, evaluation of the validity of an analysis. The specialist speaks to other specialists, who accept the same set of presuppositions; the general reader, who is apt not to accept one or more of the presuppositions, is excluded.

We have attempted in this book to include sufficient biographical and verbatim material to include the reader in the quest for understanding. Given the same data, the reader can use his/her commonsense analysis (the relations between parts and wholes) to check our interpretations. Our approach attempts to empower the reader, in contrast with specialized approaches, which tend to alienate them.

Our book begins with a review of the history of one of the main concepts in the overall theory, the emotion of shame. The second chapter states the basic theory, the relationship between shame and alienation, and how these states determine patterns of communication and social action. Chapter 3 reports two studies of videotaped interaction in television broadcasts that illustrate and provide preliminary support for our theory.

Following these introductory chapters is a series of case studies. All involve the methodology of discourse analysis—the very close interpretation of texts, word by word, line by line. Chapters 4 and 5 apply the theory and method to marital quarrels. Chapter 4 reports a study of disputes of four couples, showing how unacknowledged alienation and shame can be seen as underlying causal elements in all four quarrels. The data in these two chapters come from mechanical recordings (videotapes). Chapter 5 examines one of these quarrels in detail, calling attention to the links between alienation, emotion, communication patterns, and repetitive conflict.

Chapter 6 illustrates how the theory can be applied to a different kind of data—a work of fiction. It concerns the hidden motives of the leading character in Goethe's novel *The Sorrows of Young Werther*. This chapter illustrates the construction of meaning from extended biographical details.

Chapter 7 involves a reanalysis of the data used in a classic sociolinguistic study—the analysis of an audiotaped excerpt from a psychotherapy session by Labov and Fanshel (1977). We show how their data and interpretation provide strong support for our theory, and we point toward a modification and extension of the labeling theory of mental illness.

Chapter 8 offers a case study of a very different kind: the social and emotional bases of Hitler's appeal to the German people. Using excerpts from Hitler's writings and speeches, we suggest how a hidden thread of alienation and shame might have been causal agents in the world-encompassing violence of World War II. The last chapter summarizes the book's main ideas and ends with one last case study—an analysis of defects in Albert Speer's conscience, as inferred from passages in his memoirs. In this chapter, we offer an application of our theory for building conscience and community between nations. The theory and method outlined here suggests new directions for understanding violence and for doing something about it.

Although we have used the authorial "we" throughout, there was actually a division of labor between the two authors. Retzinger had responsibility for writing the first drafts of Chapters 4 and 5, Scheff, the other chapters. Since we each commented on the other's drafts, and discussed the succeeding versions at great length, the final chapters bear joint reponsibility.

Thanks are due to the following persons: Lori Terry, Michelle Jones, and Meline' Sarkassian provided research assistance. Joan Murdoch, Mark Schildhauer, and Lisa Daniels gave us advice and counsel on word processing and indexing. John Braithwaite, Anthony Giddens, George Ritzer, and three anonymous reviewers made helpful comments on the basis of an earlier draft. Jack Barbelet directed us to review Nobert Elias's work, which has influenced this volume, but will have still greater influence on our future work. We believe that the graceful way in which he traces sequences from verbatim texts to social structure may provide a model for future social science.

We are grateful for permission from Sage Publications (Chapter 5). We dedicate the book as a whole to those whose promise was cut short by the violent conflicts we describe here.

Part 1
Theory

Figure 1–1. Masaccio, *Expulsion of Adam and Eve*

Figure 2–1. *Doonesbury* Cartoon, by Garry Trudeau

Chapter 1
Invisible Shame and Social Structure

This book proposes an explanation of the roots of human violence. It suggests that a particular sequence of emotions underlies all destructive aggression: shame is first evoked, which leads to rage and then violence. But shame leads to violence under only one condition—that it is hidden to the point that it is not acknowledged or resolved. As we will suggest, shame occurs much more frequently in human affairs than has been recognized, but it becomes destructive only when its presence is completely suppressed. The denial of shame is institutionalized in modern societies. For this reason, the dynamics of shame are as connected to social structure as they are to individual personality.

To understand the relationship between shame and social structure, it will first be necessary to discuss shame itself and its relationship to other emotions, such as pride and guilt. This chapter introduces these topics, beginning with the Bible and classical Greek thought and progressing through early modern discussions and recent formulations. We then show the relationship between these emotions and social structure, the way shame causes and is caused by alienation, and the way pride causes and reflects solidarity.

Emotions and Shame

Although emotions have been a topic of serious discussion for thousands of years, they remain one of the cloudiest regions of human thought. Any investigation of emotion is at hazard from its beginning since the concept itself is undefined. Even the most scholarly and scientific analyses depend on the use of vernacular terms such as anger, fear, grief, shame, joy and love and on the underlying presuppositions about emotion in our society. The field of emotions is less a body of knowledge than a jungle of unexamined assumptions, observations, and theories. Some of the roots of our contemporary attitudes toward emotion, and some of the puzzles we still share, can be seen by reviewing usage in the Bible and other sources.

The issue of shame arises very early in the Old Testament. Although the word is not used, it is implied in the story of Adam and Eve. When Adam tells God that he hid from him because he was naked, God asks "Who told thee that thou wast naked?" God inferred that since Adam was ashamed of being naked, he had become self-conscious—that is, that he had eaten of the forbidden fruit. In the history, shame arises simultaneously with human self-consciousness. This event is portentous; it hints that shame may play a central role in the human drama.

The shame context of the story is depicted in most portrayals of the expulsion from the Garden, with both Adam and Eve showing embarrassment or shame. In the fifteenth-century painting by Masaccio Eve shows her embarrassment by covering her breasts and loins, but Adam covers his eyes with both hands. (For a contemporary example of the same gesture, see figure 3–2.) Perhaps Adam is more profoundly ashamed than Eve, since she covers only parts of herself. Adam, by covering his eyes so that he won't see or be seen, like a child, may be trying to escape entirely from regarding God and from being regarded by him.

Adam and Eve are completely submissive to God's punishment: they are silent in the face of his harsh judgment. The very possibility of standing up to authority has not yet arisen. Their silence implies not only that God has condemned them but that they have condemned themselves; their shame is complete.

The Book of Genesis implies two crucial episodes in human development: the physical creation of humans by God, and the shift from the paradisiacal life of human animals to that of self-conscious human beings. A third significant episode occurs in the Book of Job. The protagonist does not suffer in silence under God's wrath, as Adam and Eve did. Rather, he confronts God with his misery, questioning the justice of his fate. The story of Job provides the first suggestion that hierarchy in the human social order is not inexorable, as it is in animal societies, but can be challenged. Job's confrontation with God is a stirring toward freedom from rigid compliance to the status quo, just as the birth of self-consciousness created the potential for freedom from animal existence.

A historical equivalent can be found in Vico's 1744 pronouncement "the social world is the work of men" (rather than of God or nature). Unlike all other living creatures, humans have the potential to create their own existence. Vico's statement was courageous; by making it, he endangered his life for challenging the absolute authority of the Church and the state.

Even today, escape from inexorable authority is still only partial. Most of us, most of the time, are emeshed in the *status quo*, the taken-for-granted social arrangements of our society, which seem to us absolute and unchangeable. Even though the existing status quo is only one of many possible social orders, to those emeshed in it it seems eternal. To a great degree, human beings, like other animals but for different reasons, are cogs in a social machine. "Not for me the dark ambiguities of flesh. My maker gave me but one command: mesh," as John Updike wrote.

The three biblical episodes can be taken as emblematic of the physical, psychological, and cultural evolution of human nature. Shame may be intimately connected with all three of these steps. First, shame has a basis in biology as one of what William James called the "coarse" emotions; it has a genetically inherited component (Scheff 1987a). Second, shame has a psychological component. Shame arises in situations of self-consciousness, seeing oneself from the viewpoint of others. Finally, shame has a cultural component. The situations that produce shame, the labeling of shame, and the response to it show immense variation from one society to another. Shame may be the most social of all emotions, since it functions as a signal of threat to the social bond.

In the Old Testament there are references to pride and shame but very few to guilt. In the New Testament this ratio is exactly reversed: there are many more references to guilt than to shame. One possible interpretation of this would be to see it in terms of "shame cultures" and "guilt cultures." That is, the writers of the Old Testament were members of a completely traditional society in which shame was the major emotion of social control. By contrast, the writers of the New Testament were members of a society in transition to its current form, in which the social control of adults involved guilt. This interpretation proposes that there is external control, through shame, in traditional societies, and internal control, through guilt, in modern societies (as in Benedict 1946; Dodds 1951).

This book, however, offers a different explanation. We argue that the distinction between shame cultures and guilt cultures is misleading since it assumes that shame states are infrequent among adults in modern societies. It is possible that the role of shame in social control has not decreased but has gone underground. In traditional societies, shame is openly acknowledged; the word itself is used frequently in everyday discourse. In modern societies, references to shame still appear frequently but in a disguised form. (We suggest in chapter 2 that since guilt is a shame-anger sequence, the concept of guilt itself serves to deny shame.)

There are hundreds of words and phrases that seem to be substitutes or euphemisms for the words *shame* and *embarrassment*. For example, we may say, "It was an awkward moment for me." Such a statement usually refers to a feeling of embarrassment. It contains two movements that disguise emotion—*denial* of inner feeling, and *projecting* it onto the outer world: *I* was not embarrassed, it was the *moment* that was awkward (Scheff 1984). In modern societies our very language conspires to hide shame from display and from our consciousness. Traditional societies acknowledge shame, modern societies deny it.

A second issue is the meaning assigned to pride in the Old Testament. Virtually every reference there casts pride in a disparaging light. Perhaps the most familiar example occurs in Proverbs 16–18: "Pride goeth before destruction, and an haughty spirit before a fall." (In everyday usage, this quotation is often shortened to "Pride goeth before a fall.") A similar use occurs in 16–19: "Better it is to be of a humble spirit with the lowly, than to divide the spoil with the proud." Many similar examples could be cited.

This usage might be one source of a particular contemporary inflection—that the word *pride* itself often carries a negative connotation. To escape that connotation, it is necessary to add a qualifier, such as *"justified* pride." As we explain in chapter 2, there might be less confusion if it were the other way around, if *pride* alone signified normal or justified pride. In this usage, it would be necessary to add a qualifier, such as *"false* pride," to refer to the kind of pride so prominent in the Old Testament. There is a hint of this usage in the passage from Proverbs cited above, when it is quoted in full: the kind of pride that leads to a fall is the kind that is marked by haughtiness. Perhaps false pride is related not to normal pride but to its antithesis, shame. Insolence and haughtiness may mask deep-seated feelings of inferiority, that is, shame.

False pride corresponds exactly to the meaning of the Greek word *hubris*, the kind of pride that leads certainly to *nemesis*, or punishment by the gods. Pride and shame appear to have played key roles in Greek thought since there are many shadings of each word in classical Greek language. In contrast to *hubris*, Aristotle described a kind of pride that he saw as the supreme virtue—the interest in honor above all else, a pride that means "greatness of soul." (For a fuller discussion of Aristotle's conception of pride as a virtue, as well as many other classical and medieval treatments of pride, see Payne 1951).

Among the various kinds of shame in the Greek language, the distinction between shame as disgrace (*aischyne*) and shame as modesty or shyness (*aidos*) has survived in all European languages except English:

	disgrace	modesty
Greek	aischyne	aidos
Latin	foedus	pudor
French	honte	pudor
Italian	vergogna	pudore
German	Schande	Scham

Schneider (1977) has urged the importance of *shame* in this second meaning, "a sense of shame." The connotation of this type of shame, especially in its root in the Greek word *aidos*, connotes not only modesty or shyness but also awe and reverence. Perhaps the closest equivalent in English is *humility*. It should be noted that David Hume, in his eighteenth-century treatise on the passions (1739), devoted considerable space to pride and shame. He noted the relationship of shame to humility and also made a distinction between normal pride and false pride. (He called the latter "vanity.") A very precise analysis of Hume's approach to the emotions can be found in Taylor (1985).

Ovid (A.D. seven) depicted a relationship between shame and the stages of society in his Four Stages of the World. His first stage, the Golden Age, corresponded to the Garden of Eden, a world without fear and punishment. But this paradise was disturbed in the succeeding stages until the last stage, an age of wickedness, in which "every species of crime burst forth" and "shame [*pudor*], truth and honor took flight." This passage suggests that wickedness involves, among other things, shamelessness, a loss of the sense of shame.

The connection between shamelessness, evil, and self-destruction is made quite explicit in the Greek myth of the goddess Aidos, as told by Hesiod and others (Heller 1984). This myth makes clear that Nemesis is the avenger of Aidos. That is, a shameless attack on decency, personified as the goddess of shame, is tantamount to self-destruction. Surely the story of Hitler we tell in chapter 8 emblazons this idea on the universe.

In the nineteenth century, the issue of shame arose in debate over blushing: Do dark-skinned persons blush? In his lengthy discussion of blushing and the emotions related to it, Darwin (1872) concluded that dark-skinned races do indeed blush, that all humans do, and that blushing is a central feature of humanity: "Blushing is the most peculiar and most human of all expressions. . . . Monkeys redden from passion, but it would require an overwhelming amount of evidence to make us believe that than any animal could blush."

Darwin went on to state that blushing is caused by shame—the kind of shame that arises out of self-consciousness, or seeing oneself from the viewpoint of others. The idea that emotions can arise in seeing ourselves from the viewpoint of others, even if only in our imagination, plays a central role in Cooley's analysis (1902) of the nature of the self. He proposed that human consciousness is *social* in that we spend much of our life "living in the minds of others" without realizing it. Self-monitoring from the viewpoint of others gives rise to self-regarding sentiments:

> As is the case with other feelings, we do not think much of it (that is, of social self-feeling) so long as it is moderately and regularly grati-fied. Many people of balanced mind and congenial activity scarcely know that they care what others think of them, and will deny, per-haps with indignation, that such care is an important factor in what they are and do. But this is illusion. If failure or disgrace arrives, if one suddenly finds that the faces of men show coldness of contempt instead of the kindliness and deference that he is used to, he will perceive from the shock, the fear, the sense of being outcast and helpless, that he was *living in the minds of others* without knowing it, just as we daily walk the solid ground without thinking how it bears us up. (208; emphasis added)

Cooley placed total emphasis on two particular emotions that arise out of social self-monitoring, pride and shame. He implied in the passage above that when we are adequately deferred to by our fellows, we are in a state of normal pride. If we do not receive adequate deference, we enter a state of shame as suggested in his discussion of the "looking-glass self":

> The thing that moves us to *pride or shame* is not the mere mechanical reflection of ourselves, but an imputed sentiment, the imagined effect of this reflection upon another's mind. This is evident from the fact that the character and weight of that other, in whose mind we see ourselves makes all the difference with our feeling. We are *ashamed* to seem evasive in the presence of a straightforward man, cowardly in the presence of a brave one, gross in the eyes of a refined one, and so on. We always imagine, and in imagining share, the judgments of the other mind. A man will boast to one person of an action—say some sharp transaction in trade—which he would be *ashamed* to own to another. (184–85)

Cooley's statement suggests that pride and shame are virtually ubiquitous. We are accustomed to considering them as unusual, arising infrequently—pride at rare occasions of triumph, and shame on occa-sions of disgrace. But Cooley implied that we are virtually *always* in a state of either pride or shame. These ongoing states have very low visibility, however, to the point that they are seldom noticed or mentioned. Cooley's approach suggests that normal pride and shame are existential states: they arise out of the innately social character of human nature. (This idea anticipates Lewis's [1971] approach to shame.)

The work of Goffman, who like Cooley was a sociologist, also implied a premier role for shame and embarrassment in human conduct. In his earliest approach, Goffman only implied the role of emotion. He focused on a type of *behavior*, rather, "impression management", which seems to imply that a sense of shame determines most of our actions (1959). Goffman's actors are obsessed with their image in the eyes of others, with the impression they are making. His actors seem to constantly fear being seen negatively in the eyes of the other, which many writers have defined as the source of shame (as in Sartre 1956).

In a later treatment of social interaction (1967), Goffman made the role of shame more explicit, proposing that *embarrassment* (and anticipation of embarrassment) is a central ingredient in human contact. In presenting ourselves to others, we run the risk that our presentation will not be adequately accepted, that we will not receive the kind of response our presentation requires. Goffman analyzed not just flagrant insults but more subtle forms of disrespect, even a missed beat in the rhythm of conversation, or an averted glance or direct stare held a fraction of a second too long. Goffman's work implies that emotion—particularly embarrassment—is the fuel that drives the social machine (Scheff 1988, 1990).

The treatment of shame that has the broadest scope is that of Norbert Elias, in his historical analysis of what he calls the "civilizing process" (1978, 1982). In a study that shows extraordinary insight, he traces changes in the development of personality in the onset of modern civilization. Like Weber, Elias gives great prominence to the development of rationality. Unlike Weber, however, he gives equal prominence to changes in the threshold of shame: "No less characteristic of a civilizing process than 'rationalization' is the peculiar moulding of the drive economy that we call 'shame' and 'repugnance' or 'embarrassment' " (1982: 292). Using excerpts from advice manuals from the Middle Ages to the nineteenth century, Elias outlines a theory of modernity. By examining instance after instance of advice concerning etiquette—especially table manners, body functions, sexuality, and anger—he suggests that a key aspect of modernity involves a veritable explosion of shame.

Although Elias's language differs from ours, his analysis parallels ours. His central thesis is closely related: that decreasing shame thresholds at the time of the breakup of rural communities, and decreasing acknowledgment of shame, have had powerful consequences on levels of awareness and self-control.

The following excerpt gives the flavor of Elias's study and suggests some of its power. He first presents a lengthy excerpt from a nineteenth-century work, *The Education of Girls* (von Raumer 1857), that advises mothers how to answer the sexual questions their daughters ask:

> Children should be left for as long as is at all possible in the belief that an angel brings the mother her little children. This legend, customary in some regions, is far better than the story of the stork common elsewhere. Children, if they really grow up under their mother's eyes, will seldom ask forward questions on this point . . . not even if the mother is prevented by a childbirth from having them about her. . . . If girls should later ask how little children really come into the world, they should be told that the good Lord gives the mother her child, who has a guardian angel in heaven who certainly played an invisible part in bringing us this great joy. "You do not need to know nor could you understand how God gives children." Girls must be satisfied with such answers in a hundred cases, and it is the mother's task to occupy her daughters' thoughts so incessantly with the good and beautiful that they are left no time to brood on such matters. . . . A mother . . . ought only once to say seriously: "It would not be good for you to know such a thing, and you should take care not to listen to anything said about it." A truly well-brought-up girl will from then on feel shame at hearing things of this kind spoken of. (1978:180).

Elias's commentary on this excerpt is masterful. First he interprets the repression of sexuality in terms of unacknowledged shame.

> In the civilizing process, sexuality too is increasingly removed behind the scenes of social life and enclosed in a particular enclave, the nuclear family. Likewise, the relations between the sexes are isolated, placed behind walls in consciousness. An aura of embarrassment, the expression of a sociogenetic fear, surrounds this sphere of life. Even among adults it is referred to officially only with caution and circumlocutions. And with children, particularly girls, such things are, as far as possible, not referred to at all. Von Raumer gives no reason why one ought not to speak of them with children. He could have said it is desirable to preserve the spiritual purity of girls for as long as possible. But even this reason is only another expression of how far the gradual submergence of these impulses in shame and embarrassment has advanced by this time. (1978:180)

Elias raises a host of significant questions about this excerpt, concerning its motivation and its effects. His analysis goes to what we consider the central causal chain in modern civilization—denial of the emotion of shame and of the threatened social bonds that both cause and reflect that denial.

We fully concur with Elias's analysis of the causal process in repression, the arousal of shame and the denial of this arousal:

> Considered rationally, the problem confronting him [von Raumer] seems unsolved, and what he says appears contradictory. He does not explain how and when the young girl should be made to understand what is happening and will happen to her. The primary concern is the necessity of instilling "modesty" (i.e., feelings of shame, fear, embarrassment, and guilt) or, more precisely, behavior conforming to the social standard. And one feels how infinitely difficult it is for the educator himself to overcome the resistance of the shame and embarrassment which surround this sphere for him. (1978:181)

Elias's study suggests a way of understanding the social transmission of the taboo on shame and the social bond. The adult—the author von Raumer, in this case—is not only ashamed of sex, he is ashamed of being ashamed, and he is probably ashamed of the shame that he will arouse in his reader. The nineteenth-century reader, in turn, probably reacted in a similar way—being ashamed, and being ashamed of being ashamed, and being ashamed of causing further shame in the daughter. Von Raumer's advice was part of a social system in which attempts at civilized delicacy resulted and continue to result in an endless chain reaction of unacknowledged shame. The chain reaction is both within persons and between them—what we call a "triple spiral" (Scheff 1990).

Elias's analysis is so broad and so trenchant that it takes us beyond the scope of the present book. Here we focus on another kind of chain reaction—shame-anger spirals. Elias's analysis suggests the need for an explanation of the social transmission of patterns of shame management in terms of shame-shame spirals, just as in this book we explain interminable conflict in terms of shame-anger spirals.

Certainly Elias understands the significance of the denial of shame in the same way that we do: shame goes underground, leading to behavior that is outside of awareness and compulsive: "Neither rational motives nor practical reasons primarily determine this attitude, but rather the shame of adults themselves, which has become *compulsive*. It is the social prohibitions and resistances within themselves, their own superego, that makes them keep silent" (1978:181; emphasis added).

His analysis suggests some of the negative—indeed, destructive—effects of secrets and secrecy, in a way that directly contradicts Simmel's famous essay (see chapter 2). We believe that understanding the dynamics of unacknowledged shame will lead to exact models of repression and to precise and reliable methods of understanding behavior that is unconsciously motivated and compulsive.

At first glance, psychoanalytic theory gives the impression that it has all but ignored shame. Freud's primary emphasis was on anxiety and guilt. His approach implies that shame is "infantile" and "regressive." Schneider (1977) makes a strong case that Freud was insufficiently sensitive to patients' desires to hide their secrets, their embarrassment, and their shame about their thoughts, feelings, and actions. He argues that Freud was shameless (in the sense of being disrespectful) in his relentless attack on what he thought of as the patient's "resistance" to knowing themselves. Schneider illustrates the problem with Freud's mishandling of the case of Dora, showing how Freud's irreverence toward Dora's sense of shame led him to make a classic blunder. The downplaying of shame maybe one of the key flaws in orthodox psychoanalytic theory and practice.

Although shame is largely ignored in orthodox psychoanalytic theory, however, it emerges as central in several variant psychoanalytic theories. Adler's approach (1907–37) centered on "feelings of inferiority"—a phrase that seems to refer to shame. His theory pivots about a crucial phase in a children's development, when they need a secure bond with their parents. Adler argued that children prefer love, but if it is unavailable to them, if they feel abandoned or rejected, their adult personality will develop in one of two ways. Either they will form an "inferiority complex"—that is, develop chronic feelings of shame (low self-esteem)—or they will manifest a "drive for power." Both of these paths may be interpreted in terms of chronic shame: the inferiority complex as *overt* shame, the drive for power as *bypassed* shame.

In Horney's approach to psychoanalysis (1950), pride and shame play a central role. Horney termed the neurotic part of the personality the "false self," proposing that it is organized around what she called the "pride system." In her system, pride seems to be false pride, and in her analysis, the system is driven by a sense of humiliation, or shame. She placed considerable emphasis on a particular *sequence* of events: honor, insult, vindictiveness, revenge. Her analysis of this sequence anticipated the proposition that unacknowledged shame causes destructive aggression.

Piers and Singer (1953), Lynd (1958), and Tomkins (1963) also developed important analyses of shame and humiliation, based in part on psychoanalytic ideas. In terms of our purpose here, however, the most important psychoanalytic approach is that of the late Helen Lewis. Her magnum opus, *Shame and Guilt in Neurosis* (1971), sets forth the theory, method, and findings upon which much of this book is based.

Lewis's most important contribution was the discovery of *unacknowledged* shame, the kind of low-visibility emotion predicated by the work of Cooley and of Goffman. By patiently analyzing the transcripts of hundreds of psychotherapy sessions, moment by moment, Lewis demonstrated that patients are often in a state of shame. This state is virtually always overlooked by the therapist and the patient. Many of the patients' statements show concern for the therapists' view of them: "I'm wondering how you are thinking about me after telling you all this." Both the manner and the content of these statements suggest shame states, but these are seldom made explicit.

Lewis's work suggests that shame is a haunting presence in psychotherapy, a presence that is usually hidden, disguised, or ignored by both patient and therapist. Mindful of Cooley's conjecture on low-visibility pride and Goffman's on embarrassment, one might infer that unacknowledged pride and shame are ubiquitous in all human encounters, not just in psychotherapy. This conjecture would explain why most therapists are unaware of pride and shame in therapy, even though they may be crucial elements in treatment. Like patients and most other adults, therapists are accustomed to ignoring the manifestations of these emotions.

Lewis also noted that shame usually occurs as a part of *sequence* of emotions. Her analysis of the quotation in the secod-to-last paragraph is an example. That patient may have been imagining that he was seen in a negative way by the therapist. First a brief moment of shame was evoked, then it was quickly followed by anger at the therapist, and then it was followed, just as quickly, by guilt about the anger. That is, imagining a negative image of self in the eyes of the therapist, the patient first felt shame, then anger at the therapist, then guilt about feeling angry at the therapist. This whole sequence might have occurred rapidly, lasting only fifteen or twenty seconds.

One important implication of Lewis's discovery of shame and shame-anger sequences concerns the emotions of guilt and resentment. Guilt is usually thought of as an elemental emotion like shame, and resentment as a form of anger. But Lewis's analysis suggests that both of these emotions are *shame-anger variants*: guilt is a shame-anger sequence in which the anger is directed back at the self, and resentment is a shame-anger sequence in which the anger is directed out at another. In this conception, guilt and resentment are isotopic variations of the basic shame-anger molecule. The sequential nature of this model suggests how guilt and resentment can last indefinitely as chains of emotional reactions to one's emotional reactions.

That is to say, sequences of this kind can loop back on themselves, as when a patient feels ashamed for being upset over "nothing," then angry because of the shame and so on and infinitum. Lewis suggested that such sequences form *feeling traps*, or self-perpetuating chains of emotions. The idea of feeling traps may point toward a solution of the puzzle of lifelong guilt, resentment, and hatred (see chapter 2).

Finally, Lewis developed a method of detecting low-visibility shame in discourse. She noted that in a *context* in which the patient sees himself from the therapist's point of view in a negative way, both the patient's *words* and *manner* (tone of voice, loudness, speech static, self-interruptions, and so on) suggest a state of shame. These three contributions can be used as a foundation for investigating the role of shame in conduct.

The Social Bond

Our earlier discussion about shame cultures and guilt cultures raises a crucial question about the connection between shame and social structure. Why are references to shame virtually absent in the New Testament, replaced by references to guilt? That is, what is the relationship between emotion and social structure? We propose that pride is the emotion that corresponds to secure bonds (social solidarity) and that shame corresponds to threatened bonds (alienation). Social structure and pride and shame are reciprocally related: the repression of shame causes and is caused by alienation. (The following section is based on the senior author's earlier discussion [Scheff 1990].

Sociology as a discipline arose out of the idea that modernization—the rise of urban industrial societies—is destructive of *community*. With social and geographic mobility and the free flow of information, modern societies have a potential for change that is unthinkable in a traditional society. Although limitless change has many advantages, it also gives rise to a substantial disadvantage: *All social bonds are at risk.* Not just one bond or another is threatened, but all bonds. For many members of modern societies, perhaps even the majority, their connections to others are never quite safe.

Suppose, as a basic premise, that everyone requires a minimal sense of belonging, a web of secure social bonds, and that for the average person, this minimum is never quite achieved. If so, the human condition in modern societies is like that of a fish out of water. The sustaining web has been lost. If one were to allow oneself to be aware of the loss, every moment of daily existence would be exquisitely painful.

We are not claiming, as Cooley and others have, that social bonds in traditional society are necessarily more secure than they are in modern societies. Our argument does not require the idealization of traditional society. In his analysis of suicide, Durkheim (1905) made the very important suggestion that closely knit communities do not necessarily guarantee adequate bonds: what he called "altruistic" and "fatalistic" cultures may produce suicide rates as high as or higher than anomic or egoistic ones.

Bowen (1978), who originated the family systems approach in psychotherapy, makes a similar distinction. He characterizes a well-ordered family system as one that is "differentiated"—that is, one in which the needs of each member can be negotiated, as can those of the family as a group. In families marked by what he calls *isolation*, there is inadequate negotiation because family members are rigidly separated as individuals. The culture in this type of family is characterized by what Durkheim called anomie or egoism. In families marked by what Bowen calls *engulfment*, there is also inadequate negotiation, but for the opposite reason: the family members are insufficiently differentiated as individuals. Instead there is "fusion": members find it difficult to negotiate their individual needs because of the demand for conformity and loyalty. Such a system corresponds to the type of society that Durkheim thought produced altruistic or fatalistic suicide.

We suggest that modern societies are characterized by isolation more than by secure bonds or engulfing bonds. From this point of view, it doesn't matter whether premodern societies were based on secure or engulfing bonds or on some mixture of the two. Bonds threatened because of isolation are continuously painful, regardless of the antecedent conditions.

How might a society defend its members against such pain? One defense would be to deny the very existence of the social bond. In an anomic society, a rigid *individualism* provides a defensive myth for organizing experience: the myth that the isolated individual is the only conceivable unit of human existence. Given this presupposition, the need for social bonds would become an unmentionable secret, even an unthinkable one.

We propose that modern societies have institutionalized the myth of individualism, as well as the denial of pride and shame, as defenses against the pain of threatened bonds. The beginnings of rigid individualism can be seen in children who have undergone the loss of parental care at an early age. These children take steps to defend themselves against the pain of further separation. The case of "Reggie" (Burlingham and Freud 1942) illustrates the point. Separated from his parents at five months of age, he formed a passionate attachment to his nurse in the orphanage. This attachment was suddenly broken when Reggie was two years, eight months old: his nurse, Mary-Ann, left to be married.

> He was completely lost and desperate after her departure, and refused to look at her when she visited him a fortnight later. He turned his

head to the other side when she spoke to him, but stared at the door, which had closed behind her, after she had left the room. In the evening in bed he sat up and said: "My very own Mary-Ann! But I don't like her." (p. 114)

Reggie defended himself against the pain of his second separation; he has rejected the rejector.

Burlingham and Freud, as well as Bowlby (1969, 1973, 1980) and others who have studied the effects of broken bonds, repeatedly report the same syndrome. After a lengthy period of futile calling for the missing loved one, these children learn their lesson. In effect they say, like Reggie, "Very well, if you are not coming, then I don't need you anyway. I am sufficient unto myself. I don't need anyone. *Ever.*" This defense is what Bowen (1978) calls "cut-off." In effect, it is a self-inflicted wound in response to a wounding social environment. Since one has suffered from separation in the past, one protects oneself by giving up hope, producing a self-perpetuating system.

The Microworld of Social Interaction

An important limitation of the reports in developmental psychology requires mention. Bowlby and other researchers seem to assume that bonds that are severed create more disruption than bonds that are threatened. In effect, they suggest that being a member of physically intact household, no matter what its emotional dynamics, is less damaging than being an orphan. But as Bowen's (1978) analysis of family systems suggests, this may not be the case. The threat to bonds in an engulfing or isolating family system are hidden and confusing. The disruption caused by such a family may be more enduring than the disruption suffered from severed bonds.

Extreme ideation of severed bonds can be found in the culture of peoples who have been enslaved. A spiritual of the southern black slaves provides an example:

Sometimes I feel like a motherless child.
Sometimes I feel like a motherless child.
Sometimes I feel like a motherless child.
A long, long way from home.
A long, long way from home.

The slaves were wrenched not only from their families but from their cultures; all their bonds were severed. When the destruction of bonds is unmistakable, however, it may be possible to form new ones.

In a white middle-class family that is physically intact, isolation or engulfment can occur even though it is hidden behind a facade of polite words. Conflict between members may be so disguised that its roots are virtually invisible to its members. These are the conditions that give rise to underground conflict in the form of "interminable quarrels" or "silent impasses" (Scheff 1987). Retzinger's (1988, 1991) analysis of marital quarrels also reports such relationships; they are marked by politeness but accompanied by emotional distance, boredom, lack of trust, and withdrawal of affection.

In a classic study (Labov and Fanshel 1977), two sociolinguists made a detailed, moment-to-moment examination of conversations that an anorexic psychotherapy patient reported having with her family. They showed how the daughter and mother were locked in a hidden system of mutual threat: the daughter threatened self-starvation, and the mother threatened abandonment. Their threats, recriminations, and insults were exchanged through innuendo, seemingly outside the awareness of the family members. To find the sources of conflict, Labov and Fanshel had to examine the dialogue utterance by utterance—not just the words, but the nonverbal gestures that accompanied each word, and the combination of words and gestures for their implications. (For our review and extension of this study, see chapter 7.)

In relationships marked by hidden conflict, the bond is continually threatened in a way that makes understanding and repair of the bond extremely difficult. Since their prototypic bonds are inadequate, the typical individual in such a family might find it just as difficult to form new bonds as to repair the old ones.

Is it possible for the relationships in a whole society to be physically intact but based on threatened or inadequate bonds? In such a society, we would expect to find individuals willing to accept relationships that do not meet their needs but that they tolerate because these relationships are felt to be better than isolation. In such circumstances, nationalism and other kinds of sectarian grouping may arise, providing what may be thought of as "pseudo-bonds." Rather than an attunement that balances the needs of the individual and the needs of the society, pseudo-bonds in nations, sects, cults, and other exclusive groups furnish only the semblance of community. In such sects, the members give up significant parts of themselves and their own needs, feelings, and points of view; they are engulfed. Engulfment damages both the individual and the group, because distinctive points of view may be needed for group survival.

The ideology of individualism and its subsidiaries—such as the myth of the "self-made man"—obscure the part/whole nature of social systems. *Such an ideology may be an adult parallel to a child's defenses against the intense pain that follows severed or threatened bonds.* Approaches that insist on viewing human issues in terms of isolated individuals may be defenses against the anomic conditions in our society. In modern societies, manifestations of the social bond are supressed, and the emotions that signal the state of the bond—pride and shame— are denied and disguised. (Calling attention to the subtle signs of the state of the bond will be the focus of chapter 2.)

Repression of Emotion: Anger and Shame

A good case has been recently made concerning the consequences of the repression of anger in modern civilization. We will use aspects of this study to illustrate the insidiousness of the repression of shame. Stearns and Stearns (1986) showed that there has been a change in the "advice" literature concerning anger over the last three hundred years. Using religious texts from the eighteenth century, educational and child-rearing texts from the nineteenth, and psychological and managerial advice from the twentieth, they demonstrated that attempts to control anger have become increasingly forceful and insistent.

The Stearnses showed that religious advice before the eighteenth century was aimed not at anger per se but only at *excessive* anger. The typical advice in sermons was not against getting angry, which was often even encouraged (righteous anger), but against excessive anger and against aggression. The authors showed that beginning in the eighteenth century, there was a gradual shift toward a more restrictive stance, ending in what they call the modern ambivalence toward anger: it is not just excessive anger and aggression that are forbidden, but *all* anger.

It would be difficult to overstate the importance of the Stearnses' findings. They can be interpreted as supporting and expanding a well-known theory that connects civilization with repression—the Freud-Reich-Marcuse thesis. This thesis has always remained at the hypothetical level, even for individual cases much less for a whole society. Inadvertently, the Stearnses found massive support for Elias's thesis connecting shame and the repression of anger (1978: 191–205). The Stearnses' findings may be the first convincing documentation of the civilization-repression thesis.

Although the Stearnses do not link shame and anger, as we do, their study can be used to show this link. Following Lewis (1971), we propose that anger is repressed because of shame. That is, all anger— not just excessive anger—is forbidden in modern societies, because people have been socialized to be ashamed of it. The Stearnses come very close to making this statement, but they never make it explicit. Instead, they use what we call code words for shame (see chapter 2) in describing people's feelings about anger in modern societies. They say that increasingly, over the last three hundred years, people are "anxious" about anger, or "uncomfortable," "embarrassed," or "guilty" about it. (For several examples of these terms in a single chapter, see pages 232, 234, 235, 236, and 239.)

These are some of the very emotion-words that we believe to be glosses for the more primitive emotion, shame. Inadvertently, in the very act of revealing the repression of one emotion—anger—the Stearns study continues the repression of another—shame—by using code words that disguise references to shame. Repression depends upon the use of language as part of an inadvertent conspiracy of silence.

Our discussion of shame to this point has been a brief review of an emotion that we suggest is much more complex and pervasive than contemporary usage would have it. Several points deserve reiteration. First, shame appears to be ignored and denied in modern civilization. It is openly considered in traditional societies but is hidden in modern ones. But there is a fugitive literature on shame, and we suggest that this literature contains powerful hints as to its importance in the human scene.

One of the implications of the scholarship of Cooley, Lewis, and other writers is that pride and shame are intimately connected with the structure and process of social bonds. We propose that these emotions are facets of social relationships. This proposal, we argue, provides a way of integrating psychological and sociological analysis, of connecting momentary personal events with social structure.

The last section of this chapter noted an affinity between shame and anger that is usually ignored. This affinity is central to our explanation of aggression and violence, both at the interpersonal level and at the societal level.

If we are to understand the role of shame in our civilization, a vital new language is needed—an emotion language that calls shame and other primitive emotions by their proper names. Contemporary language elides emotions, particularly the emotion of shame. In some ways, every theory is merely a verbal shorthand for a new language with which to name the universe. Such a language will be suggested in subsequent chapters. The next chapter provides a general theory that connects emotion, thought, social bonds, communication, and behavior.

2

Attunement, Emotion, and Communication: A Theory of Social Action

What forces bind members of a society together? What forces tear them apart? What forces cause cooperation and conflict? To understand violence, it is probably necessary to go beyond the local causes of each case and ask such foundational questions. The foundations have been prepared by classic and modern social theory, but they have not been fully explicated. In this chapter, we outline a micro-macro model of social action, that is oriented both to process and to structure. This model points toward *part/whole analysis* of systems and subsystems, from the largest wholes to the smallest parts.

In conjunction with chapter 3, this chapter illustrates what may be a new genre of sociology: not a separate theory or method or empirical study, but combination theory-method-empirical-study. Giddens's (1984) demand for instantiations of theory was a first step toward this new approach. We propose that by using a theory-driven systematic method—analysis of discourse—it may be possible to resolve the tensions between the micro and the macro, between art and science.

In our proposed theory, solidarity and alienation are poles of the extent of cognitive and emotional *attunement* between persons or groups. Following Cooley, Goffman, and Lewis, we propose that two emotions—pride and shame—play a crucial role. The level of attunement and emotion both cause and are caused by communication tactics. In this model, attunement and cooperation are interdependent; each is a cause and an effect of the other. The theory suggests that attunement, emotion, communication, and cooperation are constitutive elements in social systems.

The theory outlined here connects social structure with emotion and communication. First, it proposes that the level of social solidarity—alienation can be defined as the degree of *attunement* (mutual understanding and mutual ratification) between persons, and between groups as well. Second, it proposes that the degree of attunement and emotion are reciprocally interrelated: that solidarity causes and is caused by shared pride and that alienation causes and is caused by shared shame. Third, it proposes that the level of attunement and its accompanying emotional state causes and is caused by communication tactics between the persons or groups in the system. And fourth, it proposes that this system determines the level of cooperation and conflict. After reviewing the classic theory that is relevant, we will return to these four components of our own theory.

Classic Social Theory

Classic social theory, as represented by Marx, Durkheim, and Weber, contains a framework for understanding social structure and process, but only by implication. All three theorists were highly abstract, oriented toward macrostructure rather than microprocess. Their treatment of alienation and solidarity illustrates this point. Marx implied a distinction between alienated and solidary relationships, but at the level of whole societies. He described alienation in capitalist societies in detail. By contrast, his description of the structure of communist societies is vague. It implies that in communism, relationships to the means of production, others, and self would be solidary.

Like Marx's, Durkheim's approach is abstract and preliminary. In *The Division of Labor* (1893), he distinguished between two types of solidarity. "Mechanical solidarity," for Durkheim, suggested a small, traditional society. "Organic solidarity," he thought, was characteristic of modern industrial society. Mechanical solidarity was based on "like-mindedness," on similarity of thought and behavior. Organic solidarity, by contrast, arose out of differences and the complementarity of roles. One limitation of Durkheim's argument is that he did not explain solidarity itself, the forces that hold society together. Another is that he did not treat solidarity and alienation in a unified framework.

To locate Durkheim's conception of alienation, one must look to his empirical study *Suicide* (1905). As in his essay on the division of labor, there is no explicit treatment of solidarity. But his interpretation of his findings, which suggest two different types of alienation, points toward a definition.

Durkheim showed that the highest rates of suicide occur in two different social groups. He argued that one type of suicide is produced by a culture of anomie/egoism, in which the individual is isolated from the group. The other type of suicide, altruistic/fatalistic suicide, occurs in cultures in which the individual is overly bound to the group. His work has an important implication for a concept of solidarity: solidary relationships balance independence and attachment.

Durkheim's concept of the *conscience collective* (1961) is also suggestive for a theory of social action. The meaning of the French word *conscience* is broader than that of its English cognate: it implies not only the moral-emotional elements of our word *conscience*, but also consciousness. Durkheim's concept suggests a shared awareness that is both cognitive and emotional. This implication is important; society is not only a cognitive order, but also a moral-emotional one.

Like Marx and Durkheim, Weber did not develop a systematic theory. But his conception of social action (1947) has implications for a general theory. He proposed that actions are social to the extent that they are oriented toward the subjective intentions of the other persons involved. His methodology of the social sciences (1946) had the same implication; interpretive understanding, inferring the subjective orientation of actors, is necessary for an adequate understanding of human actions.

Like the idea of the conscience collective, Weber's concept of social action implies that intersubjectivity—mutual understanding—is the basis of social order. The approach of all these theorists to a model of social action is preliminary, however, in the sense that none of them consider the microprocesses that are necessary to arrive at mutual understanding.

Not all classic theorists have ignored the microworld of social interaction. Cooley's social psychology points toward the need for microanalysis in sociology. Like Durkheim and Weber, he emphasized intersubjectivity: we are constantly "living in the minds of others" (1902). In his description of the "looking-glass self," Cooley focused on the moral and emotional aspects of social order. Unlike other classic theorists, he specified the social emotions; either pride or shame invariably occurs when we see ourselves from the point of view of others (Scheff 1988). The theory outlined here rests upon this conjecture.

Modern Social Theory: Microprocess

Much of modern social theory continues the tradition of abstract treatments of macrostructure; Parsons's *The Social System* (1951) is one example. But the work of Goffman and Lewis suggests that microprocess is a vital part of social theory. Two themes in Goffman's work are particularly significant for the concept of attunement and its associated emotions. His careful description of a "state of talk" suggests a starting point for a concept of solidarity, and his analysis of embarrassment, for alienation.

In Goffman's formulation, "a state of talk" involves persons who "accredit each other as *legitimate* participants, . . . [a] process of *recip-*

rocal ratification. . . . A single focus of *thought and visual attention* [is] maintained" (1967: 34, emphasis added). The idea of legitimacy implies that social interaction involves a moral order: in solidary relationships participants award each other the deference appropriate to their status. Reciprocal ratification suggests that the social order is not static; status honor requires continuous affirmation. Finally, Goffman's definition of a "state of talk" points to two outcomes—a single focus of thought and visual attention. The focus of visual attention is significant for empirical research on attunement in face-to-face interaction, since it is an observable sign of an inner state (as in the studies of social bonds described in chapter 3).

Although Goffman sought only to define a "state of talk," a transitory moment at the microlevel, his definition points toward a definition of continuing solidarity at any level. We will base our definition of attunement on Goffman's idea of a "single focus of thought," although our conception is much more complex than Goffman's. To begin with, we include feeling as well as thought in attunement. Second, Goffman seemed to be thinking of a simple dichotomy: two parties are either in a "state of talk" or they are not. But level of attunment is a complex continuum involving varying degrees of mutuality about different topics.

Attunement and Social Bonding

We use the concept of attunement following Stern (1985), who has described the social bond between infants and their caretakers. Although Bruner does not use the term *attunement*, he (1983) has described a similar process. An example from Bruner: as a mother says, "See the pretty dolly!" she herself focuses her attention on the doll, wiggling it close to the baby's face to be sure of its attention. The child learns the name, but the child also learns attunment by sharing the single visual focus of attention and thought with the mother.

In his formulation, Bruner captured only the cognitive content of intersubjectivity; Stern captured both the cognitive and emotional content. Like most theorists of who have treated intersubjectivity, however (such as Schutz, Mead, and Dewey), Stern does not include the crucial social element of mutual ratification that Goffman emphasized.

In a completely secure bond, each party understands and ratifies not only the other's present thoughts, feelings, and actions but also their intentions and character—their *being*, so to speak. This distinction has considerable significance for understanding the nature of personal relations and for social structure. The quest for secure bonds, the quest to be cognitively and emotionally *connected*, appears to be instinctive in all humans and other social creatures. Hearne (1986) has argued that domesticated animals, such as dogs, horses, and cats, seek secure bonds with their human owners.

Hearne's commentary implies an important corrective to the theoretical work on attunement by Goffman, Stern, and others. Their work focuses on intersubjective accord, mutual understanding, only in the moment. In a "state of talk," the actors understand at least some of each other's words and gestures at the time they occur. This emphasis misses understanding and ratification by the interacting parties of each other's *being*, of their long-range intentions and their character.

It is important to note that not even a completely secure bond necessarily implies *agreement*. Competitors may have a secure bond but such a bond implies only that they will fight fairly. If one or both participants demands agreement and conformity, the implication, from our point of view, is that the bond is insecure: they are *engulfed*. Such bonds can give the outward appearance of intense attachment. But on close inspection one would find that engulfment always requires "de-selfing," giving up major parts of the self in order to stay in the relationship. Only similarities are tolerated; differences are seen as disloyalty or even betrayal. Bonds of this kind, according to our theory, interfere with the survival potential of the larger group in which the relationships occurs, if not with that of the relationship itself.

In a *completely* insecure bond, there is no understanding or ratification of the other; there is mutual misunderstanding, lack of understanding, and rejection of the other. In such a relationship, the parties may coordinate their behavior, but since they are intellectually and emotionally alienated, the task will be in jeopardy (as suggested in chapter 3).

Contrary to the simple dichotomy in Goffman's description of a "state of talk," actual relationships are seldom completely solidary or completely alienated, but involve varying mixtures of the two. The completely secure and completely insecure bonds described above are only limiting cases, ideal types that never appear in reality. For that reason, it is important to develop descriptions of the cues to the *degree* of attunement.

To conform to current usage, which demands different terms for microlevels and macrolevels, we refer to the degree of solidarity at the microlevel as involving the state of the social bond; we refer to a relationship involving attunement as a *secure* bond. A relationship lacking attunement involves a *insecure or severed* bond.

The bond concept originates in Bowlby's attachment theory (1969, 1973, 1988) and it is congruent with family systems theory (Bowen 1978) and with Durkheim's treatment of alienation. As in Durkheim's conception, Bowen (1978) proposed that bonds could be insecure in two opposite ways. One type of bond, characterized by *isolation*, occurs in families in which members are inadequately bound to the group. The other type, characterized by *engulfment*, occurs in families in which members are overly bound. These two types of family systems correspond to anomic-egoistic and altruistic-fatalistic groups, respectively. Although unaware of his work, modern family systems theory is Durkheimian. Like Durkheim, however, it is not specific about emotions.

Like Durkheimian theory, attachment theory (Bowlby 1980) strongly implies that the nearer people are to a state of bondlessness, the more likely it is that violent emotions and behavior will arise. To the extent that people literally have no one to turn to, they are likely to become violent or mentally ill or both. All of our case studies support this proposition, whether the relationship is at the interpersonal level or at the level of societies or civilizations.

Attunement and Emotions

Goffman's definition of a "state of talk" implies that there is a relationship between social structure and emotions. Ratification of the other party as a legitimate participant must not only be felt but expressed. If it is not expressed, the other party may be offended, giving rise to the emotions appropriate to being insulted, devalued, or rejected. Threats to the bond between persons or groups generate intense emotions. These considerations led to Goffman's analysis of the role of embarrassment in social encounters.

Goffman did not limit his analysis to thought and behavior but included emotion as an important component. His discussion of "states of talk" occurs as part of his treatment of "face," the ritual expressing the social worth of interactants. Although Durkheim had suggested that emotion is a key aspect of ritual, this element remained vague in his work since he named no specific emotions.

Goffman, by contrast, named the specific emotion that he saw at the core of ritual defining the self; he proposed that embarrassment (and anticipation of embarrassment) is the key to understanding "face-work" (1967), as well as what he had earlier called "impression management" (1959). Goffman's interactants are exquisitely sensitive to the exact nuances of how others treat them, undergoing embarrassment when they receive inadequate deference. Although he did not use the terms *pride* and *shame* as Cooley did, Goffman's analysis is in the spirit of the looking-glass self.[1]

---

[1]Although embarrassment has been considered an emotion distinct from shame, we treat both it and humiliation as shame variants, as others have done (Tomkins 1963; Lewis 1971; Elias 1978, 1982; Izard 1977; Wurmser 1981).

As we indicated in chapter 1, recent discussions suggest that shame may be as crucial an emotion in modern societies as it has long been thought to be in traditional ones (Lewis 1971, 1976; Elias 1972, 1982; Braithwaite 1989; Scheff 1990). Goffman's treatment of face and embarrassment has been supported by a large-scale, cross-cultural review of studies of politeness behavior (Brown and Levinson 1987). Brown and Levinson propose that protecting face (through politeness) is a universal feature of all known societies. They define face as Goffman did, in terms of avoiding embarrassment or humiliation (1987:61). Shame dynamics may be a universal feature of social interaction in all cultures.

The relation between social bonds and emotion was developed by Helen Lewis (1977). In her analysis of infant-caretaker relations and adult relations in modern societies, she made explicit what was implied by Cooley and Goffman: that shame and threats to the social bond are interdependent aspects of the same reality. *Shame is the emotional aspect of disconnection between persons.*

Lewis proposed that there is a universal human nature, one that unites biology and culture. She suggested that studies in infant development have demonstrated a biological initiation of social competence. The infant-caretaker studies (Bowlby 1980; Tronick, 1982; Stern 1985; and other human development studies) have established that neonates have social skills virtually at birth, including turn-taking with gaze (looking at and away from the caretaker) and giving and receiving affection (smiling behavior). This biological heritage is enormously elaborated and redirected by learning, however: social solidarity begins in the nursery. Lewis proposed that humans are social by both biological and cultural inheritance. As we indicated in chapter 1, emotions play a crucial role in her approach. Since her formulations are the starting place for this book, we must expand our review of her work.

Lewis (1976) referred to pride and shame (and associated emotions such as guilt and anger) as the *attachment emotions*. These emotions are cause and effect of moment-by-moment changes in the social relationships between persons. (Kemper [1978] make a similar claim.) This formulation is important to sociological research for two reasons. First, it points to shame as an observable indicator of alienation (as illustrated by the two studies reported in chapter 3).

Lewis's formulation is also important because it implies an answer to our central question about the forces that build and disrupt social relationships. In an apparent paradox, Lewis suggested that one form of shame is a binding force and that another is an alienating one. Independently of Lewis, Braithwaite's (1989) theory of shaming behavior proposes the same idea. To understand that the Lewis-Braithwaite formulation is not self-contradictory, it is necessary to spell it out in detail.

In her study of emotions in psychotherapy (1971), Lewis systematically rated cues for shame and anger, moment by moment, in audiotapes of several hundred sessions. For this purpose she used the Gottschalk-Gleser scale (1969) for rating emotions in verbal texts. Her method was to interpret each Gottschalk-Gleser rating in the situational *context* in which it occurred. Following Darwin, James, McDougall, Cooley, and others, she defined the shame context as one in which the client seemed to be imagining self from the viewpoint of a negative other.

The method Lewis used combines system (Gottschalk-Gleser scales) and intuition (inferring context from the client's comments, such as "You [the therapist] must think I'm crazy"). This method is a potent combination since it is systematic yet avoids decontexualizing the data. (See the discussion of context and functionalist theory elsewhere in this chapter.) Her method was a form of what is today called *discourse analysis*. It could be used to establish micro-macro linkage in discourse between individuals and between groups. In this way, it would provide instantiation (Giddens 1984) at both the micro level and the macro-level, and trace the linkage between them.

Lewis's findings can be summarized in four points. First, although her study detected many episodes of emotion, shame was by far the most *prevalent* emotion, far outranking anger, grief, and fear, for example. Second, virtually all the shame episodes were *unacknowledged* by either party. That is, neither the patient nor the therapist commented on most of the shame states that Lewis's ratings revealed, or even seemed to be aware of them. At first glance, this finding is puzzling, since other emotions, such as anger and grief, were often acknowledged by one or both parties. How could a client's state of shame go unnoticed by both client and therapist?

Third, Lewis suggested in answer to this question that adults in our society virtually always deny and disguise shame. *Denied shame* takes two forms, both of which disguise an emotion from the self and/or the other. The first form of denied shame is what she called *overt shame*. In this form, the client felt emotional *pain* to the point of slowing or disrupting his or her thought and speech. There was usually flustering and unwanted physical symptoms, such as blushing, sweating, or a pounding heartbeat. The meaning of this syndrome was disguised, however, by misnaming. Instead of referring explicitly to shame, the client used code words such as *awkward, uncomfortable, insecure, stupid, rejected,* or similar words. (A list is provided by Gottschalk et al. [1969] in their "shame-anxiety" scale.) The meaning of the experience was disguised by a coded label, a form of denial.

Lewis referred to the second form of denied shame as *bypassed shame*. This form had characteristics opposite to those of overt shame:

there was little pain, and thought and speech were speeded up rather than slowed down. In this form, the individual appeared to distract the self from pain by rapid activity. Although behavior was fluent, it was slightly off-key. This form of denied shame corresponds to Adler's (1956) "drive for power," which he thought to be a form of what he called the "inferiority complex" (chronic shame). Although behavior caused by bypassed shame is goal-oriented, it is as irrational as the behavior caused by overt shame; it is obsessive and compulsive. This finding is directly relevant to the theory of society as a moral order, since it suggests a micro-macro model of conscience and conscienceless-ness.

Even in the most technical discussions of morality, conscience is taken to be an elemental; its meaning is never unpacked. For example, instead of explaining conscience, psychoanalytic theory merely gives it another name, the superego. Lewis's discovery of bypassed shame points toward an explicit model of conscience.

The connection between shame and conscience has been implied in many discussions. As we have seen in chapter 1, two thousand years ago, the poet Ovid (A.D. 7) connected the two: "in this age of wicked-ness, every species of crime burst forth. . .[when] shame, truth and honor took flight." Wickedness involves shamelessness, a loss of the sense of shame. (Schneider 1977). Shame functions as an automatic pilot, a gyroscope. When it is bypassed, individuals and groups lose their moral direction, leading to conflict and anarchy.

The cases in this book illustrate this point. In chapter 8, for exam-ple, in our analysis of Hitler's appeal to the Germans, we show that due the circumstances in his family of origin, Hitler was virtually bond-less from infancy. His personal history shows bypassed shame in every sphere. His fantasy of national solidarity (a "folk community") and his humiliated fury had unlimited appeal to the Germans, who were also suffering from alienation and shame states. They and their leader trans-formed their experience of bondlessness and humiliation into murder-ous rage, using the bypassing operation described by Lewis. (Katz [1989], working independently, has also suggested that the transforma-tion of humiliation into rage is a cause of homicide.) The individual and collective dynamics of shame may be a key to understanding con-flict and anarchy. The social order is a moral-emotional structure, as well as a cognitive-behavioral one.

The fourth point that Lewis made was to distinguish normal shame from pathological shame. When shame is acknowledged rather than denied, it is of brief duration—usually lasting less than a minute—and serves as a signal, allowing for the repair of damaged bonds. ("When I do something stupid, if I say 'That was stupid,' everyone laughs and we get on with it.") Denial occurs when one is ashamed of being ashamed.

Under these conditions, shame becomes recursive and self-perpetuating. Unacknowledged shame builds a wall between persons and between groups. A chain reaction occurs, shame building on shame. Loops of this kind are both internal and social, occurring both within and between parties (Retzinger 1985, 1987, 1989, 1991; Scheff 1987, 1988, 1989, 1990). This formulation provides a micromodel of pathological shame.

A distinction similar to ours between normal and pathological shame forms the basis for Braithwaite's (1989) analysis of crime causation and control. Independently of Lewis, he proposed that "reintegrative" (normal) shaming leads to the effective control of crime, but stigmatization, analogous to pathological shaming, leads to high crime rates. Although Braithwaite's theory focuses on shaming behavior rather than shame itself, it is exactly parallel to Lewis's model.

Lewis found that unacknowledged (pathological) shame damages the interpersonal bond; Braithwaite found that stigmatizing shame damages the bond between the punisher and the punished, leading to the formation of criminal subgroups. Although Lewis studied discourse at the microlevel and Braithwaite studied punishment at the macrolevel, they reached the same conclusion. We will call it the Lewis-Braithwaite hypothesis: that normal shame and shaming produce social solidarity, whereas pathological shame and shaming produce alienation.

Communication

To this point, our discussion has concerned two dimensions of a new theory—social bonding and emotion. A third dimension of the theory concerns communication tactics. Secure bonds demand and are based on direct communication. Insecure bonds generate and are caused by indirect and inadequate communication (Retzinger 1991; Scheff 1987, 1988, 1989, 1990). The isolated form of alienation is usually accompanied by silence or destructive conflict; the engulfed form by conformity and the withholding of "negative" information. One obvious example of dysfunctional communication is a quarrel in which each side blames the other and neither side acknowledges its own part in causing conflict. We are prepared to argue that open communication is functional for social relationships, while indirect and inadequate communication is dysfunctional.

We argue this proposition with some trepidation, given the depth of the belief held by sociologists that full disclosure is a threat to relationships. Most sociologists currently seem to believe that Simmel based this idea on theoretical grounds, and that in her study of blue-collar marriage, Komarovsky (1967) demonstrated it to be true.

It would require at least a chapter in itself to do justice to the depth and complexity of Simmel's ideas on the social functions of secrecy. Suffice it to say here that although we believe his discussion to be a valuable source of ideas about social relationships, it confounds the very dimensions we wish to separate—that is, patterns of social bonding, emotion, communication, and cooperation.

For example, Simmel began his discussion of the social role of secrecy by contrasting the secret with what he calls "the childish stage," in which "every conception is expressed at once, and every undertaking is accessible to eyes of all" (1955:330). In our view, there are two significant confoundings in this single sentence. The first confounding is the apparent assumption that one must either be secretive or reveal everything, like a child does.

We agree with Simmel that revealing everything that one thinks or feels can be as damaging to relationships as keeping secrets. But such impulsive revelation is not the only alternative to secrecy. At the age to which Simmel's image refers, children have yet to develop a sense of the relevancy of information and its emotional impact on the other. In our society, virtually all adults are able to communicate in a way that ensures that most of the message is relevant to the particular context.

The assessment and management of the emotional impact of our messages, however, is another matter entirely. It is true, as Goffman points out, that we are frequently tactful about preserving the "face" of the other, if only to protect our own face. But Goffman hinted—and our case studies demonstrate—that one can show a kind of surface tact and still wound the other person in a most pernicious way. Because of the complexity of human communication, one can be polite and civil but still communicate various and offensive kinds of innuendo. (See our discussion of the styles of communication in subsequent chapters, especially in chapters 4 to 7).

When we speak of direct communication, what we have in mind is the revealing of one's thoughts and feelings in a way that is *respectful* of the other. Satir's (1972) concept of "leveling" comes quite close: it refers to communication between parties about thoughts and feelings that is respectful but direct (that is, avoids using subterfuges and evasions such as denial, triangling, and the like). With such communication, it is possible to disagree or even to quarrel without damaging the bond. At the same time that one is disagreeing about *content*, one's *manner* is respectful of the other. It is exactly this combination of content and manner that is absent from the conflict we examine in our cases.

The second confounding in Simmel's formulation is the dichotomy he contructed between secrecy and communication in which "every undertaking is accessible to the eyes of all." Once again he created a false opposition between secrecy and openness. In the phrase we have quoted, he drew in the difference between private and public communication, even though he was ostensibly discussing the difference between reserve and disclosure in marriages. Obviously one usually avoids public disclosure of many matters that must be revealed in private; both the avoidance of public disclosure and the necessity of private disclosure are required to maintain relationships. But this difference of venue is tangential to Simmel's basic formulation of the social functions of secrecy.

Perhaps the most damaging aspect of Simmel's analysis is his failure to take seriously some of the negative effects of secrecy. We briefly referred to this issue in chapter 1 in our discussion of the repression of sexuality; children were, and to some extent still are, kept in ignorance of and, as important, ashamed about their own natural functions. Silence and repression go hand in glove—a fact Simmel did not note.

Another kind of negative effect of secrecy occurs in the wider political arena. The Iran-Contra scandal exposed only one episode of what must be the continual secreting of vital information by governments from the public that they are supposedy serving. For democracies to be effective and just, their publics must have access to the actions that affect them. One of the tragedies of our time has been the growth of governmental secrecy, which may effectively negate the parallel growth of democratic forms. (For a scholarly discussion of some of the tragic effects of secrecy caused by conscious deceptions, see Bok, 1978).

The effect of disclosure and secrecy on the functioning of public opinion can be seen by contrasting the Salman Rushdie incident with the pattern of U.S covert action in South and Central America. Because the Ayatollah's death sentence on Rushdie was made openly, not secretly, world opinion was effectively aroused. But the death sentences on democratic reformers that is implied by U.S. policy is covert, effectively paralyzing world opinion. Hitler rose to power after World War I occurred against a backdrop of the secret negotiations that made World War II inevitable. Simmel, who had little interest in political and historical events, apparently was unaware of these issues. In our opinion, his analysis of the effects of secrecy is vitiated by his lack of awareness of macroeffects, as well as by the inconsistencies and contradictions in his interpretation of interpersonal relations.

Komarovsky argued that her findings about blue-collar marriages support Simmel's defense of secrecy in marriage: "Married partners sometimes achieve a satisfying relationship precisely because they are able to grant one another considerable privacy" (1967:142). In this brief space we cannot adequately review Komarovsky's justifiably renowned study. We will argue that because of her somewhat selective reading of Simmel and because of her methodology, her findings should be not be taken as definitive on the usefulness of secrecy.

A close reading of Simmel suggests that although he did propose that reserve may be useful in some situations, he was careful to note that it can also be damaging. For example, he noted that "the range of secrecy is often extended much too far, in clumsy and undifferentiated fashion" (1960:331). Although Simmel probably had formal organizations in mind in this passage, his observation is equally applicable to intimate relations. Furthermore, his discussion in context often suggests that he was thinking of secrecy as consciously intended; our discussion is far broader, however, since it includes both conscious and unconscious withholding of information. Indeed, our studies suggest that the unconscious withholding of information is far more consequential for social systems than is intentional reserve.

The issue of inadvertent withholding is related to a second issue— cultural conservatism and radicalism in social studies. Komarovsky seems to have thought that the verbal responses of her subjects concerning their marital satisfaction should be considered the basic data for understanding their relationship. From our point of view, however, members' conscious beliefs and feelings about their relationships are only one facet of a complex reality. Most of the alienation and shame that our approach detects are not part of the subjects' conscious awareness. Indeed, what makes alienation and shame pathogenic is their very *lack* of acknowledgment. Komarovsky's study was content with exploring the surface contours of relationships; our studies explore their depths.

The difference between studies of surfaces and studies of undercurrents is related to a very general issue in human studies—the polarity between conservative and radical approaches. Research that investigates only the surface of social life—behavior that is easily observed, subjects' conscious beliefs, official statistics, and so on—usually results in only a picture of the status quo, the social arrangements currently in place in a society. Many social theories confound the status quo, a particular social order, with the generic concept of social order. This kind of confounding is perhaps Mills's (1959) most important criticism of Parsons's theory of the social system.

Studies of surface appearances need not be conservative, but they usually are. Mannheim (1936) made a fundamental distinction between *ideological* and *utopian* attitudes. He argued persuasively that ideologues—those who uphold the status quo—and utopians—those who rebel against it—live in two different universes. Ideology, in his sense, is myopic, it can see no further than the status quo. For ideologues, whatever is, is right. Utopians are also blind, but in the opposite way: for them, whatever is, is wrong. Their consciousness is transfixed by a vision of a world different from the present one. Mannheim's definitions concern polar ideal types, of course; in real life most approaches are mixtures of the two.

We believe that Komarovsky's interpretation of her findings is a mixture also, but with a definite leaning toward the ideological. Her methodology, which is based on interview responses, limits her perspective to the conscious beliefs of her subjects. Our methodology, which allows us to make inferences about innuendo and undercurrents, pushes our approach—also a mixture—in the utopian direction.

Our use of the terms *conservative* and *radical*, like Mannheim's, is somewhat different from conventional usage. In ordinary language, *conservative* and *radical* usually refer to political and economic ideas. But our usage is much broader; we have in mind attitudes toward the whole culture, as Mannheim did. From our point of view, most political and economic radicalism is actually just as culturally conservative as its seeming opposite, conservatism. Most political radicals seem to be as emeshed in the status quo as their opposites. Their radicalism involves a single issue, such as ownership of the means of production, rather than subsuming all the fundamental issues throughout the broad spectrum of the social order.

Komarovsky's approach led her to endorse preserving the marital relations she studied, no matter what the hidden costs. Her methods gave her little access to the hidden features of marriages. For this reason, we argue, she ignored them. Our theory, by contrast, predicates that most aspects of relationships are carefully hidden—not only by the marital partners, but also *from* them. To discover the basic parameters of a relationship, it is necessary to make repeated microscopic observations of the discourse that occurs within it. (We return to the issue of appropriate methodology at the end of this chapter.)

We prepose four basic dimensions of relationships: *the state of the bond* (the degree of attunement), *the state of the accompanying emotions, patterns of communication*, and *the degree of cooperation*. The relationships among these four variables in the theory are shown in figures 2–2 and 2–3.

Note that the fact that the state of the bond is in the first position does not imply that it is causally prior to shame; each relates to the other reciprocally. Shame is the emotional aspect of alienation; alienation is the relational aspect of shame. Being connected with others is instinctive in humans and all other social creatures.

Our theory proposes that protracted destructive conflict is not caused by conflict of interests. Compromise can always be secured that

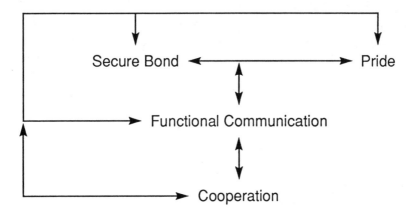

Figure 2–2. Social Solidarity and Cooperation

will maximally reward or at least minimally damage the contending parties, provided there is some bond between them. In this context, unacknowleged emotions do not interfere with direct communication and negotiation, which lead to settlement. *Unacknowledged* alienation and emotion, on the other hand, *always* lead to dysfunctional communication, which results either in separation or in protracted conflict.

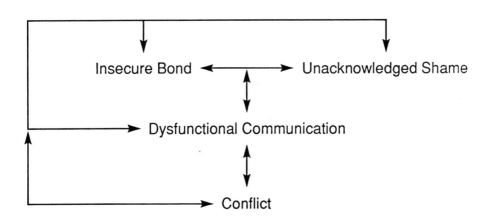

Figure 2–3. Alienation and Conflict

In order to locate our theory within existing sociological theories and methods, we have, for the most part, utilized preexisting terms, such as *social bond, solidarity,* and *alienation,* but we have given them special meanings that are uniquely our own. Our usage is a step toward specifying the meaning of these terms to the point that they can be applied to actual instances of behavior.

A Model of Social Action

The discussion so far suggests foundations for a micro/macro theory of social action, of how social process and structure interact. Social action produces and is produced by cognitive and emotional attunement between persons and between groups. Pride and shame, posited to be universal, pancultural emotions, play a crucial role in both generating and signaling solidarity and alienation. Our theory is congruent with earlier structure/process approaches. In particular, it revives and expands structural-functional ideas. A brief review will establish this connection.

The core idea of functionalism is that a working culture is a system, its components interconnected. Functional thinking postulates that elements in a viable culture are integrated, that each is linked to the whole system. Although this idea was once attractive, it was abandoned because no way was found to test it. A theory and method are needed to determine the extent to which a part of a cultural is integrated with the whole.

Like classic social theory, functionalism was stated in terms of abstract macrostructure, with no microprocess. *Discourse analysis,* however, may provide that microprocessual underpinning. The analysis of discourse between individuals and between groups can be used to demonstrate interpersonal and institutional linkages between elements of a culture.

The foundations for such a perspective were laid by Wittgenstein's (1953) discussion of the structure of ordinary language. He demonstrated that even a simple rule—"Stop at red lights"—required what he called "mastery of practice," or understanding a whole normative structure. The failure of automated translation by computer points in a similar direction. It suggests that the meaning of any word or sentence of ordinary language is ambiguous in itself; consensual meaning can be understood only in a vast matrix of words and actions. The ability of members of a group to understand ordinary language is an example of functional integration.

In recent communication theory, societies and their subcomponents are referred to as "open systems"; that is, they are composed of a very large number of items, the meaning of each being ambiguous when considered in isolation from the system. Such open systems contrast with ones that are "closed"; closed systems are games like tic-tac-toe and chess, computer programs, and mathematics. In closed systems, there is no ambiguity whatever in the meaning of the isolated components of the system. (For discussions of the usefulness of ambiguity, see Levine 1985; Scheff 1990.)

Functional thinking has important theoretical and methodological ramifications. It implies that any concept or hypothesis should be linkable. Social analysis can be seen as componential: institutions, relationships, roles, messages, even words and gestures are subcomponents of larger systems—that is, societies and civilizations. This formulation implies a metatheory that social inquiry requires *part/whole analysis*. That is, concepts and hypotheses need to be considered within a framework that connects them with the social system of which they are part.

The concept of the hologram provides a strong representation of the implications of functionalism. In open systems, each subcomponent is partially autonomous, yet also serves the larger system of which it is a part. It reproduces elements of the larger and smaller units with which it is connected, as beautifully illustrated in the study of fractals (Goldberger et al 1990). In open systems, a unit is partially autonomous, but it also serves the whole system. Each unit shares some of its characteristics with the larger system within which it is embedded, but it also has features that distinguish it from other levels.

In social systems, each relationship shares some characteristics with all other relationships, but each is also distinctive. To the extent that a viable social order exists, most relationships serve the larger society, as well as pursue their own ends. Contrary to current intellectual fashion, it is not necessarily a mistake to posit similar patterns at the micro and macrolevels. Patterns of *character*, perduring types of perception, emotion, and motivation, might well occur in both interpersonal and international relationships. They concept of national character has been rejected because it was originally employed as an *assumption*. It may be important to revive it as a *hypothesis*.

The concept of character is a part of the micro/macro theory proposed here. To avoid protracted conflict and anarchy, it may be necessary that attunement involve not only a mutual understanding of momentary meanings in discourse, but also long-term emotions, intentions, and character. This point may help to solve problems that seem otherwise intractable.

The discussion of the causes of World War I is a notorious example, since it is a continuing embarrassment in many different disciplines. Even a cursory examination of the relevant documents suggests that there was a profound lack of attunement within and among the participant nations. Although each nation understood the meaning of the others' diplomatic communications well enough, it is clear that there was little understanding of the others' character, emotions, or long-range intentions, or of those of the subgroups within their own nation.

The most dramatic illustration of this point is that each side thought that it could easily and quickly win the war, grossly misunderstanding the other side's ability and commitment—and, in the case of Russia, its own. These issues concern failure of attunement at a deep level—the level of character, a vital part of the world cultural system (Scheff 1990, chap. 5). Our theory proposes an analysis of relations between parts and wholes, within and between groups.

In this chapter we proposed a new theory of social action. We argued that the level of cooperation is determined by communication tactics, which in turn are generated by the state of the social bond and its accompanying emotions. The basic theory can be stated in the form of two propositions:

1. High levels of cooperation are based on effective communication patterns, which depend upon attunement and pride.
2. Destructive conflict is caused by dysfunctional patterns of communication, which are generated by unacknowledged alienation and shame.

All the studies reported in subsequent chapters illustrate one or both of these propositions. These studies also illustrate the application of a new method—part/whole analysis of discourse—which we argue is appropriate to our theory.

The definitions of the state of the social bond, types of communication, and types of emotions that we have provided in this chapter form the basis for our analysis of discourse. In our usage, sociological concepts such as *solidarity* and *alienation* are no longer mere metaphors, lacking in specific meaning. The definitions and propositions in this chapter specify their meaning to the point that they can be applied to specific episodes of behavior. For example, manifestations of pride are indicators of solidarity, and shame that is not acknowledged, is an indication of alienation.

Attunement is indicated by direct but respectful communication and by the absence of triangling, projection, denial, and the like. Even the particular kind of alienation can be specified, on the basis of emotion cues and patterns of communication: engulfment is usually signaled by signs of overt shame and by the absence of references to self (statements concerning "we," "us," and "ours" predominate). Obversely, isolation is signaled by signs of bypassed shame and by ideation and signs of separation ("I," "you," "me," and "mine" predominate). Such cues provide objective evidence for what have hitherto been only conceptual, visible signs of the nature of social relationships and social structure. The next chapter provides a preliminary report of two empirical studies that illustrate and provide rudimentary support for our theory and method.

3

Two Videotape Studies of Social Action[1]

This chapter introduces the first empirical studies, two investigations that illustrate and support our theory. Before we present them, we first review some issues concerning research methods.

In ordinary life, people continually make part/whole inferences; it is necessary for them to do so to get through the day. Based on observable cues, words, and manner, people make inferences about inner experiences that are not directly observable. In assessing their friends and relations, business opportunities, and world affairs, they make rapid inferences about other people's capacities, intentions, and character. An appropriate methodology for exploring our theory must follow a similar path.

In ordinary life, the problem with making such inferences is that people seldom have the skill or the time to investigate the extent to which they are true. The same limitation applies to much of the knowledge that comes through the mass media. Editors and reporters often lack the skill and the time—and in some instances, the inclination—to carefully investigate the inferences that they make and the conclusions they draw.

In our analysis we follow a method that appears to combine the strengths of intuition with those of systematic analysis, of common sense and expert knowledge, but that avoids or at least diminishes their limitations (Scheff 1990, chap. 8). We apply general concepts, such as attunement and dysfunctional communication, to actual instances, second by second. Our procedure, like any procedure, has advantanges and disadvantages. One obvious disadvantage is that we must start with the laborious analysis of single cases. For this reason, we cannot test how general our findings are.

---

[1]The studies reported in this chapter are based on research assistance at a high level of competence, resourcefulness, and creativity. For the first study, on *Candid Camera*, credit is due C. R. Macchi; for the second, on game shows, to Jillian R. Buss, Josh Miller, and Lori Terry.

Why would we want to conduct laborious studies of single cases, when we are unable to assess the generalizability of the results? Why not go immediately to the stage of aggregating cases into a sample of a respectable size? The answer to this question lies at the core of our study. We argue that in order to aggregate cases, one must inevitably shear away most of the context of the events that one is studying. But in the case of the subject matter we are studying—alienation and its accompanying emotions—the basic cues are deeply *embedded* in the context of each case. To aggregate the cases would be to cause our subject matter to vanish. Although the aggregation of data has many useful consequences, preserving the exact context is not one of them.

At first glance, our method may seem to be lacking in reliability and validity, even for the single cases themselves. But we argue that this is not the case. Because of the availability of our data to the interested reader, our findings are directly falsifiable, which gives them a warrant that is not available for most studies. Some of the discourse we analyze is publicly available, such as Goethe's novel and Hitler's *Mein Kampf.* Those that are not, such as the *Candid Camera* excerpts, we will make available to the interested reader at cost.

We argue that the availability of these tapes—the recorded discourse—gives our findings the potential for reliability and validity— a solution to the problem of "thick description." (See the extension of Geertz's methodology in Scheff 1986.) Intuitive interpretations of texts are unreliable unless the reader has access to the raw discourse. Having the same access as the author, however, empowers the reader; he or she is then free to criticize, modify, or support the author's findings.

This method has the potential to promote the interested reader to being a participant in the original research. In chapter 7, we demonstrate this process. Because the original audiotape of Rhoda's session became available to us, we were able to extend Labov and Fanshel's investigation of it, even though their study was already extraordinarily thorough and precise. We were able to build upon Labov and Fanshel's analysis by focusing on an aspect of their data and findings that they had not developed—the emotions of the subjects. In doing so we were able to provide support for many of their findings and add new findings of our own.

Our approach has a type of falsifiability that is very rare in human studies. In most reseach, the original data are not available to the reader. In order to test the findings, the reader must conduct a new study. If the new findings are negative, there is still ambiguity about the original study: Do the negative findings imply that the original study is invalid, or only that they do not hold true for the new research site? In our approach, the validity of the original findings can be tested definitively by the interested reader.

Brief descriptions of two recent studies illustrate our theory. The first concerns the close relationship between shame and the disruption of social bonds. The second shows the contexts that evoke pride and shame, and the effects of those emotions on cooperation.

Both studies use videotapes of broadcast television. The first involves the "moment of truth" on *Candid Camera*; the second, the moment when game-show contestants find out whether they have won or lost. Both situations evoke abrupt changes in social relationships and intense emotions.

One problem in studies of emotion has been the difficulty of obtaining clear examples. For ethical and other reasons, laboratory experiments and social surveys have not generated high levels of emotion. Fieldwork is more likely to find such moments, but rarely a large number of comparable moments. The subjects of *Candid Camera* and of game shows are in strictly comparable situations with high emotion potential.

The format of *Candid Camera* invariably produces a moment of rupture in the social bond between the subject and the "host"—Allan Funt or his co-workers. Subjects have been tricked into thinking they are attuned with the host, that they share the same definition of the situation as he. At the moment of truth, they find that they have been betrayed, are victims of a hoax. This realization usually gives rise to displays of intense emotion.

The format of TV game shows, too, leads to momentary changes in social relationships and strong emotions, although less intense than those on *Candid Camera*. For our study, we chose game shows that involve pairs or larger groups of contestants rather than lone individuals. Winning prizes usually produces signs of positive emotions and of solidarity, while losing produces signs of painful emotions and alienation. We first describe the methods and findings of the *Candid Camera* study.

Emotion and Attunement in Candid Camera

We collected 254 consecutive episodes from broadcasts of *Candid Camera*. We excluded only those that did not involve a moment of truth or that ended too soon to determine the participant's emotional reactions. There were many of the former (such as conversations with children), but few of the latter. Reactions to the moment of truth were usually shown for at least a minute.

In many of the episodes, the subjects showed intense arousal. In virtually all cases, the first reaction was *surprise* (a widening of the eyes, and in more extreme cases, highly visible gestures such as opening of the mouth and recoil of the head). The next phase involved *embarrassment* (shame). In addition to surprise and embarrassment, a substantial minority also *laughed* or manifested signs of *anger* (scowls, sarcasm, cursing, hitting, or throwing objects).

The subjects seemed embarrassed not only because they had been tricked, but because they had been tricked in public, a humiliation. Additionally, they may have felt they had allowed themselves to be completely taken in, without any redeeming suspicion on their part. In the words of several of the subjects, they felt "like idiots," "foolish," or "stupid." (Gottschalk et al. [1969] rate such phases as shame cues.) For shame to occur, one must place at least part of the blame on oneself. In these cases, apparently, the subjects blamed themselves for being taken in rather than the perpetrators for betraying them.

Our interpretation is supported by a deviant case, an episode unlike the others, in which the subjects were skeptical from the start. In this case there were two subjects; they discussed their suspicions when Allan Funt's confederates were absent. They sensed that something was wrong, even though they couldn't identify it. Neither showed shame at the moment of truth. There was brief and slight laughter, but no intense emotional arousal. Perhaps these subjects felt intelligent—that is, proud—because they had not been taken in, thus avoiding shame.

Most signs of embarrassment can be interpreted as types of *hiding behavior*. Obvious manifestations of hiding are bodily movements such as covering all or part of the face. More subtle kinds of hiding behavior are gaze aversion and manner of speech (such as speaking so softly as to be inaudible).

Because the hiding behaviors were so frequent and dramatic, we classified them. A rater divided the more obvious movements into six groups, as shown in table 3–1. Gestures were so flagrant that no explicit coding instructions were needed. As can be seen in table 3–1, the majority of cases, 211 (83 percent), showed at least one of these cues. Of the 43 remaining cases, virtually all showed either verbal cues for shame or a break in the social rhythm of gaze:

Language:	"I feel like a perfect idiot!" (Gottschalk et al. 1969).
Paralanguage:	Long pauses, abrupt drops in audibility and pitch, repetition, and fragmentation of speech (Pittenger et al. 1960; Lewis 1971; Labov and Fanshel 1977).
Visual:	Gaze aversion (Tomkins 1963; 119–20; Izard 1977: 386; Retzinger 1988).

Most of these cues were not ambiguous. Often they occurred in combination; for example, drops in loudness of speech usually occurred

Table 3–1
Number of Subjects Who Exhibited Nonverbal Hiding Behavior in *Candid Camera*, with Percent of Total

Gestures	Figure	Once	Twice or More	0	Episodes
A					
Hand over face	3–1	28	7	219	35 (14%)
Hand over eyes	3–2	19	6	229	25 (10%)
Hand over mouth	3–3	28	11	215	39 (15%)
Both hands over face	3–4	15	9	230	24 (9%)
		90 (19%)	33 (30%)		123 (48%)
B					
Hand(s) touch face		39	8	207	47 (19%)
Hand(s) touch hair		27	10	217	37 (15%)
Hand(s) touch neck		3	0	251	3 (1%)
Hand(s) touch chest		22	4	228	26 (10%)
		91 (20%)	22 (20%)		113 (44%)
C					
Head down (chin on chest)	3–5	32	5	217	37 (15%)
Head turned to the side		71	17	166	88 (35%)
Head and body turned around		51	9	194	60 (24%)
		154 (33%)	31 (28%)		185 (73%)
D					
Hide behind an object or fixture		6	0	248	6 (2%)
Run out of frame		25	3	226	28 (11%)
		31 (7%)	3 (3%)		34 (13%)
E					
Bend over (waist level)		24	9	221	33 (13%)
Bend knees		7	2	245	9 (4%)
		31 (7%)	11 (10%)		42 (17%)
F					
Eyes closed or partially closed	3–6	67 (14%)	9 (8%)	178	76 (30%)

Note: N = 254 episodes

along with gaze aversion, giving an overall effect of "sheepishness." But four of the cases (2 percent) involved changes in the rhythm of gaze that were ambiguous. Finally, in five of the cases (2 percent), there were no obvious shame cues. We return to these cases presently. This description will focus on obvious gestures involving bodily movements.

The most extreme behaviors were attempts to hide behind furniture (2 percent) or to run away (11 percent). (One man crawled under a desk.) Hiding the face with one hand (14 percent) or both hands (9 percent), eyes (10 percent), or mouth (15 percent) were other blatant gestures (see figures 3–1 to 3–4). Another extreme movement was bending forward at the waist (13 percent). Covering part or all of the face, combined with bending over, was a double hiding movement. (See figure 3–3; the subjects in figures 3–4 and 3–6 also bent over in subsequent frames, not shown.)

The most common large gesture was turning the head away (35 percent), illustrated by figure 3–5. Other similar movements were bending the head down (15 percent) or turning the head and body away (24 percent). Head movements could be accompanied by other hiding gestures, such as covering the face. The combined gestures of turning the head and covering all or part of the face are particularly suggestive of hiding.

An unexpected gesture that we interpret as hiding behavior was bending the knees (4 percent). Bending in this way moved the face and eyes away from the field of vision of the camera and/or the other person(s) onstage.

Figure 3–1. *Candid Camera* Subject: Hand over Face

Figure 3–2. *Candid Camera* Subject: Hand over Eyes

In addition to these blatant movements, there were smaller gestures, such as touching the face (19 percent), head or hair (15 percent), neck (1 percent), or chest (10 percent). Such touching could be a "miniaturized" version (Tomkins 1963; 56) of covering the face or body. Indeed,

Figure 3–3. *Candid Camera* Subject: Hand over Mouth

Figure 3–4. *Candid Camera* Subject: Both Hands over Face

the initial movements often suggested that the hand was to be used to cover the face, eyes, or mouth but ended in only touching. The subjects seem to become self-conscious during the time that the hand(s) moved toward the head.[2]

Figure 3–5. *Candid Camera* Subject: Head Turned to the Side

---

[2]Independent support for face-touching as a shame cue comes from a survey of the experience of embarrassment in five European countries (Edelmann 1987). In each country, some of the respondents mentioned face-touching when asked how they behaved when embarrassed, ranging from 2 percent (Greece) to 16 (Russia).

Figure 3–6. *Candid Camera* Subject: Eyes Closed

Another movement suggestive of hiding was the full or partial closing of the eyes (30 percent; see figure 3–6). Instead of covering the eyes with the hand or averting the eyes by turning, they are covered or partially covered with the eyelids. This gesture, like the others, shields the eyes from seeing and being seen.

A majority of the subjects (57 percent) displayed two or more of the six gestures. The second-largest group (31 percent) displayed only one. As already indicated, one group (17 percent) displayed none. The rest displayed three or more, and two of the subjects displayed gestures of all six kinds (see Table 3–2).

The movements of one of these latter subjects conveys the intensity of her display. Allan Funt, in disguise, was playing the role of a clerk. He told the subject that he could not return her photographs, implying that they were pornographic. She insisted that he was mistaken; he repeated his refusal. Finally, she indicated that she was angry and would talk to the manager. As she began to turn away, Funt shed his disguise. In the ensuing thirty-five seconds, she enacted a dramatic dance of shame and alienation.

As she turned away, laughing, she covered her face with one hand. Funt caught her other hand to keep her from moving off-camera. She said, "Oh my God," turned toward him, and hid her face in his shoulder. As she turned to escape again, she touched her hair and face, with her eyes closed. She went through this cycle or ones similar to it (some involving bending movements) several times before the segment ended. All told, she displayed hiding gestures twenty-two times, more than one every two seconds.

Table 3-2
Number of Joint Occurences of Gestures, with Percent of Total

Gesture A	Gesture B	Gesture C	Gesture D	Gesture E	Gesture F	Number of Gestures	
A ONLY 6	B ONLY 13	C ONLY 32	D ONLY 2	E ONLY 3	F ONLY 9	1 Gesture	65 26%
AB 9	BC 14	CD 8	DE 1	EF 1		2 Gestures	80 31%
AC 11	BD 0	CE 5	DF 0				
AD 1	BE 2	CF 16					
AE 2	BF 4						
AF 6							
ABC 8	BCD 2	CDE 1	DEF 0			3 Gestures	39 15%
ABD 0	BCE 1	CDF 1					
ABE 1	BCF 7	CEF 2					
ABF 2	BDE 1						
ACD 0	BDF 1						
ACE 2	BEF 0						
ACF 9							
ADE 1							
ADF 0							
AEF 0							
ABCD 3	BCDE 0	CDEF 0				4 Gestures	18 7%
ABCE 3	BCEF 2						
ABCF 8	BDEF 0						
ABDE 0							
ABDF 0							

ABEF	0						
ACDE	0						
ACDF	0						
ACEF	2						
ADEF	0						
ABCDE	4	BCDEF 0				5 Gestures	7	3%
ABCDF	0						
ABCEF	3						
ACDEF	0						
ABCDEF	2					6 Gestures	2	1%
NONE	2						43	17%
Total	83	90	144	28	39	75	TOTAL	254	100%
% of episodes	33%	35%	57%	11%	15%	30%		

Key: Gesture A: Hand over face, eyes, mouth
Gesture B: Hand touches face, hair, neck, chest
Gesture C: Head movements
Gesture D: Running or hiding movement
Gesture E: Bending movement
Gesture F: Eyes closed or partially closed

The virtually perfect association we found between shame and hiding behavior provides support for the emphasis Tomkins (1963) and Izard (1971, 1977) placed on visual behavior as crucial in shame states. Persons in this state seem to want to escape from the gaze of the other (also central to formulations by Sartre [1948] and Lynd [1958]). The emphasis on making oneself smaller, as in Izard (1977), seems to be only a special case of the more general process of hiding.

Our data suggest that the intensity of embarrassment is related to the number and size of the gestures involved. Masaccio's painting of the expulsion from the Garden of Eden (figure 1–1) suggests an additional dimension: Eve covers her breasts and pudenda. (The derivation of this word is relevant, since the Latin meaning is "the shame part.") But Adam covers his eyes, suggesting shame about the whole self rather than just a part. (Note the similarity of the placement of his hands to those in figure 3–4.) Perhaps Adam wants to escape from God by not seeing Him or being seen by Him. Shame about a part might be less intense than shame about the whole.

The process of making oneself smaller or larger depending on one's emotional state seems to play a role in the human world. The winning contestants on TV game shows, for example, appear to swell in size when they learn of their good fortune, as we shall see. (Shrinking in defeat is less obvious.) Allusions to this phenomenon occur in the vernacular: "swelling with pride" or being "crestfallen" with shame. Retzinger (1988), on the basis of her moment-by-moment analysis of videotapes of marital quarrels, has characterized the total effect of verbal and nonverbal cues of intense shame as one of "implosion," the blatant withdrawal and shrinking of oneself. A typical sequence: In response to his wife's contemptuous anger, a husband stops smiling, narrows his eyes, and lowers his head, his verbal responses shortening to barely audible single words and phrases. Visually and verbally, he becomes smaller.

The description of the "giant/dwarf" relationship among chimpanzees (de Waal 1982: 87–88) suggests an animal analogue. The dominant ape makes itself large by standing erect, raising its arms, puffing up its hair; the submissive ape makes itself small by bending low or bowing. Perhaps in the evolution of social behavior, pride and shame were once connected with dominance and submission. In humans, however, to the physical movement of shrinking or bowing has been added the *idea* of becoming smaller to the point of disappearing, averting one's attention from an embarrassing moment, or the other's attention from the self. In the human context, what was once a very limited domain of actions has been vastly extended to the realm of thoughts and feelings.

Signs of shame or embarrassment in outer behavior need not be flagrant in order to be clearly recognizable. Most of the embarrassment manifested by gaze aversion alone was unambiguous. The pattern of prolonged looking away, with only a furtive or very brief direct gaze, could usually be distinguished from the normal cycle, a rhythm of direct and averted gaze.

What Eibl-Eibesfeldt (1975) calls "coyness behavior" can be interpreted in terms of embarrassment (or in some cases, the feigning of embarrassment), since the subject typically alternates between direct and averted gazes. The normal cycle of direct and averted gazes, unlike coyness behavior, is subtle and undramatic; it usually occurs without mention or even notice. In coyness behavior, the alternation between direct and averted gazes is flagrant and is accompanied by a smile.

In the *Candid Camera* subjects, in addition to physical hiding behavior, there were also paralinguistic suggestions of hiding, like those specified by Lewis (1971) in her description of nonverbal markers of shame: decreases in sound volume, in some cases to the point of inaudibility; speech disruption (long pauses, stammering, and repetitions of words or phrases); and speech filler ("well," "uh," and so on). Like the visual gestures of covering the face or body, and averting or lowering the gaze, these nonverbal behaviors can be interpreted as hiding behaviors. The silence of long pauses, inaudibility, speech disruption, and filler can be seen as ways of hiding one's thoughts and feelings from oneself and from others.

Although none of the subjects in our sample used this language, verbal evocations of hiding sometimes accompany shame, such as "I wanted to disappear" or "I wished that the earth would have opened up and swallowed me." This ideation, together with the verbal and nonverbal cues discussed, suggests that hiding behavior may subsume many different types of shame behavior.

We have been assuming that all 254 cases involved moments of truth, since all the subjects were told they were on *Candid Camera*. The issue that remains concerns five exceptional cases, who did not manifest hiding behavior. One of these cases, the skeptical pair, has already been discussed. In the remaining four cases, it is possible that although they were *told*, they didn't *understand*. Two of these subjects were informed over the telephone. Lacking any visual cues, they seemed not to grasp the message. The other two cases lacked this excuse, however. Perhaps one or more of them were unaware of existence of *Candid Camera*. We cannot clarify these five cases any further since the relevant process is completely internal. In any case, in the overwhelming majority of episodes (96 percent), the disruption of the social bond, of attunement, was marked by clear shame cues, as suggested by our theory.

Context, Emotion, and Cooperation in TV Game Shows

In the second study, we used seven sets of episodes from two different game-show formats. In the first, there were five pairs of contestants; in the second, there were two familial groups of five persons. The descrip-

Figure 3–7. Game Show Pair 1

tion of the results here will be brief; they are preliminary to a longer report.

The reactions of the contestants *to winning* were almost identical. In five of the seven groups, the contestants consistently showed the same set of reactions—pride and joy in their facial expressions and comportment, and signs of increasing solidarity and attunement. (See figures 3–7 to 3–11; for brevity, only photos of the five pairs are

Figure 3–8. Game Show Pair 2

shown. The larger groups require more complex and lengthy descriptions). Two of the pairs, numbers 2 and 3, showed slight deviations from this pattern. Deviations by pair 2 were infrequent and faint; those by pair 3 were more frequent and marked. But even pair 3 conformed

Figure 3–9. Game Show Pair 3

most of the time. In victory, direction of gaze was either mutual, as in pairs 1, 2, and 3, or when not facing each other, indicated a single visual focus or attention, as in pair 5. Pair 4 were too close to meet either condition, but they did both before and after their embrace.

At the moment of victory, the contestants showed other movements indicative of solidarity besides visual attunement. First, most of them moved closer together. An extreme example is pair 1; they are sisters. The men in pair 4 moved still closer, even though they were unrelated strangers. More typical distances in victory are those of 2 and 5. The contestants in pair 3 usually conformed to this movement but sometimes did not. In figure 3–9, they are slightly closer in defeat than in victory. This pair and pair 2 retained faint smiles in defeat, but infrequently.

In six of the seven groups, moving closer resulted in episodes of touching, as shown in figures 3–7, 3–10, and 3–11. Pair 3, once again, was an exception. In six of the groups, touching was mutual. Figure 3–11 shows a form of mutual touching. His hand can be seen around her shoulder. Her hand is off-camera, but it is around his waist.

In all seven groups, the contestants leaned toward each other during moments of victory, and they were erect or leaned away during defeat. This pattern can be seen most clearly in pairs 1 and 5, but it occurred in all cases. Pair 3 was an occasional exception, as shown in figure 3–9, but their direction of lean usually followed the same pattern as the others. There was also a brief exception in the defeat of one of the family groupings. The eye of the man who had given the wrong answer was caught by another contestant (his wife). He quickly looked away, however, and both resumed their erect stance.

The contestants' reactions to defeat were initially as uniform as their reactions to victory. All showed clear signs of shame and alienation. Gaze aversion, erect stance or leaning away, and greater physical distance were indicative of alienation; hiding behavior was indicative of shame. (In figure 3–8, the woman is moving her hand toward covering her mouth; in figure 3–10, the contestant on the left is shielding his face from his partner.)

In the game-show episodes, hiding behavior was much less extreme than it was in *Candid Camera.* Many of the gestures were miniaturized; there was much touching of face and hair and fewer gross bodily movements of hiding. These differences suggest lower levels of humiliation and alienation. Perhaps giving a wrong answer is less humiliating than being tricked. Also, the contestants observed were all in groups; they were thus not alone in their defeat.

Beyond the uniform initial response to defeat, there were two different patterns of reaction. In three of the groups, the duration of the moment of shame and alienation was quite brief—less than thirty seconds. After this initial reaction, at least one of the contestants would seek eye contact with the other(s). In three of the groups, this quest was successful. In these groups (represented in figures 3–7 and 3–9), the contestants rapidly reestablished a single visual focus of attention, followed by other signs of solidarity and group laughter.

Figure 3–10. Game Show Pair 4

In the other four groups, however, seeking eye contact did not occur or was unsuccessful. These groups continued to exhibit signs of alienation, marked by physical distance, erect posture or leaning away, gaze aversion, and miniaturized forms of hiding behavior.

These two different patterns of reaction to defeat had strong consequences for the level of cooperation. All three groups in which the bond was repaired went on to subsequent success. In the four groups with no repair, indications of tension and flustering were clear. Three of these groups were immediately defeated. One of the groups avoided

Figure 3–11. Game Show Pair 5

immediate defeat, but they won less than the least successful of the "repair" groups. The relationship found between repair and success supports our theory: attunement leads to effective cooperation, while failure of attunement interferes with cooperation.

This chapter has illustrated our theory of the role of the social bond and emotion in social structure and process with two studies of the connection between emotional states and social relationships. At the heart of our theory is the interrelation between attunement, emotion, communication, and cooperation.

The key concept is attunement. When persons or groups are mentally and emotional connected, when they understand each other, many consequences are likely to follow: shared pride, trust, mutual identification, and social solidarity. Under these conditions, a common language is likely to develop, as well as a sense of community. These are the conditions for effective cooperation.

The failure of attunement sets the stage for shared shame. If shame is acknowledged, the threatened bonds can be repaired and solidarity sustained. If shame is not acknowledged, separation and/or destructive conflict are likely to follow. The two case studies illustrate some of the main elements in our theory and instantiate it by showing that basic concepts like solidarity and alienation need not be mere metaphors but can be applied to concrete episodes of behavior.

In our theory, mutual understanding of beliefs, emotions, intentions, and character—since it is a condition for effective cooperation—has survival value for any group, from marital couples to the largest civilizations. Solidarity and alienation can be systematically studied through analysis of discourse. Our theory points toward describing and understanding the structure and process of social order, conflict, and anarchy by a close reading of cues for the state of social bonds and emotion. At the microlevel, such cues can be found in precise recordings of discourse. The study of marital quarrels reported in the next two chapters illustrates this type of investigation.

Part II
Case Studies of Violence

4
The Role of Shame
in Marital Conflict[1]

As we indicated in chapter 2, a theory of social bonds and emotions may help to explain protracted conflicts. Conflict theorists dealing with macro-issues have discussed the importance of the social bond, but work in interpersonal conflict has virtually ignored their advances. This chapter further develops a theoretical relationship between social bonds, shame, and conflict, as well as an explicit methodology so that the theory can be applied to concrete examples.

To be applicable to actual behavior, the concepts in a theory must be specified in voluminous detail. In our theory, we claim that protracted conflict is marked by alienation and unacknowledged shame, leading to anger, which in turn is expressed with disrespect, which leads to further separation, and so on. To see if this formulation fits actual sequences of behavior, we have explicitly defined each of these concepts.

Shame in Classic and Modern Social Theory

While early theories have mentioned emotions that occur in conflict, they have not focused on them; nor have they been applied to microanalyses. Our approach differs from constructionism (Gordon 1981; Hochschild 1983; Thoits 1989), incorporating both biological and cultural components of emotion. An organic conception of emotion follows from Cooley:

> When our individual life begins the two elements of history from which it is drawn, the heredity and the social, merge in the new whole and cease to exist as separate forces. Nothing that the individual does

[1]We are greatly indebted to Melvin Lansky for his comments on this chapter.

can be ascribed to either alone, . . . the real thing is a total organic process not separable into parts (1902:15).

Lewis (1971) maintained that human beings are social by biological origin. The social and biological are not separate entities; rather human beings are born able to respond socially. In this formulation, emotions, although socialized and managed as the constuctionists have observed, are also functional. They serve to regulate social interaction in the interest of maintaining social bonds.

In all interaction, either the social bond is being built, maintained, or repaired, or it is being damaged. Distinct emotional responses occur in different states of the bond. The building of bonds is accompanied by pride. When bonds are being damaged, anger, shame, and/or grief ensue. These responses mobilize the persons involved to attend to the bond.

Macrotheories of conflict can be combined with a theory of emotion by considering responses to separation and alienation to be functional. That is, emotions serve to signal the state of the social bond and the need to readjust behavior in relation to the other. Emotions communicate to the self and to the other that the bond is either intact or threatened.

Many writers have focused on the importance of the social bond. In discussing "species needs," Marx (1844) suggested that the most important human need is connection with other human beings. He went on to discuss alienation—not only from the mode of production but from others and self. Although the state of the bond is largely invisible, Marx noted two observable emotional responses to alienation: "impotence" and "indignation" (Tucker 1978: 133–34).

For more than a century theorists have argued that separation induces conflict (Marx 1844; Simmel 1955; Coser 1956; Coleman 1957; Kreisberg 1973). As Simmel put it, "separation does not follow from conflict . . . conflict [follows] from separation" (1955: 47)—that is, conflict results from lost social bonds.

Recently, studies of both animals and human beings have shown the effects of inadequate bonds (Adamson et al. 1977; Bowlby 1973; Brazelton et al. 1974, 1982; Harlow 1962; Massie 1982; Spitz 1965; Stern 1971; Tronick 1980). They report how aggressive or destructive behavior occurs during a period of separation. Bowlby (1973) stressed that in children, separation from a caretaker can lead to angry protest. Cooley (1922) observed how his four-month-old infant behaved to get herself noticed, and the rage she expressed when she was ignored.

A further step in the separation-anger link is found in Cooley's (1902: 269–70) work: the most common form of hostility is rooted in social self-feeling. He focused on the importance of the social bond: "we live in the minds of others," we feel *pride* when we are noticed favorably, and we feel *shame* when our bonds are threatened (p. 208). More recently, others have observed the co-occurrence of anger with other emotions involved in social self-feeling, such as shame and humiliation.

Lewis (1971, 1976) also emphasized the co-occurrence of shame with anger. She first observed unacknowledged shame in patients' anger toward the therapist. She traced sequences of emotion, as manifested in transcripts of sessions, back from the moment anger first appeared and found that shame, caused by a real or perceived injury or injustice, always preceded anger. Because a major reaction of shame was to hide from the hurt, the anger was often turned back on the self or thrust outward subtly or vehemently toward the other in a disrespectful manner, continuing and escalating in a cyclical pattern.

Cooley's idea of social self-feeling suggests that every word, gesture, facial expression, action, or implication gives some message to persons about *their worth*. If the message imputes low worth to a person, shame results; if the message indicates high worth, pride occurs. Goffman (1967) focused on deference and demeanor, which he treated as means of communication. Deference (respect) involves one's *manner*, which goes beyond speech (the *topic* of dispute) in understanding escalation. All social interaction involves obtaining respect and avoiding "embarrassment" or *loss of face*. (Embarrassment is a variant belonging to the shame family, a response to disrespect.)

Shame in our Theory

We use the word *shame* to refer to a family of emotions that include a wide range of variations, from mild embarrassment and social discomfort to intense forms such as humiliation. Unlike other emotions, the primary characteristic of shame is that it is always social: it involves the simultaneous involvement between self and other, concern about other's images of oneself.

The context for shame is a message perceived to involve separation (or threat of separation) and injury to self: insult, rejection, rebuff, disapproval, unrequited love, betrayal, unresponsiveness, disrespect, and the like. Shame is intricately connected with *social separation* and threats of abandonment—responses to *alienation* from others.

When shame is ignored, not only does one feel separated from the other person and hurt, but identification with the other becomes difficult. The *other* person is then experienced as the source of the hurt; only the part the other person plays may be seen. Each person reciprocates with a more vehement assault against the perceived attack: withdrawal, sarcasm, blame, demeaning criticism, threat, or worse. Each tactic communicates disrespect and separates them further from one another, generating strong emotion. This formulation should not be taken lightly. People kill for social reasons: lost affection, lost honor, and other highly moral reasons (Lewis 1976; Katz 1988).

In this framework, anger can be viewed as an attempt to ward off perceived attack and "save face," or to remain attached in the face of threats to basic emotional ties. Rage, a reaction against an injury to oneself, is a protective measure used as an insulation against shame.

Several studies have explicitly shown the prominence of shame and its role in conflict and violence, each of which developed its formulation independently of the others. Katz (1988) has suggested that humiliation often underlies violent crime and homicide. Lansky (1987) has shown that violent marriages are rampant with shame, that couples in violent relationships are particularly prone to shame. Johnston and Campbell (1988) have found shame to be a central component in angry impasses during divorce. Elsewhere, we have suggested that unacknowledged shame is an important cause of quarrels in marriages, psychotherapy sessions, prison riots, and warfare (Scheff et al. 1989; Scheff 1989; Retzinger 1991).

Characteristics of Shame

Lewis's (1971) working concept is used here for identifying shame. Table 4–1 summarizes the characteristics of a shame experience. These include: stimulus (context), experience of a shame state, relationship between self and other, hostile reactions, and defenses. Table 4–2 depicts the perceived relationship between the self and other during a shame experience. Note the position of the self in relation to the other; the self is always perceived to be in the inferior position.

In addition to physiological changes and conscious content, there are many cues for shame and anger states: verbal, paralinguistic, and visual gestures all provide cues to emotion.

Toward a Theory of Conflict

Several components are evident in conflict. One, a threat to the social bond arises (separation/alienation). Two, shame is (evoked but *not acknowledged*), and the bond is not discussed. Three, anger follows as a defense against perceived attack. It is often communicated disrespectfully, leading to a perpetuating series (figure 4–1). The first triad of figure 4–1 represents a conflict-free situation, interaction within an intact bond. The manner between the persons is mutually responsive and respectful. Each feels connected; there is solidarity.

The second triad shows the initial cause of conflict. The manner is perceived as unresponsive or disrespectful—each person feels

Table 4–1
Summary of Working Concept for Shame

Stimulus	1. Disappointment, defeat, or moral transgression 2. Deficiency of self 3. Involuntary; self feels unable 4. Encounter with other
Conscious Content	1. Painful emotion 2. Autonomic reactions 3. Connections with past feelings 4. Many variants of shame feelings 5. Fewer variations of cognitive content (the self) 6. Identity thoughts
Position of Self in Field (see table 4–2)	1. Self passive 2. Self focal in awareness 3. Multiple functions of self at the same time 4. Vicarious experience of other's view of self
Nature and Discharge of Hostility	1. Humiliated fury 2. Discharge blocked by guilt and/or love of other
Characteristic Defenses	1. Denial 2. Repression of ideas 3. Affirmation of the self 4. Affect disorder: depression 5. Negation of other 6. Anger, disrespect, violence

Source: Adapted from Lewis (1971a). Shame & Guilt in Neurosis. *Psychoanalytic Review*, 58, no. 3.

Table 4–2
Self and Other in Shame

Self (Unable)	*Other*
1. Object of scorn; contempt; scorn, ridicule; reduced	1. The source of contempt, ridicule
2. Paralyzed; helpless; passive	2. Laughing, powerful ridiculing, active
3. Assailed by noxious stimuli; rage; tears; blushing	3. Appears intact
4. Childish	4. Adult; abandoning
5. Focal in awareness	5. Also focal in awareness
6. Functions poorly as agent or perceiver; divided between imaging self and the other; boundaries permeable; vicarious experience of self and other.	6. Appears intact

Source: Adapted from Lewis (1971a).

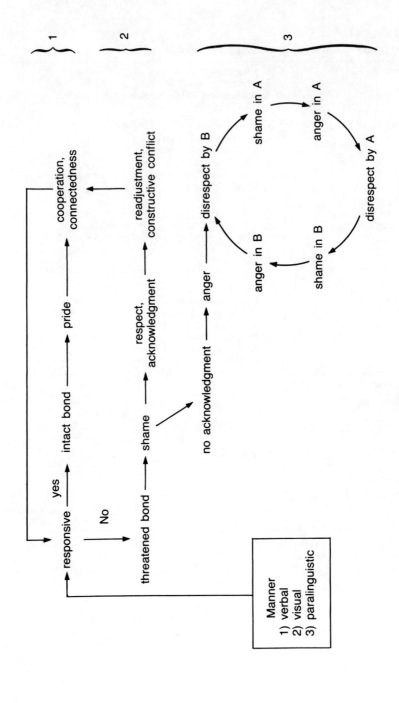

Figure 4–1. Toward a Theory of Conflict

separated from the other. This is the crucial point at which either conflict will arise or resolution will occur. Anger may arise, but if there is no further shaming, if feelings are acknowledged and the interpersonal manner communicates respect, negotiation, readjustment, and change can occur with minimal damage to the relationship. This is a functional conflict.

Escalation is portrayed in the third triad. Escalation is triggered when the bond is threatened and when feelings are not commented on; behavior is likely to be interpreted as an attack. The greater the parties' inability to communicate needs and feelings, the more likely it is an impasse will develop. Disrespectful behavior elicits further shame; each person feels alienated, in a recurring loop. This loop can occur and reoccur within seconds.

Method

The method we have developed to use with our theory differs from others that have been used for studying emotion in that it is interdisciplinary and multileveled; it combines methods from psychology, linguistics, and sociology. While most studies on emotion use surveys (Thoits 1985), field methods (Hochschild 1983), or experiments (Gottman 1979), we use sequential analysis of discourse.

What follows is an analysis of the discourse between married couples who agreed to hold a forty-five-minute discussion in a video lab. Twelve couples were recruited through flyers and word of mouth. An analysis of discourse is presented here for four of the couples. Following Gottman's (1979) technique, the couples were asked to discuss three different topics for fifteen minutes each. First, they discussed the events of their day—a *neutral* condition. Second, they discussed a topic of frequent argument—a *conflict* condition. This second instruction always led to an actual quarrel. (Levenson [1986] has indicated to us in a personal communication that he and Gottman never found a couple who did not quarrel using this technique.) In the third fifteen-minute period, they discussed activities they enjoy doing together as a couple— a *positive* condition.

We used verbal and nonverbal cues for inferring emotion. *Verbal* cues include the explicit naming of emotions and indirect references to emotions, as well as thought processes involved in emotional experiences (Gottschalk, Wingert, and Gleser 1969; Lewis 1979). *Nonverbal* cues include paralinguistic behaviors such as voice tone, loudness, and pitch (Labov and Fanshel 1977; Pittenger et al. 1960). *Visual* cues include facial and bodily movements (Darwin 1872; Edelmann 1987;

Ekman and Friesen 1978; Izard 1971, 1977; Retzinger 1985, 1987, 1989, 1991; Scheff, Retzinger, and Ryan, 1989; Tomkins 1963). All three categories of behavior were used for identifying sequences of emotions.

The tapes were encoded with a time frame representing the minute, second, and frame number (there are thirty frames per second in videotape) as 00:00.00. The tapes were transcribed to include all vocal utterances and gestures, including emphases, pauses, and the like. Table 4–3 shows the conventions used to transcribe the tapes (see Heritage 1985).

This method allows for a validity check. Because the tape will be made available to interested parties, the reader can check the validity of our ratings and interpretations.

Verbal References

Gottschalk, Wingert, and Gleser's (1969) content-analysis scale identifies low-visibility shame and anger. Their categories for shame include references to being ridiculed and to feelings of being inadequate, ashamed, embarrassed, humiliated, exposed, or deficient. They also include references to oneself in relation to another in which a negative evaluation is placed on the self, as well as references to feelings of disconnectedness to significant others, such as rejection, desertion, abandonment, ostracism, or loss of support or love. Negative ideation about one's appearance in relation to another, and obsessive ideation about what one might have said or done, also indicate shame.

Table 4–3
Meaning of the Conventions of Transcription

Convention	Meaning
boldface	= anger
italics	= shame
underlined bold	= shame-rage
[ ]	= interruptions
- between words	= rapid, condensed speech
(inaud)	= inaudible
< >	= words laughed
CAPITAL LETTERS	= heavy emphasis; loud
( )	= untimed pause (under 1 second)
(0.00)	= timed pause (seconds and 1/100 of sec.)
: :	= previous syllable drawn out
00:00.00	= time code in minutes, seconds, and frames
=	= the second speaker begins speaking at precisely the end of the first speakers utterance

Behaviors that identify anger include references to aggravation, annoyance, criticism, blame, dislike. The Gottschalk-Gleser scale provides extensive lists of verbal behaviors that indicate the presence of shame and of anger.

Labov and Fanshel (1977) provide further methods for identifying emotion in discourse. (They used the term *embarrassment*, a shame variant.) Some of the behaviors indicating shame include vagueness or oblique, suppressed references (such as "they"); mitigation, or attempts to diminish severity (such as "it was *just*"); defensiveness, exaggeration, and expansion; and denial and verbal withdrawal. Each of these behaviors implies the presence of shame through verbal *hiding* behaviors (see chapter 2). Anger cues include interruption, challenges, sarcasm, blame, and complaining.

Paralinguistic Cues

Emotions can also be detected in vocal *manner*. Labov and Fanshel (1977) and Pittenger et al. (1960) provide paralinguistic cues indicating shame. These cues involve vocal withdrawal or hiding behaviors and disorganization of thought: oversoft speech, irregular rhythm, hesitation, self-interruption, self-censorship, pauses and filled pauses ("uh"), stammering and stuttering, fragmented speech, rapid condensed speech, and laughed words. Indications of anger include: staccato speech (with distinct breaks between successive sounds), loudness, stress on certain words, a sing-song pattern (ridicule), and strident (harsh) voice qualifiers.

Visual Gestures

Shame can also be detected by visible bodily manifestations (Darwin 1872; Edelmann 1987; Izard 1977; Lewis 1971, 1979; Tomkins 1963; chapters 2 and 3 in the present book). Such visual gestures for shame include (1) hiding behavior: One may hide with one's hands, as when the hand covers all or parts of the face or simply touches the face. One may also hide with one's eyes, by averting the gaze or by lowering and averting the eyes. A second type of visual gesture that indicates shame is (2) blushing. A third type are (3) visual gestures that indicate a struggle for control, such as turning the lips in, biting them, or licking them, or biting the tongue; false smiling (Ekman and Friesen 1982) or other masking behaviors; and fidgeting.

Visual gestures can occur alone or in combination. In combination, they often occur in sequences: biting the lip may be followed by false smiling, followed by covering the face. In such sequences, one gesture may follow another so rapidly as to seem simultaneous. Often verbal and nonverbal cues occur simultaneously (such as when covering the face with hands, a person says "I feel like a fool").

Visual cues for anger include (1) brows lowered and drawn together, while vertical lines appear between them; (2) eyelids narrowed and tense in a hard fixed stare, and eyes with a bulging appearance; (3) mouth closed with lips pressed together, the corners straight or down, or mouth open but tense and square (The closed-lip position may occur in an attempt to control shouting or hostility. Open lip anger occurs during speech [Ekman and Friesen 1975, 1978; Izard 1971]; (4) leaning forward in a challenging stance; (5) clenched fists, waved fists, and hitting motions.

These cues are *context-related*; their relevance to shame and anger depends on the relationship between self and other, as expressed verbally: a client might say to a therapist "you must think I'm crazy." The more visual, verbal, and paralinguistic categories that are involved, and the more cues from each category, the stronger the evidence for a particular emotion. Dense constellations of cues are stronger evidence than are single occurrences. Based on constellations of cues, emotions are inferred as they are being expressed and exchanged between husband and wife.

Results

Although these results are preliminary, several patterns emerge. Each quarrel is marked by lack of respect. There is a high frequency and prominence of shame cues. The quarrels begin with shame and separation rather than anger. And the quarrels contain rapidly alternating sequences of shame and anger in escalation.

These patterns differ from couple to couple. They involve variations in the style of emotional expression (verbal, visual, paralinguistic) and in dispute style: impasse or quarrel. An impasse can be likened to a cold war, in which there is little or no overt anger but withdrawal, avoidance, and coldness instead. In a quarrel, there may be shouting, name-calling, and other overt signs of conflict. These stylistic differences mask underlying similarities; we will not go into the differences here. Each pattern will be illustrated with examples from four cases. (All names given are pseudonyms.)

Disrespectful Manner

In these quarrels, each spouse is disrespectful toward the other, either subtly or vehemently. The disrespectful manner of a dispute is important because it is a major source of shame. Unacknowledged shame results not only in disrespect but in indirect anger. Couple 1, David and Colleen, for example, blame, interrupt, placate, and interrogate each other. Couple 2, Roxanne and Brian, call each other names, blame, interrupt, and exaggerate. Couple 3, Rosie and James, use implicature and innuendo, disguising their hostility with smiles. Couple 4, Randy and Karin, put each other down in demeaning ways, both directly and through implication. In the following excerpt from couple 1, David interrogates Colleen, Colleen tries to withdraw and placate.

David and Colleen quarrel over the remodeling of their house. David implies that he alone bears the burden, that Colleen has not been involved. (Transcripts written in ordinary English can be found in appendix 4A.) Early in the quarrel, David questions Colleen relentlessly.

Excerpt 1a

27:33.13 D: I'm *jist saying it it* do you KNOW what you WANT () cause you can't GET there if you don't know what you WANT=

40.11 C: =right ya=

D: =an the other part is () why after fifteen years if

45.25 you KNOW what yu want () if you can desCRIBE it or visualize it in yer head

C: um hm

50.24 D: why ya haven't implemented it

C: umhm

53.09 D: an if the MOney wasn't there that's just an excuse its just a roadblock=

C: =umhm=

57.01 D: =tu

overcome=

C: =umhm=

58.05 D: =why didn't yu do something tu get the money together ta decorate just

28:01.07 the way that yu wanted=

C: [ya] =ok so what I've done

07.00 *an uh* is tu decorate just with what I've got=

D: =right ()

an thats satisfactory ()

10.20 C: *well* () it's been practical

13.10 D: an that's satisfactory

C: uh hu () *I mean um ye-yes an no*

18.00 D: it hasn't been for me . . .

Less than two minutes later, he asks the same question again.

Excerpt 1b

30:15.20 D: has it been satisfactory to you () all this time () to decorate with your history () instead of () making your history (1.70)

Questioning, rather than making a direct statement, is often disrespectful because there may be a hidden message behind the question. In this instance, Colleen is in a double bind: if she says no, he could ask, "Why didn't you do something to get the money together to decorate just the way you wanted?" (27:58.05). If she says yes, he could say, "It hasn't been for me" (28:18.00). "Is it satisfactory to you?" seems not to be a real question. Behind his question, he is making a statement about his own dissatisfaction with the relationship and his feeling of powerlessness. David and Colleen ended up divorced. At the time of the quarrel, neither stepped out of the frame to comment on the *manner* of the discussion between them. Like the other couples, they are fixated by the *content* of the quarrel, which is a form of triangling away from discussing their actual relationship.

Lack of respect is the medium for exchange of shame-rage between partners. Shame is present in each case, but is seldom acknowledged. The manner of each person is degrading toward the other. Anger is expressed indirectly and alternates rapidly with shame; each is disrespectful toward the other but also feels put down (shamed) by the other, which leads to further anger in a cyclical pattern. Disrespectful manner perpetuates feelings of separateness and shame.

Prominence of Shame

Each conflict is marked by a high density of shame cues; overall, there are twice as many cues for shame as for anger. Shame is consistently high across all persons and relationships, while anger is not. The two couples that exhibit the most shame at the start of their quarrel are the couples whose conflict reaches the highest level of intensity: David and Colleen, and Randy and Karin.

Etiology

Each conflict begins with ideation of isolation, separateness, and other sources of shame. Roxanne and Brian's argument involves the division of household duties. The initial topic is Brian's feeling of isolation. The quarrel begins with Brian:

Excerpt 2a
16:17.05 B: It's the times when you *feel like you're the only soldier on the field () and you come ho-I come home*

26.20 R: [*hhh*]   [*hhh*]
        B: and **you're going OH MAN, I've done E::VERY-THING today I've jis done e::verything I've dealt with this and that and this and that and now it's**

	R:	*[laugh]* *[ah]*
36.05	B:	YOUR-TURN to deal with it () an here take
	R:	[cough]
	B:	Christopher (the baby) () an here change his diaper
		an let me eat an give me two minutes-uh-peace an
		I'm burned out (2.85)
16:43.15	R:	<u>OH I do that every day (2)</u>
	B:	<u>Mo:r:e often than not</u>
48.05	R:	<u>Bull <shit> (1.75)</u>
	B:	<u>More often than not</u> <softer)
	R:	[-uhuh]

Brian begins with a strong ideation of being *alone* in a harsh environment (being the only soldier on the field), but he attributes these feelings to Roxanne, denying his own feelings behind the image. (Later in the interview, at 22:47.10, he says that it is *he* who feels like the only soldier doing battle.) The ideation of separation marks a shame state that is not acknowledged. The disparaging manner that follows damages the bond.

From a state of isolation, Brian launches directly into a long demeaning complaint about Roxanne, using sarcastic gestures and an imitative voice tone. (He twists his face and waves his arms like an ape.) He uses exaggerated terms ("everything").

At first, as Brian begins to complain, Roxanne smiles and laughs tensely. When he begins to complain about her handing over the baby to him, the tense smile fades from her face and is replaced by a cold, silent glare; she appears to be insulted and angered. There is a long pause before she answers with a sarcastic remark ("Oh, I do that *every*day"). Roxanne responds defensively (16:43.15). They continue, tit for tat:

Excerpt 2b:

	B:	You're tired you don't wanna deal with it ()
16:52.05	B:	You're tired you don't wanna deal with it ()
	R:	[ya/ I am tired]
	B:	you don't <u>wanna deal with Christopher</u> () You feel
		<u>like () YOU'VE</u>
	R:	[nah () not all the time]
58.28	B:	had tu-do everything in the house an pick up
	R:	[hhhhhh]
17:02.00	B:	everything an clean everything an you SAY::!
	R:	[YA I] GOTTA PICK up AFTER YOU
		ALL THE TIME you're such a SLOB you *jis* take
		your clothes off in the <*middle*> of the floo::r
05.22	B:	[an () you say that I] () [don't] do
		any:thing
09.09	R:	you don't if I don't move *(R&B slight laugh)* your

shoes out of the middle of the living room, they just stay there, if I don't pick up your clothes in the middle of the floor they'll stay

17.06   there. you'll walk all over them. You'll walk over em when you get home from WORK. Your MESS in the CLOSET, it's still there you don't put ANY- THING away. I fold your laundry, I wash it

28.05   and put it some where where you can put it away and you don't put it away. *It's more work for me (slight laugh)*

38.08 B: I NEVER put it away. <oversoft)

R: WELL, before OUR parents come you usually tidy up a little.

45.00 B: its not the only time () <oversoft)

R: and once in a blue moon, when you get the urge to uh pick up

They continue quarreling, switching roles: Roxanne is now the aggres- sor, and Brian becomes defensive. She ends up calling Brian a "slob" (17:02.00). Brian becomes very uncomfortable, displaying behavior that was not previously present (face touching); his response becomes mini- mal (withdrawal) as she begins to complain vehemently.

Another example of the origin of conflict in unacknowledged shame comes from David and Colleen. Disconnectedness is seen in her verbal statement at the start of their quarrel.

Excerpt 1c
  26:01.00 C: . . and um, but in general I think what I'm comfort- able with is not what you're comfortable with.

The ideation is of being "two different people" (which she actually says later). This utterance is surrounded by cues for shame—hesitation, miti- gation, and other paralinguistic and visual cues—before anger emerges.

Shame and ideation of separation precede anger in each case. This finding is consistent with Simmel's suggestion that conflict follows sepa- ration rather than the other way around. Shame marks damage to social bonds, a state of alienation; anger is not only a protest against the loss of affectional bonds but a means by which to protect the vulnerability of the self in the face of a perceived attack—that is, to save face and defend against shame.

Shame and Anger Alternation

When shame occurs and is not acknowledged, anger is quick to follow in these couples. Rapidly alternating sequences of shame and anger are found in each case. Often the brevity of the two emotions makes it necessary to view the sequences in slow motion. In a six-second time span, there can be a change of emotion each second.

Couple 3, Rosie and James, are involved in an impasse about an airplane that they own. It is his "pride and joy," but Rosie hates it. Their relationship is marked by emotional distance and a lack of affection. Their quarrel involves a brief outburst, then hiding emotions. Rosie begins in a soft, sweet voice:

Excerpt 3

22:23.25a	R:	*so what-aspect of the plane do you wanna talk about?*
b	J:	*oh jis airplanes in general it doesn't have to be ()*
c	R:	[oh]
d	J:	*specifically the one we have now (laugh)*
30.09e	R:	\<no:: NARROW it RIGHT down TU that one\>
34.15a	J:	[\<be]cause\> **I don't plan on it being the <u>las-the end</u> of the line** *ha*
37.07c	R:	NO:: *well,* I don't either () **not for you** ()
d	J:	<u>**Oh good**</u> \<soft)
40.28a	R:	**no- I wouldn't take yer toy from you**
b	J:	<u>**alright**</u> \<over soft)
22:42.14	R:	**I-I sacrificed a LOT for you to have toys** *(1.8)(both laugh tightly) but you-didn't-ask-for-it-an-I-resent later an-we're-still-going-over-it*\< *almost inaud) () ok".*

Rosie and James begin their quarrel with hesitation, mitigation, vagueness, avoidance, tense laughter, and false smiling. They seem to be colluding in avoiding the subject. Both are evasive; neither wants to be the one to begin. In their first utterances, their bond is being maintained at an arm's distance—neither wants to discuss the issue.

There is rapid alternation between shame and anger within and between Rosie and James. Alternation first becomes evident *between* them when James interrupts Rosie "[\<be]cause\> **I don't plan on it being the las-the end of the line** *ha*." He not only shows disrespect by interrupting her, he challenges her by implying that it doesn't matter what she thinks—he is going to continue to have airplanes. The indirect manner and disguised threat could damage the bond.

Rosie's response may first appear to be agreement ("NO:: *well* I don't either"), but after a short pause she retaliates ("**not for you**"). Her manner is derogatory, with an emphasis on *you*; her eyes and mouth are narrowed and tight, displaying anger. She may be implying,

"It might not be the last plane for you, but it is for me" (threatening abandonment).

Although James had been talking in full sentences, his response now becomes minimal ("**Oh good**"). Although the word *good* itself is affirmative, his voice is now very quiet; he withdraws from interaction (hiding behavior), cutting Rosie off from his inner world (anger). The conflict rapidly escalates, and the bond disintegrates.

Rosie's next response is more vehement: "**no I wouldn't take yer toy from you.**" Her response marks escalated anger and disrespect (like a mother talking to a child); it is sarcastic, demeaning, and condescending. Her face looks angry and tight and her eyes are narrowed, but she doesn't directly voice her anger—it seeps out. Visually, James implodes: his tense smile fades, and he appears to shrink in his seat. He withdraws—his response becomes minimal, and his voice is almost inaudible. Rosie's next response is vehement.

Unacknowledged shame was followed by anger in Rosie, which was followed by disrespect toward James. This in turn led to James's state of shame, angry withdrawal, and so on. (Rosie's shame as a starting point here is arbitrary, since the sequence is circular.) She seems to sense his disapproval because she quickly takes it all back in an attempt to repair the damage, displaying cues for both shame and anger in her last two lines.

Alternation of shame and anger *within* Rosie can be seen in the last three lines. Rosie stutters, complains, emphasizes, uses a degrading term ("toys"), pauses, laughs tensely, quickly changes the topic, speaks very rapidly, uses a code for shame-anger ("resent"), and becomes oversoft and inaudible. Five alternations occur in six seconds; there is shame and rage within and between them. This rapid alternation is followed by a change to an intellectual level of discussion. The conflict goes underground, emerging periodically throughout the remainder of the fifteen-minute quarrel.

Returning to Roxanne and Brian's conflict (excerpt 2a): Brian originally feels isolated, which is followed a demeaning complaint about Roxanne's behavior. His tone becomes sarcastic and belittling (anger). While he complains, Roxanne smiles and laughs tensely (shame cues). In turn, as she begins to speak, her voice is harsh and loud: "**OH I do that every day**," marking anger. Her response is also indirect; she hides her feelings behind a half question–half statement comment rather than directly stating her feelings, suggesting the presence of shame.

Brian's response defends his position: "**more often than not**," spoken very quietly. Roxanne's anger increases: "**Bull shit** *ha ha*," but includes tense laughter (shame). Roxanne launches into a long complaint about Brian's messiness, calling him a slob. As she complains loudly, Brian's response becomes minimal; he becomes tense, partially covering and touching his face with his hand. Face touching is something he had not done previously. When shame is present but not acknowledged, lack of respect and anger emerge.

Escalation

Not only is shame involved in the etiology and not only does it alternate with anger, but *in all cases shame precedes each episode of angry escalation*. As shame increases and is not acknowledged, anger emerges in indirect and disrespectful ways. The clearest illustration is the case of Randy and Karin. Their quarrel involves Karin's weight. She is about a hundred pounds overweight, and Randy harps about it. He seems to take her weight as an assault; he is also embarrassed by it. He also appears to be overweight, but his weight is not discussed.

The start of the quarrel is rampant with shame, before anger becomes visible. The utterances on the part of both parties are marked by lack of eye contact, fidgeting, avoidance, frequent pausing, mitigation, whining, defensiveness, and vagueness; all are manifestations of hiding behavior. There is a very high proportion of shame to anger in this couple, compared with the other couples (more than five times more shame than anger at the start of the quarrel).

At one point, Randy and Karin argue about where the weight problem originated. She complains that it stems from his lack of support; he claims that he gives her support. Randy complains that "the problem has gone too far, you have to lose weight." She counter-complains, "Support has to come from you." Randy responds, "I gave you five years of support." Karin says, "Obviously I wasn't getting ENOUGH support or I wouldn't have gained all this weight." Randy continues, "There's a million times you walked up to the corner to Swensens and I asked you () 'leave the damn ice cream alone' () and you would get an ice cream cone to spite me." Karin responds, "Ya but the support doesn't come in telling me not what to eat, but realizing I have some problems an I'm internalizing 'em, is where the support an YOU should come in." They're in a blame-blame cycle, tit for tat.

The segment that directly follows this exchange occurs less than a minute before intense escalation. Randy responds:

Excerpt 4a
    10:23.34 R: *ya but I can't get into yer mind*
             K: *well I-I you know I ()* **fairly read you well**

Randy's remark is an indication of separation. Karin follows with repetition, hesitation, and pausing, but finishes with a comparison with Randy in which he comes out deficient. She says she is able to do something he is unable to do—she can understand, and he can't. This comment seems to affect Randy intensely—his next response is defensive and dense with shame cues:

Excerpt 4b
29.52 R: well I fairly read you well too and *it it and I don't know I don't know whats going on it seems like ()* I *mean* we're both gonna be sixty five someday ()

This segment is marked by gaze aversion, as well as repetition, fragmentation, and self-interruption. All indicate disorganized thought processes involved in shame states. This segment is rapidly followed by escalated anger:

Excerpt 4c
R: an I'm not going to *you know* I'm not gonna
10:40.64 () mind livin with a **sixty-five year-old broad when I'm sixty-five** () **but we're in our thirties**
48.57 K: *I don't think I look like I'm sixty-five* (defensive) (said in a soft sweet voice)
R: (*clears throat*) **you have the same silhouette as a sixty-five-year-old broad**

Randy's verbal attack is preceded by a constellation of shame cues. His words and manner humiliate Karin, who responds defensively, and so on. Neither party steps out of the frame and comments on what is going on between them; they're caught up in the topic. Each escalation follows the same pattern across couples.

These findings suggest that escalation involves stages. First, there is a preexisting alienation. Second, shame is evoked but is not acknowledged; nor is the relationship discussed. Third, anger results as a defense against a perceived attack. It is often communicated disrespectfully, leading to a perpetuating series (figure 4–1).

Although the couples presented are not physically violent, there is verbal and emotional violence. They are alienated from each other. They deal with *what* was said—the topic—and not the manner or *how* it was said, which involves the bond between them; their emotions were not acknowledged. The tactics they used showed disrespect, and feelings escalated; the bonds were further damaged. Although preliminary, these results suggest that inadequate bonding and unacknowledged shame play a central role in destructive conflict.

Escalating conflict can be viewed as a reaction to inadequate bonds. Emotions signal the state of the bond, as well as the need for readjustment and change. Conflict is functional to the extent that it repairs the bond; it is dysfunctional to the extent that it creates further alienation. On a macro level, alienated societies may be at risk not only for suicide, as Durkheim's findings suggested, but also for higher rates of violence of all kinds.

Chapter 4 further examines the escalation of conflict. Randy and Karin's quarrel is used because it escalates seven times during the course of fifteen minutes, each point of escalation more intense than the previous one. The rapidity and complexity of this escalation suggests why the causal process is mysterious to both participants and analysts alike.

Appendix 4A

David and Colleen:

27:33.13	D:	I'm just saying do you know what you want () cause you can't get there if you don't know what you want
40.11	C:	right yeah
	D:	an the other part is why after fifteen years if you know what
45.25		you want, () if you can describe it or visualize it in your head
	C:	um hm
50.24	D:	why you haven't implemented it
	C:	umhm
53.09	D:	an if the money wasn't there that's just an excuse it's just a roadblock
	C:	umhm
57.01	D:	to
		overcome
	C:	umhm
58.05	D:	why didn't you do something to get the money together to decorate just
28:01.07		the way that you wanted
	C:	[yeah] ok so what I've done
07.00		an uh is to decorate just with what I've got
	D:	right () an that's satisfactory ()
10.20	C:	well () it's been practical
13.10	D:	an that's satisfactory
	C:	uh hu () I mean um yes an no
18.00	D:	it hasn't been for me . . .

30:15.20 D: has it been satisfactory to you () all this time () to decorate with your history () instead of () making your history (1.70)

Roxanne and Brian

16:17.05 B: It's the times when you feel like you're the only soldier on the field () and you come home-I come home

26.20 R: [hhh]   [hhh]

B: and you're going OH MAN, I've done EVERY-THING today, I've just done everything, I've dealt with this and that and this and that and now its

R: [laugh]   [ah]

36.05 B: YOUR-TURN to deal with it () an here take

R: [cough]

B: Christopher (the baby) () an here change his diaper, and let me eat, and give me two minutes of peace, and I'm burned out (2.85)

16:43.15 R: Oh I do that every day (2)

B: More often than not

48.05 R: Bull-shit (1.75)

B: More often than not

R: uhuh

16:52.05 B: You're tired, you don't wanna deal with it ()

R: yeah I am tired

B: you don't wanna deal with Christopher () You feel like () YOU'VE

R: no () not all the time

58.28 B: had to do everything in the house an pick up

R: [hhhhhhh]

17:02.00 B: everything an clean everything an you SAY!

R: YEAH I GOTTA PICK up AFTER YOU ALL THE TIME, you're such a SLOB you just take your clothes off in the middle of the floor

05.22 B: an () you say that I () don't do anything

09.09 R: you don't if I don't move (both slightly laugh) your shoes out of the middle of the living room, they just stay there, if I don't pick up your clothes in the middle of the floor they'll stay

17.06   there, you'll walk all over them. You'll walk over them when you get home from WORK. You're MESS in the CLOSET, its still there; you don't put ANYTHING away. I fold your laundry, I wash

28.05   it and put it some where where you can put it
away and you don't put it away. It's more work for
me (slight laugh)

38.08 B: I NEVER put it away.

R: WELL, before OUR parents come you usually tidy
up a little.

45.00 B: it's not the only time ()

R: and once in a blue moon, when you get the urge to
pick up

Rosie and James

22:23.25a R: so what aspect of the plane do you want to talk
about?

b J: oh just airplanes in general it doesn't have to be ()

c R: [oh]

d J: specifically the one we have now (laugh)

30.09e R: no NARROW it RIGHT down TO
that one

34.15a J: because I don't plan on it being the last,
the end of the line

37.07c R: NO, well I don't either () not for you ()

d J: Oh good

40.28a R: no I wouldn't take your toy from you

b J: alright

22:42.14 R: I I sacrificed a LOT for you to have toys (1.8)
(both laugh tightly)
but you didn't ask for it, and I resent later, and
we're still going over it () ok

Randy and Karin

10:23.34 R: yeah but I can't get into your mind

K: well I-I you know, I () fairly read you well

29.52 R: well I fairly read you well too and it it and I don't
know, I don't know what's going on, it seems like
() I mean we're both gonna be sixty-five someday ()
and I'm not going to, you know, I'm not going to

10:40.64 () mind living with a sixty-five-year-old broad when
I'm sixty-five () but we're in our thirties

48.57 K: I don't think I look like I'm sixty-five

R: you have the same silhouette as a sixty-five-year-old-
broad

5
Emotional Violence: A Case Study

T his chapter demonstrates in detail our theory and method for understanding conflict. In earlier chapters, we have proposed that *protracted* conflict may be a result of social-emotional separation and unacknowledged shame. A single case is used here to demonstrate the dynamics of marital conflict. The discourse of an actual quarrel is analyzed; sequences of emotion prior to moments of escalation are traced. The results indicate that angry escalation is always preceded by unacknowledged shame. Sequences within and between spouses move from emotional separation and shame, to anger, to disrespect, to further separation and shame, and so on. Interaction in this couple is marked by alienation rather than solidarity.

Case studies are perhaps an endangered species, but they nonetheless may fill a knowledge gap. Intensive case studies using sequential analysis may provide a significant contribution since they lend themselves well to expanding studies of emotion, and since they show moment-by-moment sequences of causation.

In this chapter, the quarrel between husband and wife that shows many instances of escalation is investigated for hidden patterns. Rather than relying on anecdotal material, an intensive method detects emotions in discourse as they occur in moment-by-moment sequences. The framework for analysis is built around our theory of the social bond and emotion.

In chapter 2, we discussed the importance of the social bond and the fact that separation is an important element in conflict. For the purposes of this book, we view separation as social-emotional alienation rather than as physical alienation. Conflict results from lost or threatened emotional bonds.

The context for shame is important because shame involves a message perceived as emotional separation (or as a threat of separation) and as an injury to the self: insult, rejection, rebuff, disapproval, unrequited love, betrayal, unresponsiveness, disrespect, and so on. The context in which shame occurs reveals its intricate connection with *alienation* and threats of abandonment.

In other studies using video techniques and photographs, Retzinger (1985, 1987) has shown the rapidity with which shame and rage alternate. Retzinger used still frame and slow motion to capture these events. Photographs were used to illustrate six alternations between shame and rage in a time span of seven seconds. A further finding was that when shame co-occurred with anger, the anger expression was drawn out to extended periods of time, whereas when no shame was present, anger expressions were short-lived. The following analysis shows how the shame-anger spiral can develop in a particular quarrel.

Randy and Karin

Randy and Karin, a couple first mentioned in chapter 4, are both in their thirties. He is a college student, an artist and sculptor; she is employed as a manager. They are both unhappy about the state of their relationship, and they are destructive toward each other verbally and emotionally. There has been no reported physical violence.

Karin and Randy's quarrel is intense, characterized by covert and overt hostile criticism on the part of both, and "character assassination" by Randy toward Karin. Their tactics include name-calling, demeaning criticism, interruptions, and blaming. Randy's hostility to Karin is very overt, evident in comments such as "You have the same silhouette as a sixty-five-year-old broad" (10:48.57). Karin's anger is more subtle, emerging in disguised forms, such as in her innuendo that Randy is a sexist.

The main focus of their quarrel is the weight that Karin has gained: "since the death of the last baby alone I've gained eighty pounds." She appears to be greatly overweight. Although Randy also appears to be quite overweight, little mention is made of his weight. During the fifteen-minute quarrel that was videotaped, they moved from topic to topic: who gives who support, their sex life, Randy's friends, and Karin's father. Each blames the problem on the other, and neither takes responsibility for his or her own role. Randy and Karin's bond seems to be quite fragile, and their disrespectful manner of communicating their grievances damages it further. This quarrel escalates eight times in fifteen minutes; it ends with cursing and a very high level of anger.

The excerpts below show behavior patterns at different points of escalation. (The uncoded transcript using standard English spelling can be found in appendix 5A). The transcript is broken into nine excerpts for analysis, using the conventions of transcription (table 4–3). These conventions are based on those used in conversation and discourse analysis.

Randy and Karin are entrenched in the type of quarrel where each seems to know what the other will say and that it will be futile, but neither can stay out of it. The quarrel is already in process at the beginning, as Randy mentions "Joseph." The feelings are already high; Karin is quite fidgety—behavior she did not display previously. Karin and Randy's quarrel begins.

Excerpt 1

05:10.60a	R:	So yer brother Joseph () was gonna talk to me at
b		one point in time (3.75) *ya-remember* you were gonna tell
21.63c		me that *uh* (2.60) he's saying that *um* (1.25)
d		men in () *what S::amoa or something*
26.35e	K:	**Jamaica**
f	R:	In Jamaica () would prefer () overweight women
30.65g	K:	**they-don't preFER-it they jist accEPT it** (1.69)

In excerpt 1, Randy begins by tiptoeing into a sensitive issue— Karin's weight. He is cautious and avoidant, pausing frequently; his first step is to triangulate (Bowen 1978) on to a third party, "Joseph," instead of talking directly about what is going on with their own relationship. Bringing a third person into the conversation is a maneuver used to avoid feelings and increase the distance between them—that is, to separate them.

At this point there is no evidence of anger, but Randy displays many cues for shame in his hiding behaviors: he averts his gaze, leans away, hesitates, triangles, makes frequent pauses, uses filler words, mitigates, and generalizes. His shame is also evident in his attempt at casualness or indifference. Indifference can mark a state of bypassed shame; "it succeeds in warding off feelings of humiliation in the self and it can succeed in evoking them in others" (Lewis 1981:12).

Randy pauses after he says "one point in time" (05:10.60b), giving Karin a cue to speak. Karin does not take the cue. Instead, she closes her eyes, nods her head affirmatively, but barely observably, and averts her gaze. She avoids or relinquishes her turn, avoiding the topic.

Although Randy is doing the speaking in excerpt 1a–d (as well as during the 3.75-second pause), Karin silently reveals many cues for shame. First, she doesn't take up the cue from Randy to speak, although she nods her head very slightly, acknowledging what Randy is saying. Her refusal to engage and her withdrawal from interaction suggest avoidance (hiding) behavior. Shame also is seen in her constellation of visual cues during the entire time Randy speaks: her gaze aversion, false smiling, fidgeting, and vertically wrinkling forehead are recurrent.

Karin's silence and withdrawal indicate the presence of anger as well as shame. Withdrawal can be interpreted as passive-aggressive—a hostile gesture of cutting off emotionally from Randy. While evidence of anger is only slight and indirect, the evidence of shame present is strong.

After the long pause, Randy continues, cueing her further: "ya-remember . . . (2.60)." Karin looks down at this point, displaying a false smile, avoiding further involvement—even visual involvement—with Randy (that is, she separates herself visually). Randy pauses and stalls, manifesting his discomfort. Both continue to avoid being the first to mention "weight."

As Randy speaks, Karin displays many nonverbal cues for shame, but when she actually speaks, the emotion manifest in her first utterance is anger. Karin whines the word *Jamaica*, which indicates a state of "helpless anger" (Labov and Fanshel 1977). Helpless anger is a state of shame-rage, helplessness being a shame variant. Anger is also present in the implication of the "other correction"; she is terse and to the point—he was mistaken: it was not Samoan women, but Jamaican women.

Karin's emotions are first manifest vocally as she corrects Randy's error: she averts her gaze, whines, and bluntly corrects him; her response is minimal. (Compare this line of Karin's with her other utterances in the dialogue; she is usually not at a loss for words.) She fidgets, and her mouth becomes tense and square.

One implication of Karin's correction might be "I am right, you are wrong"—that is, one-upmanship: she knows better than he. Karin also shows disrespect in her correction with her matter-of-fact tone:* "any fool would know it was Jamaica and not Samoa."[1] She averts her gaze as she corrects Randy and again when Randy says they "prefer" overweight women in Samoa. Karin displays cues for both shame and anger.

In excerpt 1, Karin is disrespectful toward Randy, as if he were putting her down. She appears to be acting in accordance with her past experience and her future expectations, rather than the present interaction. In excerpt 1g, Karin attacks Randy, implying that *he* doesn't accept *her* weight gain—not that he should *prefer* it, but he should *accept her* in spite of the weight. Karin and Randy are not talking about "other" women but about her weight, using third persons (Jamaicans) and whether they accept it or not. Putting a third party between them symbolizes separation.

---

[1] A *counterfactual* is something that could have or might have been said, but that was not said. Counterfactuals are marked with an asterisk in this book.

Randy corrects himself and completes his idea, displaying further cues for shame: pausing, hesitation, indifference, question/statement. He attempts to remain casual and indifferent. He pauses before he says "overweight" and ends his sentence with a question, as if asking permission for a go-ahead, or reassurance about discussing the issue. Karin does not give him either but looks away as he speaks and correct Randy's error a second time.

To summarize excerpt 1, Karin is filled with feelings about being overweight. She is defensive and acts as if Randy is going to blame her for their problems. There is helpless anger in her manner, as seen in the alternation of the cues for shame and rage in the transcript conventions: *she averts gaze*, **other correction, staccato, heavy emphasis, whine, heavy emphasis**, *long pause, averts gaze*. She strikes out at Randy by correcting him at every opportunity. Randy does not show cues of anger, but many cues of shame.

As we have seen, when shame is not acknowledged, hostility is perceived as coming from the other. Here, Karin attacks Randy as if she were being attacked by him. Although he does not *appear* to be showing any hostility in this first excerpt (and in fact he *appears* to be attempting to show indifference), later in the interview he puts her down in the most hostile and demeaning ways.

Karin's anger increases as she puts Randy down in a disguised way.

Excerpt 2

05:35.00a	K:	**jis-tryin-tu-say-that Madison Avenue type** (.85)
b		stereotype () of what American women should look
40.49c		like *(2.00) I mean-jis* **ALL**
d	R:	umhm
46.90e	K:	*right now (1.8) (inaud)* what Madison Avenue
f		thinks women should look like-*hhh I mean* not all
g		women are () five () feet six inches high (/) *I-mean*
h		tall an *you know know* weigh 123 pounds (1.10)
i		there's a lot of women because they weigh 160 or
59.60j		because *they weigh 250 are not acceptable* because
06:03.00k		they're overweight () but *society doesn't accept them*
l		*(1.05) yer not accepted on job interviews yer not*
m		*accepted (1.06)* you know with MO::ST () **so called**
n	R:	*umhm* [*uhm*]
11.20o	K:	**elitist type men an stuff so (1) who-who needs it**
p		*(1.3 an if yu* happen tu have gained weight because
q		*you've* got problems in *yer* life then *yu* gain weight

r   because *you* got problems in yer life *that-doesn't-*
s   *mean-yer any less of-a-person ()*

To understand why Karin attacks Randy with a long monologue, later exchanges need to be invoked. In an excerpt that occurs seven minutes later, Randy completely denies any responsibility for the problems they have: he assumes that their problems exist entirely because of Karin's weight:

13:53.00 K: . . . that sex isn't the greatest, could any of it be your fault

R: NO

56.62 K: NONE of it

R: uhuh

K: none of it in BED was your fault it was all my fault that it wasn't the greatest (1.8) ya see what yer saying

R: ya I do () and that's what I'm saying

. . .

14:10.00 K: wel-I mean but let's be honest about it () I'm THAT horrible in bed tha-and yer that exciting () is that what yer saying

R: umhmm

Randy's attitude may help explain Karin's earlier behavior in excerpt 2. His conviction seems to be that if she would just lose weight, *everything* would be better:

15:00.52 K: [cause all that stuff (their problems)] would disappear? yer gonna care more if I weighed a hundred an twenty-five

03.92 R: [HELL:: YA]

Returning to excerpt 2, Karin triangulates onto further topics: "Madison Avenue" stereotypes, society (not accepting overweight), job interviewers, elitist men (as well as using *you* rather than *I*). These are important social issues about the stigmatization of overweight people, but a subtle world of gestural interaction is occurring between Karin and Randy that is not being dealt with: the distance between them, their manner toward each other, and their unacknowledged emotions.

Karin's actual utterances avoid the feelings between them, creating further distance. Excerpt 2 is filled with emotion, as seen in many cues. To illustrate the density of cues in this utterance, each is presented in order of occurrence. Each cue corresponds to the actual line of the

verbal dialogue in excerpt 2. This excerpt takes place in a fifty-second
time span; in that period there are nine cues for anger; and sixty-eight
cues for shame.

a) *mitigate avert gaze rapid/condensed triangle pause*
b) **hostile** *pause avert gaze lean away fidget triangle*
c) *long pause justify mitigate* **emphasis** *expansion*
e) *avert gaze* **fidget** *fragmentation long pause inaudible
lax articulation triangle*
f) *avert gaze* **forced outbreath** *justify generalize pause*
g) *pause avert gaze pause self-correction avert gaze filler*
h) *long pause fidget avert gaze generalize triangle*
i) *avert gaze fidget wrinkle forehead*
j) *wrinkle forehead pause ideation isolation*
k) *wrinkle forehead ideation isolation pause avert gaze
ideation isolation emphasis*
l) *avert gaze ideation of isolation*
m) *long pause filler avert gaze* **heavy emphasis** *pause* **hostile**
implication
o) **heavy emphasis** *avert gaze generalize filler pause oversoft*
repetition denial pause
p) *avert gaze denial* **blame**
q) *avert gaze* **heavy emphasis**
r) *avert gaze*
s) *ideation of being insignificant pause*

Excerpt 2 provides a massive constellation of cues that indicate
evidence for shame: visual, paralinguistic, and verbal, with the ideation
of the possibility of being "less of a person" and "unacceptable."
Although there are fewer cues for anger, they are present and increasing: Karin challenges and insults Randy by implying that he is like
"elitist type men" (she looks directly at him as she says "elitist"); she
emphasizes certain words and implies that he is a sexist. There was no
forewarning that Karin was going to change the subject from Samoan
women to Madison Avenue women, marking flagrant disrespect. It is
not direct, but her anger seeps out in a demeaning way. She acts as if
she were talking not about Randy but about everyone else.

During her long vocalization, Randy's response becomes minimal,
signaled only by infrequent *umhum*'s, as if he were politely listening to
what Karin has to say. As Karin begins to say that overweight women
are socially unacceptable, Randy exhibits shame cues: scratches his
chin, covers his mouth (28.84), leans away, and averts his gaze (22.45,
15.00) until the end of her speech. Karin's message affects Randy
strongly, as evidenced by his reaction as he begins to speak.

Excerpt 3

06:25.87 R: *(4) YA we::ll () (long sigh) (8.26)*

34.38 K: **ya-well-wha** *(3.70)*

R: *ya but I hesitate ta get into this at all I ()*

K: **well**

42.30 R: ([**AHH!**] -guttural noise) *() cause I (3) you know I
don't wanna () get into yer ()* **character assassination**
but I usually do (3.20)

58.80 K: you-don't-have-tu say anything *SUPER* personal but

Randy is hesitant, and his cues for shame become increasingly dense:
he covers his mouth with his hand and averts his gaze; there is a long
pause, then a mitigation, then a very long pause. Randy hesitates before
starting the topic of Karin's weight. There is a sigh that seems to be a
precursor to going into the inevitable battle. There is an unusually long
silence (8.26 seconds)—the longest in the entire dialogue.

As Randy speaks, anger flashes across Karin's face as her eyes and
mouth tighten, lasting two seconds, followed by gaze aversion, followed
by another anger expression one second later, as she begins to speak
(06:34.38). She has taken more than eight seconds to respond to Randy's utterance. When she does, she challenges him. Cues for anger
increase in frequency, particularly in Karin: tight eyes and mouth, challenging words, direct hard gaze, rapid/condensed words. She also displays cues for shame toward the end of her utterance as she averts her
gaze, fidgets and pauses, displays a false smile, and licks her lips.

Another long pause occurs before Randy explains his reluctance to
enter the topic. He does not want to go into it, he knows what will
happen: he will assassinate Karin's character. Many cues for shame are
exhibited in Randy before he brings up this violent image, character
assassination. Karin tries to diminish the threat of getting personal
(06:58.80).

In excerpt 4 Randy pays no attention to her suggestion but reacts
to what Karin said in excerpt 2. He defends his ground, as though
Karin had been talking about him rather than "elitist type men."

Excerpt 4

R: [but] ya
have   tu   understand   that-*ah*   *um(2.40)if-uh-you-
know-tha-tha*

07:02.00 *I mean* yer living with one of the most anti-social
men in the world *(1.50)* that anything that society

		would do I would AUTOmatically try to find a a completely different way tu go about anything
13.30	K:	but NOT when women are concerned
	R:	[but you also] *we-* that's not true
17.50	K:	ya it is

Randy interrupts Karin, showing disrespect. Although several exchanges have occurred since excerpt 2, Randy perseveres. He is insulted by Karin's insinuation that he is one of those "elitist type men," like the rest of society in how they treat overweight people. Randy defends himself. Karin challenges Randy further (07:13.30); they respond tit for tat: "yes you are," "no I'm not."

Although Randy says he does not want to get into Karin's "character assassination," he cannot stay out of it. The next and remaining excerpts indicate rapidly rising anger. The last five excerpts are episodes of angry escalation, each more intense than the preceding one. (Visually compare the italicized type with the boldfaced type in excerpts 1 to 9).

Excerpt 5

R:	its not true *I mean* () I think *every* man has th
07:21.29	dream woman () *every* man has th-their dream nuh silhouette () dream () shape *() you know uh* dream eyes *uh:: you know* whatEVER **(2.35) and um (3.15) an I I hate tu put it you this uh you know I hate tu (2.62) to always harp on the same stuff but- tuh (2.75) I mean** at your weight now: **(2.35) you're**
50.36	**just not doin-it for me** *(2.50) and uh (4) I know that its been really shitty of* me *to (2.10)*
08:00.00	**not touch you and not be romantic with you an not** *(2.50)* **sometimes even be kind to you** *(2.10) but uh (3) I don't-know-yu-know* it started out
15.50	about about a year ago that *uh () yu know I I* suddenly felt *very very* hemmed **very frustrated** by it *(3.53)* and tu begin with if () we're both down to
33.17	our proper weights *(2.59)* **sex would be much better**

Cues for anger multiply and alternate rapidly with shame cues. A characteristic feeling associated with shame-rage is that the situation is endless or hopeless. Four minutes and eighteen seconds into the quarrel, Randy expresses this feeling: "[this one seems] like a never ending one (2.75)" (09:17.51). By now the level of anger is very high, but one minute and five seconds later, the quarrel escalates further:

Excerpt 6
09:39.03 R: *you have you you* have tu lose some weight
   41.30 K: I agree but the support from you should come =
         R: = I
         gave you five years of support =
   46.31 K: = can't say that
         because I mean obviously
         R: [with every damn diet]
   48.40 K: I wasn't getting ENOUGH support or I wouldn't
         have gained all this weight
   51.90 R: [well] then you would
         need to have married FIFTY men and had them all
         sort of *u u u*
   55.50 K: *thats not fair* <softly)
         R: telling you that "you kin do it, you kin do it" the
         support doesn't necessarily *jus* come from without ()
         there's a million
10:03.90 K: [I wouldn't]
         R: times you walked up to the corner tu Swensen's
         an I
    8.20 asked you () leave the damn ice cream alone () an
         you would get an ice cream cone tu spite me
   13.50 K: ya but the support doesn't come in telling me not
         what tu eat but realizing that I have some problems
         an I'm internalizing em is where the support an
         YOU should come in
   23.34 R: *ya but I can't get into yer mind*
         K: *well I-I you know I () fairly* read you well
   29.52 R: *well* I fairly read you well too and *it it and I don't
         know I don't know whats going on it seems like ()
         I mean* we're both gonna be sixty-five someday ()
         an I'm not going to *you know* I'm not gonna ()
         mind livin with a sixty-five-year-old broad when I'm
         sixty-five () but we're in our thirties
   48.57 K: *I don't think I look like I'm sixty-five*
         R: (*clears throat*) you have the same silhouette as a
         sixty-five-year-old broad
   53.71 K: that doesn't matter

Randy and Karin argue about where the weight problem originated. She complains that it stems from lack of support; he claimed
that he has given her support. There are complaints and countercom-
plaints; each judges the problem as due to the other. They are now in a
blame-blame cycle, each putting the responsibility on to the other.
Alternations of emotions continue.

Intense escalation occurs in less than a minute as Randy responds
to Karin's complaint about his lack of support: (*"ya but I can't get into
yer mind"*—ideation of separation). Karin responds with one-
upmanship: *"well I-I you know I () fairly read you well."* She starts
out with repetition, hesitation, and pausing but finishes with a criticism
of Randy. She says she is able to do something he is unable to do—she
can understand and he can't.

Randy is affected intensely. His next response is defensive and
dense with shame cues: gaze aversion, repetition, fragmentation, and
self-interruption. All indicate the disorganized thought processes involved in shame states. Escalated anger rapidly follows as he demeans
Karin as "**a sixty-five-year-old broad.**" His verbal attack is preceded by
shame cues, as it is in each instance of escalation. His words and
manner humiliate Karin in turn, who responds defensively, and so on.
They continue to blame each other in excerpt 7.

Excerpt 7
14:21.61 K: *(laugh)* **yu see yer not even FACING the problem
               an maybe thats where the problem lies**
  24.78 R: [what do you mean] not no
              no see the problem is (1.63) jis-visualize () **you at a
              hundred and twenty-five**
  31.59 K: **EVEN IF I WEIGHED** a hundred and twenty-five
              we'd still have a problem in bed
  32.63 R: [wait a second I'm not finished talking] thats not
              true () <u>what kind of a problem would we have</u>
  38.40 K: the same problem we have NO::W because of the
              way you ARE
       R: what do you mean that I don't kiss you
  43.97 K: <u>you don't yer not really</u>
       R: <u>[that I] don't that I don't get into</u>
  46.21   <u>foreplay that I don't get into um:: being kind an an
              um being uh () watchful for your own *um* () yu
              know</u>
       K: *[laugh]*
       R: **climaxes** an yer own () uh

Their quarrel is out of control. Randy has become extremely personal about the details of the problems in their sex life. Cues for overt
anger are now predominant where earlier unacknowledged shame was
in the fore. Randy continues claiming that the problem is Karin's
weight. Karin now says the problem is that Randy doesn't face the
problem, and that the problem won't end if she loses weight because
it's Randy's denial that causes the problem. They interrupt and criticize

each other frequently and vehemently, both showing more disrespect than previously.

Shame remains unacknowledged; neither person levels, commenting either on their manner or on the bond. Rather, the tactics they use erode the bond between them. Although shame cues are still present, anger is now the predominant emotion.

Excerpt 8

16:40.49 R: . . . simply
because **I don't want tu kiss you or spend time kissing you** *doesn't mean* <u>**I don't like YOU**</u> *() yu see* **you got that backwards**

50.06 K: [yes it does] =

R: = no you got that backwards ()
what that means *is* () *is* that I don't like yer FACE

54.40   () *right now* () *I mean* it used tu be that had some actual lips () NOW::yer there's-ther there's very

17:01.31 K: <u>[you don't have any upper lip]</u>

R: <u>little definition</u>

K: <u>don't talk about my lips</u>

Randy and Karin continue to interrupt each other and show increased signs of anger; they use tactics that blatantly insult and humiliate each other. Although the topic seems trivial (lips), it is discussed with great vehemence. The quarrel escalates to include a friend of Randy's (as in, K: "look at Kevin and his relationship. . .he's entering his fourth marriage; his ideal of women is only looking through the magazines and not caring about their character") and Karin's father, putting the friend and father down in demeaning and hostile ways. Excerpt 9 is the last episode of escalation before the session ends.

Excerpt 9

19:57.12 R: **I don't know how the hell you were raised that way I mean your father is <u>the mo-is</u> the biggest liar () I mean you could ask yer father what day it was** . . .

As another third party is drawn in, the gap between Randy and Karin is widened; nothing about the relationship is addressed, nor the emotions between them. When outside parties get involved, polarization of positions can solidify into tribal warfare (Neuhauser 1989).

The quarrel continues to escalate at intervals as illustrated. Each incident of escalation brings the quarrel to a higher level of anger; the increase in cues for anger parallels the increase in shame cues.

The level of anger and hostility becomes very high as the 15-minute session comes to a close. As a timer signals the end of the session, Randy cannot stop "harping"; he finally ends with the line, "**GOD DAMN KARIN** *I'm jis gonna go the rest of my life with. . . .*" Continued cursing and hopelessness is an indication that shame-rage is present at a high level.

Conclusion

Randy and Karin's quarrel began with a dense cloud of shame cues but few anger cues. Alternation between anger and shame steadily increased, reaching a high level of emotional violence; the quarrel ended with intense anger. Although the quarrel began with the topic of Karin's weight, it shifted from topic to topic; shame preceded each topic change. It was never acknowledged and was followed by an increase in anger—paralleling the increasing shame. The rapid change of topics showed disrespect; it was used to blame, to overwhelm the other, and it served to avoid the isolation that each felt in this relationship. Throughout the quarrel the bond was being damaged; there were no moments of repair or building bridges. Each was alienated from the other.

Randy and Karin were not physically violent, but they were verbally and emotionally violent, as seen in their demeaning comments. They dealt only with *what* was being said—the topic—and not with the manner or *how* it was being said, which involved the bond between them; emotions were not acknowledged. The tactics they used showed disrespect, and feelings escalated—the bonds were further damaged in each case. Although the results are preliminary, they suggest that inadequate bonding and unacknowledged shame play a central role in destructive conflict.

Conflict and escalation can be viewed as a reaction to inadequate bonds; feelings are signals that communicate the state of the bond and the need for readjustment and change. At all times, bonds are being *built, maintained, repaired,* or *damaged.* When important bonds are damaged, shame results; when shame is not acknowledged, the attack is warded off with anger. Anger, according to Bowlby (1973), is functional to the extent that it repairs a bond; it is dysfunctional to the extent that it creates further alienation, shame, and anger.

The findings show that escalation involves several stages. First, the bonds are inadequate or threatened in emotional separation/alienation. Second, shame is evoked but is not acknowledged; the bond is not discussed. Third, anger follows shame, as a defense against an attack (that is, to save face), often expressed disrespectfully, leading to self-perpetuating sequences. This finding supports Lewis's formulation of the relationship between shame and rage.

The next chapter uses a quite different source of information—a classic novel. Our analysis of Werther's emotions suggests that biographical and verbal data can be used to understand motivation in much the same way that verbal and nonverbal data have been used in this chapter.

Appendix 5A

Randy and Karin:

05:10.60 R: So your brother Joseph () was gonna talk to me at one point in time (3.75) you-remember you were
  21.63   gonna tell me that uh (2.60) he's saying that um (1.25) men in () what Samoa or something
  26.35 K: Jamaica
          R: In Jamaica () would prefer () overweight women
  30.65 K: they don't prefer it they just accept it (1.69)
05:35.00   just trying to say that Madison Avenue type (.85) stereotype () of what American women should look
  40.49   like (2.00) I mean just ALL
          R: umhm
  46.90 K: right now (1.80) what Madison avenue thinks women should look like I mean not all women are () five () feet six inches high () I mean tall and you know weigh 123 pounds (1.10) there's a lot of women because they weigh 160 or because they weigh 250 are not
  59.60   acceptable because they're overweight () but society
06:03.00   doesn't accept them (1.05) you're not accepted on job interviews you're not accepted (1.06) you know with MOST () so called
          R: umhm   [uhm]
  11.20 K: elitist type men an stuff so(l) who-who needs it (1.3) an if you happen to have gained weight because you've got problems in your life then you gain weight because you got problems in your life that doesn't mean your're any less of a person ()
  25.87 R: (4) YOU well () (long sigh) (8.26)
  34.38 K: you well what (3.70)
          R: you but I hesitate to get into this at all I ()
          K: well

42.30 R: [AHH!] (guttural noise) () cause I (3) you know I
don't wanna () get into your () character assassination but I usually do (3.20)
58.80 K: you don't have to say anything SUPER personal but
R: [but] you have to
understand that ah um (2.40) if uh you know
07:02.00 that I mean your living with one of the most anti-
social men in the world (1.5) that anything that
society would do I would automatically try to find
a a completely different way to go about anything
13.30 K: but NOT when women are concerned
R: [but you also] that's not true
17.50 K: yeah it is
R: its not true I mean I think every man has their dream
21.29 woman () every man has their dream nuh silhouette
() dream () shape () you know uh dream eyes uh
you know whatever (2.35) and um (3.15) an I I
hate to put it you this uh you know I hate to
(2.62) to always harp on the same stuff but uh
50.36 (2.75) I mean at your weight now: (2.35) you're
just not doing it for me (2.50) and uh (4) I know
that it's been really shitty
08:00.00 of me to (2.10) not touch you and not be romantic
with you an not (2.50) sometimes even be kind to
you (2.10) but uh (3) I don't know you know it
15.50 started out about about a year ago that uh () you
know I I suddenly felt very very hemmed very
frustrated by it (3.53) and to begin with if () we're
both down to
33.17 our proper weights (2.59) sex would be much better

. . .

09:39.03 R: you have you you have to lose some weight
41.30 K: I agree but the support from you should come=
R: =I gave you five years
of support=
46.31 K: =can't say that because I mean
obviously
R: [with every damn diet]
48.40 K: I wasn't getting ENOUGH support or I wouldn't
have gained all this weight
51.90 R: [well] then you would need to have married

		FIFTY men and had them all sort of u u u
55.50	K:	that's not fair <softly)
	R:	telling you that "you can do it, you can do it" the support doesn't necessarily just come from without () there's a million
10:03.90	K:	[I wouldn't]
	R:	times you walked up to the corner to Swensen's and
8.20		I asked you () leave the damn ice cream alone () an you would get an ice cream cone to spite me
13.50	K:	you but the support doesn't come in telling me not what to eat but realizing that I have some problems an I'm internalizing em is where the support an YOU should come in
23.34	R:	yeah but I can't get into your mind
	K:	well I I you know I () fairly read you well
29.52	R:	well I fairly read you well too and it it and I don't know I don't know what's going on it seems like () I mean we're both gonna be sixty-five someday () an I'm not going to you know I'm not gonna () mind living with a sixty-five-year-old broad when I'm sixty-five () but we're in our thirties
48.57	K:	I don't think I look like I'm sixty-five
	R:	(clears throat) you have the same silhouette as a sixty-five-year-old broad
53.71	K:	that doesn't matter

. . .

14:21.61	K:	(laugh) you see you're not even FACING the problem an maybe that's where the problem lies
24.78	R:	[what do you mean] not no no see the problem is (1.63) just-visualize () you at a hundred and twenty-five
31.59	K:	EVEN IF I WEIGHED a hundred and twenty five we'd still have a problem in bed
32.63	R:	[wait a second I'm not finished talking] that's not true () what kind of a problem would we have
38.40	K:	the same problem we have NOW because of the way you ARE
	R:	what do you mean that I don't kiss you
43.97	K:	you don't your not really
	R:	[that I] don't that I don't get into
46.21		foreplay that I don't get into um being kind and an

um being uh () watchful for your own um () you
know

K: [laugh]

. . .

R: climaxes an your own () uh

16:40.49 R: . . . simply
because I don't want to kiss you or spend time
kissing you doesn't mean I don't like YOU () you
see you got that backwards

50.06 K: [yes it does]=

R: =no you got that backwards () what
that means is () is that I don't like your FACE

54.40   () right now () I mean it used to be that had some
actual lips () NOW your there's-there there's very

17:01.31 K: [you don't have any upper lip]

R: little definition

K: don't talk about my lips

. . .

19:57.12 R: I don't know how the hell you were raised that way
I mean your father is the mo-is the biggest liar () I
mean you could ask your father what day it
was . . .

6

"Love" and Revenge: Hidden Shame-Rage in a Classic Novel[1]

T his chapter proposes a model of unconscious motivation in infatuation and in revenge. Using the theory of alienation/ shame and the method of discourse analysis, we interpret sequences of events in Goethe's novel *The Sorrows of Young Werther*, and its parallels in Goethe's life. The concept of the social bond provides a framework for understanding the effects of alienation at the levels of society, personal relationships, and the self in the novel. Alienation from others and self gives rise not only to shame and anger but to unending chain reactions of these two emotions.

The concept of unconscious motivation is central to psychoanalytic theory, but it has never been accepted in the wider world. The difficulty may be less due to the idea itself than to Freud's presentation of it. Freud's theory of the unconscious is only an outline. His case histories are evocative, but the idea of unconscious motivation remains hypothetical and elusive in them.

Even the longest of Freud's cases is relatively brief; he never dealt with the masses of detail found in biographies and novels. His analyses are sketches in that they do not describe *sequences* of events showing, moment to moment, chains of cause and effect. In such brief sketches, both cause and effect remain hypothetical. For example, Freud's (1911) analysis of the Schreber case did not show *how* the son's unconscious homosexual feelings toward his father caused paranoia. Not only is the causal chain missing, the basic elements in the theory are vague. Both the putative cause, unconscious feelings, and the effect, paranoia, are treated abstractly.

---

[1]The advice of Harry Steinhauer has been invaluable in the writing of this chapter.

Unacknowledged Shame

To be applicable to sequences of events in a life, a theory needs explicit concepts and a precise description of the links between them. As indicated in earlier chapters, the theory of emotional dynamics proposed by Lewis (1971) contains these elements. The theory proposes *unacknowledged shame* as a crucial but hidden causal agent, leading to irrational and destructive behavior. (Lewis's work also suggests that shame plays a central role in maintaining *normal* social relationships. Shame causes pathological behavior only when it is *denied*.)

At the center of Lewis's theory is the idea of a "feeling trap," or having emotional reactions to one's own emotions, and reactions to the reactions, and so on. A "feeling trap" involves a series of loops of shame (being ashamed of being ashamed), which causes further shame, which can continue indefinitely. Such loops are recursive; there is no limit to the intensity and duration of the resulting emotions. This idea spells out a moment-to-moment causal chain in a way that earlier theories did not. The theory of "feeling traps," when applied to sequences from shame to anger to shame, may explain chains of behavior that erupt in violence (Scheff 1987, 1988; Katz 1988; Lansky 1988; Scheff, Retzinger and Ryan 1989).

As we have seen in chapter 2, Lewis's concept of bypassed shame seems to correspond exactly to Adler's (1956) concept of the "drive for power." And the speeded-up thought and speech processes, the empty, numb or hollow feelings, and the preoccupied obsessiveness typical of bypassed shame are familiar from descriptions of the personalities of very successful obsessive-compulsive men, the so-called Type A personality (Friedman et al. 1984).

Lewis's theory suggests that bypassed shame can take another route, in addition to the one specified by Adler: infatuation. Several of Lewis's cases (1971) suggest that infatuation occurs under the compulsion of unidentified shame. A person with chronic feelings of low self-esteem (shame) may seek attachment with a person who appears to exemplify desirable qualities. Rather than acknowledging their shame, the infatuated person acts it out, but not in terms of a drive for power.

Lewis's approach represents an advance over Adler's both in theory and in method. As a theory, it explicitly describes its basic concepts and the links between them. Like most other theories of human behavior, Adler's is only schematic; the concepts are "black boxes", neither their internal structure nor the causal links between them are specified.

In contrast to Adler and other theorists, Lewis provided a method for applying her theory to concrete episodes. Her method, which she does not name, would today be called *discourse analysis*. That is, she proceeded through transcripts, word by word, from beginning to end, applying precise concepts. She defined the context that was likely to give rise to shame and the outer indications of unacknowledged shame. It is possible to judge how closely her theory and method apply to episodes of behavior, whether factual events or in episodes taken both from fact and fiction.

In this chapter we use a model of a specific kind of "feeling trap,"—shame leading to anger—which in turn leads to further shame, creating unending feedback loops. Unlike most sociobiological processes, this one appears to have no natural limit to its intensity and duration. It can lead to explosive violence, and it can persist over a lifetime as what is called bitter hatred. (In Lewis's theory, hatred and resentment are interpreted as shame-anger sequences, with the anger directed outward. Guilt is seen as a shame-anger variant with the anger directed at the self.) Indeed, shame-anger chains can last even longer than a lifetime, since hatred can be transmitted from generation to generation in the form of racial, religious, and national prejudice.

According to this scheme, unalloyed anger is not damaging; it is rapidly and almost invisibly discharged as body heat or in other harmless ways (Scheff 1984). But when anger is bound by shame, it takes the form of "humiliated fury"; in this form, it refuses to subside (Lewis 1981).

It should be noted that Kohut was apparently referring to the same process with what he called "narcissistic rage," since he specified that it was a shame-anger compound (1979). But, like Adler's concept of the inferiority complex, the concept of narcissistic rage is a black box: Kohut doesn't spell out the details. In this chapter, we specify a structure/process model that shows how both rejection and revenge are motivated by a "triple spiral" of shame-anger: one spiral of shame-anger is *within* each party, and one spiral is *between* them as each person's angry shaming of the other intensifies the inner spirals (Scheff 1987).

The purpose of this chapter is to bring to life the idea of unconscious motivation, to show how it is positioned within an actor's matrix of thoughts, feelings, and actions. How do unconscious motives function in lived experience, in the "life world"?

Understanding the place of the unconscious and of repression in experience remains vague in psychoanalytic writing. Even Lewis (1971), in the course of showing unacknowledged shame in actual discourse, said little about the degree of repression, the mix of understanding and denial. Part of the problem is the breadth of the concept of unacknowledged shame. She usually did not specify the extent to which lack of acknowledgment was intentional or unconscious, or a mixture of the two.

Lewis's reticence on this point may have resulted from the type of data available to her—transcripts of therapy sessions. Although the transcripts were verbatim, her access to the persons involved was quite limited since she had no direct contact with them. She knew nothing about the overall lives of her subjects, only their behavior in a series of dialogues. By using Lewis's theory and method to interpret sequences of events in a novel and in its author's life, a precise theory of unconscious motivation can be illustrated.

Goethe's *Werther*

It has long been customary to view Goethe's *The Sorrows of Young Werther* (1774) as a romantic tragedy: because of unrequited love, the passionate Werther is heartbroken to the point that he takes his own life. But we suggest a different motive; that the emotions responsible for his suicide are shame-anger rather than love-grief. We propose that Werther's suffering originates in humiliation, which leads to unconscious revenge. A humiliation-revenge sequence can also be detected in Goethe's own life.

Our analysis unifies what have heretofore been considered two disparate themes in the novel: the romance, Werther's relationship with Lotte; and its political theme, his relationship to the Count. Werther's situation is one of profound alienation, not only from his society but in his personal relationships and from himself. Lotte is also alienated, but in a less obvious way than Werther. The concept of alienation provides a bridge between the romance, which we characterize as infatuation rather than love, and the embassy incident, which leads to Werther's break with the Count.

At first glance, an exacting interpretation of a work of fiction might seem futile from a scientific point of view. But in this case, literary scholarship has established that most of the plot is not fictional. Goethe spliced together two actual episodes—one autobiographical, the other biographical (Rose 1931; Reiss 1971). The first half of the novel is based largely on the twenty-three-year-old Goethe's summer in the city of Wetzlar (called "Wahlheim" in the novel), focusing on his relationships with Charlotte Buff and her fiancée, Johann Kestner. Like Werther, Goethe became attached to a woman who was promised to another man. But unlike Werther, Goethe broke off when he established himself in another city.

The second half of the book shifts from Goethe's life to that of Karl Jerusalem, an acquaintance of Goethe and Kestner. Like Werther, Jerusalem suffered an attachment to a woman who did not return his love and a social rebuff from a social superior. (Both Jerusalem and Goethe were novice lawyers.) Like Werther, Jerusalem took his own life. Not only are the main lines of the plot based on episodes from Goethe's and Jerusalem's lives, but so are many of the smallest details.

In later life, Goethe indicated that he had had intensely suicidal feelings after he left Wetzlar. To write the novel, he imagined how he might have taken his own life as Jerusalem did, calling upon his own experiences of defeat and humiliation. In a tour de force, Goethe integrated a torrent of details, real and imagined, into a single dramatic vision. As was readily apparent in Goethe's vastly productive later life, he was able to fashion the smallest *parts*—dense clouds of events—into the largest *wholes*, artistic and scientific creations.

Not only was Goethe able to connect *parts and wholes*, he was also able to describe this crucial process explicitly:

> In every living thing, what we call the parts is so inseparable from the whole that the parts can only be understood in the whole, and we can neither make the parts the measure of the whole nor the whole the measure of the parts; and this is why living creatures, even the most restricted, have something about them that we cannot quite grasp and have to describe as infinite or partaking of infinity. (Goethe 1787:195)

This statement is taken from Goethe's botanic studies, which are informed by his part/whole understanding: the smallest unit, the cell, must be understood in its relation to the plant, and the plant must be understood in its relationship to its cells. Goethe's analysis seems more coherent and forceful than current attempts to treat the part/whole issue. (For example, see Lerner 1963.) Modern scholars and scientists are so *specialized* that they usually ignore the problem of parts and wholes. Theorists and critics deal with wholes, while scientists and artists deal with parts (and parts of parts); there is little congress between the realms.

Goethe was a phenomenom even in the relatively unspecialized eighteenth century. His accomplishments in the arts and sciences are too extensive even to summarize here (Amrine et al. 1987). One example from his science must suffice. His work on relating form and function in plants seems more sophisticated than the current standard in botany. It connected the smallest details of plant structure to the largest theories of development and function. Modern botanic classification still shows substantial traces of its Linnaean heritage—that is, it is limited to the purely classificatory mode. Goethe combined in his own person the best features of general and particular understanding.

In *Werther*, Goethe forged an integrated whole from factual parts of two lives, as well as fictional parts. Goethe's ability to relate parts and wholes may have been greater than that of anyone before or since. This is not to say that he was aware of all the parts and wholes in his own work, or in his life. Although our analysis of the novel shows that

Werther has an overarching motive—*unconscious vengeance*—there is no evidence that Goethe was aware of it. As we will show at the end of this chapter, Goethe himself may have been unconsciously vengeful in the writing and publication of the novel.

Unlike the brief and abstract case histories written by Freud and others, *The Sorrows of Young Werther* makes available whole episodes, concrete events which often involve moment-to-moment sequences. The factual events from Goethe's and Jerusalem's lives also furnish such episodes. To the extent that Lewis's theory is true, there should be a correspondence between it and the details in both the novel and in Goethe's life.

Goethe's access to his subjects was quite different from that of Lewis (1971). Although he had no exact recording of their discourse, his information was rich in another way. The report of the events leading to Jerusalem's suicide was not firsthand but was conveyed to him in a very lengthy and detailed letter from Kestner. Kestner was in Wetzlar at the time, and he knew Jerusalem personally and others who knew him. He was in a position to glean a very exact description of the events leading to Jerusalem's suicide in the context of Jerusalem's whole life. Goethe also had the advantage of himself knowing Jerusalem and his ambience.

The other subject that provided the basis for the novel was Goethe himself. Many of the conversations in Book 1 may have been verbatim. Goethe's access to his subjects was rich in that it provided him with detailed information about particular episodes, like Lewis's accounts, but in the context of an entire life. The fullness of biographical context adds a dimension that is missing in most scientific and scholarly studies. Such studies usually provide either parts *or* wholes but seldom parts *and* wholes: discourse in the context of an entire life. Using Lewis's theory of feeling traps and her method of discourse analysis, we relate parts and wholes in the novel and in Goethe's life.

Unconscious Revenge

Part/whole analysis suggests the *insidiousness* of unconscious motives. This feature is particularly flagrant in the character of Werther. His conscious thought about suicide invokes religious themes and themes of self-sacrifice: he professes that by taking his own life, he is clearing the way for Lotte and Albert, and he says that he will see Lotte in the afterlife. But the text suggests an alternative motivation: rejection-humiliation-revenge. Werther's conscious thoughts are rationalizations that serve to further disguise his already well-hidden feelings. The possibility that Goethe himself harbored unconscious motives makes the same point: vengeful feelings may be acted upon, even though outside of one's own awareness.

There are many suggestions of Werther's vengefulness in the text. Most are indirect or disguised; only two are overt. Revenge against Albert and Lotte is mentioned in his last letter to her: "In this torn heart the frenzied thought has prowled about, often—to murder your husband—you—myself!" (81). The other overt indication of vengefulness occurs shortly after Werther suffered a social slight: the embassy incident. At the Count's prompting, Werther took himself off from a gathering of aristocrats because they were outraged that a commoner was present. After learning the next day that the incident was common knowledge, Werther states in the letter of March 16: "I am still in an inner rage. I wish someone would dare to reproach me, so that I could run a sword through his body; at the sight of blood I would feel better" (54).

There are many other manifestations of vengefulness in the novel, but they are all hidden or indirect. The most dramatic involves Werther's actions immediately following the embassy incident, described in his letter of March 15. (For further analysis, see Scheff and Mahlendorf 1987.) After leaving the reception, Werther reports: "I quietly slipped away from the distinguished company, . . . drove to M— to watch the sun set there from the hilltop, and to read that glorious Canto in Homer in which Ulysses is entertained by the excellent swineherd. It was a satisfying experience" (52). On the surface, the only emotion reported is a pleasant one; satisfaction. Werther's choice of reading matter points to a hidden emotion, however.

The canto that he reads in the *The Odyssey* (Book 14) raises the possibility that although Werther is not aware of it, he may be harboring resentment. In this passage, Ulyssess finds more courteous treatment from a swineherd than from the noble suitors, the aristocrats who are courting his wife and wasting his possessions. In context, Werther's selection of this passage suggests covert revenge upon the count: he is being compared unfavorably to a swineherd. Hidden in his reading matter is an implied sequence: insult-resentment-revenge.

Not only the particular passage but Werther's choice of the book from which it comes is redolent of unexpressed feeling, for the story culminates in bloody revenge. After the swineherd passage, Ulyssess kills all of the unarmed suitors one after another. After that, he continues the bloodbath by killing all the collaborators among the servants. Little wonder that Werther finds his reading a satisfying experience.

After he leaves the scene of his humiliation, Werther's reading allows him a fantasy of revenge, but outside of his own awareness. The text makes clear that if left to himself, Werther would have forgotten the incident and swallowed his feelings. But encounters with acquaintances (Adelin and Fraülein von B—) force him to recall the incident and experience the bitter feelings that result from it.

There are many other intimations of covert revenge in the text, but we will focus our attention on one—the effect of Werther's suicide on Lotte. Unlike the other hints, which involve single episodes, this one can be seen as pervading the entire story: Werther's hidden humiliation and anger at Lotte.

The first indications of the effect of Werther's death on Lotte are not unexpected. Lotte faints when she hears the news that Werther has shot himself. The "editor" (that is, Goethe) reports a further reaction after his death: "I shall say nothing of Albert's consternation nor of Lotte's grief" (96). But the last four sentences of the novel, with their death march cadence, hold a shock: "The old man and his sons followed the body; Albert was unable to do so. *Lotte's life was feared to be in danger.* Workmen bore him. No clergyman was present" (emphasis added). The reader is unprepared for such an intense reaction by Lotte. What could endanger her life? In romances, the heroines may die of grief, but slowly; they waste away, they languish. What crisis could threaten her life so rapidly? To answer this question, it is necessary to reread the text, starting with Lotte's involvement in Werther's suicide.

In the course of their final meeting, Lotte had a strong sense that Werther intended to kill himself. Werther was reading a passage from Ossian: "But the time of my fading is near, the blast that shall scatter my leaves. Tomorrow shall the traveler come;. . . His eyes will search the field, but they will not find me" (88). These words have a powerful effect on Werther: "The full force of these words descended on the unhappy man. He threw himself down before Lotte in all his despair, grasped her hands, pressed them to his eyes, against his forehead, and a premonition of his terrible resolve seemed to rush through her mind." (88) Lotte, in turn, responds emotionally: "Her senses became confused, she pressed his hands, pressed them against her breast, leaned toward him with a mournful movement, and their glowing cheeks touched. The world ceased to exist for them." (88) Werther then loses all restraint: "He threw his arms about her, pressed her to his breast, and covered her trembling, stammering lips with violent kisses." (88) He has gone too far, much too far:

> —"Werther!" she cried in a suffocating voice, turning from him, "Werther!" and with a weak hand she pushed his body away from hers. "Werther!" she cried in the steady tone of the noblest emotion.—He did not resist, released her from his arms and threw himself before her, senseless. She jumped up, and in confusion and anxiety, quivering between love and anger, she said, "This is the last time, Werther. You shall not see me again."—And, casting a look full of love at the wretched man, she hurried into the next room and locked the door behind her. (88–89)

Her indignation at his advances has overcome her pity; she cuts herself off from him.

Goethe's plot ensnares Lotte: she feels compromised to the point of paralysis. She fears that Werther will kill himself, but she cannot tell Albert because of the circumstances under which she has realized Werther's intention. She tells Albert nothing of her fear or of the tempestuous scene with Werther.

Her silence continues even in the face of Werther's request to borrow Albert's pistols (92).

> The appearance of Werther's servant threw her into the greatest embarrassment. He handed the note to Albert, who turned calmly to his wife and said: "Give him the pistols."—"I wish him a happy journey," he said to the boy. The words struck her like a thunderclap; she staggered to her feet, not knowing what she was doing. Slowly she went to the wall; she trembled as she took down the weapons, dusted them off, and hesitated, and she would have hesitated longer still if Albert had not pressed her with a questioning look. (92)

She understands what she must do, but she cannot bring herself to do it: "Her heart foretold her every possible terror. At one point she was on the verge of throwing herself at the feet of her husband, and disclosing eveything to him: the events of the previous evening, her guilt, and her forebodings." The plot is a trap for Lotte from which she cannot escape. Goethe has constructed her character and her relationship with Albert in such a way that she will feel irretrievably implicated in Werther's suicide.

Relentlessly, Werther's final letter presses home her complicity in his death. He explains that he is sacrificing himself to insure her happiness with Albert. He reminds her that she herself handled the pistols to be sent to him. (He interprets her action as indicating consent to his intention to commit suicide: "And you, heavenly spirit, favor my resolve!") Finally, he tells her that he will be waiting for her in Heaven. These elements in his letter, together with her own actions (and inaction) may explain Lotte's extreme reaction to Werther's death: she could be suffering from an unbearable sense of *guilt*.

Although attention in the novel is focused on Werther's actions and character, it also provides, in smaller space, enough of Lotte's discourse and actions for an analysis of her character. For brevity, we only summarize findings, which parallel those for Werther. Like him, Lotte is unable to acknowledge and discharge her shame and its variant, guilt, which would explain her inability to confide in her husband at the crucial moment. (Further comment on Lotte's management of her emotions are found at the end of this chapter.)

If we assume that Werther's suicide, in combination with her guilt, might endanger her relationship to Albert, her standing in the community, and even her life, it becomes necessary to reconsider the entire relationship between Werther and Lotte.

Love and Infatuation

Love and infatuation are often treated as synonyms, but it is possible to distinguish between them. The latter usually involves feelings of attraction that have little to do with their object. The infatuated person is mostly unaware of the actual person, but rather projects onto her desirable qualities; she is *idealized*. Love, on the other hand, involves knowledge of and sympathy for qualities of the loved person, even undesirable ones. Infatuation is delusional; love is not.

Lewis's theory suggests that unacknowledged shame lies at the root of infatuation. By idealizing another person, the shame-prone person seeks to dispel shame by attaching to someone imagined to have the virtues lacking in oneself. But the outcome is usually the opposite; difficulties in the relationship, arising out projections on one or both sides, increase shame. This conjecture illuminates many aspects of the relationship between Werther and Lotte.

The text makes clear that Werther idealizes Lotte. In the letter of July 16, Werther confides: "She is sacred to me;" he calls her his angel, his goddess, his "heavenly spirit." He says that she is "perfect" (twice). He consistently denies his own sexual feelings toward her and protests her virtue and innocence. The text, however, contains numerous incidents that suggest that Werther has erotic feelings toward Lotte and that Lotte doesn't always discourage them (for example, the letter of July 16 and the incident of the canary's kiss on September 12).

There is an air of unreality about their entire relationship, an unreality caused not by inaccurate details, but on the contrary, by details all too revealing of the shallowness and self-deceptiveness of the two characters. The text suggests that both Werther and Lotte continuously deceive themselves—and, inadvertently, each other. Their relationship is characterized by what Sartre called "bad faith." They deceive each other unintentionally because each of them is self-deceptive.

Virtually all of the dialogue between the two suggests bad faith. One of many possible examples will give the flavor. Their first meeting involves their participation in a village dance. Lotte has not come with Albert, her fiance, because he is away on business. While dancing with Lotte, Werther notes that another dancer "wagged a threatening finger" at Lotte and "spoke the name Albert twice, with much emphasis." Werther asks, "Who is Albert, if it is not impertinent to ask?" (18). The conversation is briefly interrupted because of a separation required by the dance. Then Lotte responds, "Why should I keep it from you? Albert is a worthy man to whom I am as good as engaged."

Both utterances involve a modicum of both deception and self-deception. Werther has already been told that Lotte is engaged. Smitten (infatuated) at first sight, he has forgotten (repressed) this information. His question has introduced a false note. An utterance like*2 "I have been told you are engaged. Is Albert your fiance?" might have led the dialogue into a different path from the one it took.

Lotte's response falls short of being completely candid. First she delays, answering a question with a question. This delay follows another, longer delay, occasioned by the dance. (The dance required separation for the Grand Figure Eight, in which each dancer goes around in large circles, each circle only tangential to the other. This detail could serve as a metaphor for their relationship.)

When Lotte answers, what she says does not correspond exactly to what the reader has been told earlier. Werther had been warned by Lotte's cousin not to fall in love with Lotte: "She's already engaged." The cousin doesn't qualify the engagement as Lotte does. Like Werther's question, Lotte's answer seems to introduce a false note.

There is another demi-quaver in Lotte's initial response. The question she asks him, "Why should I keep it from you?" suggests that during the pause caused by the dance, Lotte may have briefly considered concealing the fact of her engagement. (During the Figure Eight, Werther notes that "her brow looked pensive.")

The context for her response is provided by Werther's manner toward her; he has fallen head over heels, and his manner probably betrays this fact. During an earlier dance, he indicates, "I (Heaven knows with what bliss) clung to her arm and gazed into her eyes." Even the slightest ambiguity in Lotte's response, in words or manner, might then encourage Werther.

Both Lotte's words and manner are ambiguous. The combination of her delay in answering his question, her pensive look, and her description of her relation to Albert, in context, suggests that she might have a romantic interest in Werther, as he clearly does in her.

Two further features of this passage can be noted. In context, her question "Why should I keep it from you?" might be read as self-congratulatory. She could have apologized to Werther for keeping him waiting for her answer or *sub voce* berated herself for disloyalty to Albert. Instead, she asks a rhetorical question. In a way that evades exact specification, she seems to make her hesitation a virtue rather than a fault. This is only the first of many hints of smugness in Lotte's character.

Returning from their circular dance figure, Lotte offers her hand to Werther for the promenade. The offering of her hand is required by the

---

2As already indicated, an asterisk * is the conventional symbol in linguistics for a *counterfactural*, a hypothertical utterance.

dance, yet in context, it can have an additional meaning. Just before revealing that she is engaged—which might increase the emotional distance between her and Werther—she also extends her hand to him, decreasing their distance. This double movement introduces ambiguity into her actions, a feature of Goethe's descriptions of Lotte.

Lotte's behavior is consistently described in a way that hints that she has two contradictory faces. One persona is the soul of propriety; the other is more adventurous. Goethe gives her the ability to conform perfectly to social mores but at the same time to use them for her own ends. The text suggests that Lotte is able to eat her cake and have it too. Werther's character notoriously lacks this ability. He is the disruptive outsider, even as Lotte is the harmonious insider. His behavior flaunts social mores both intentionally and out of ineptitude, just as hers usually give the appearance of exact conformity.

Conformity, Alienation, and the Social Bond

Werther's nonconformity and Lotte's conformity introduce an issue broader than those considered so far: the existential positions of Werther and Lotte and their relationships to their society, to each other, and to themselves. Alienation from each other is suggested by our discussion of infatuation and by our discussion of their self-deceptiveness, alienation from self. The concept of the social bond unifies all three levels—their relationships to self, each other, and society.

The sociological paradigm assumes that every human being requires a sense of belonging, a network of close bonds with others (Scheff 1990). Following Bowlby (1969, 1973, 1980), three levels of bondedness will be considered here: secure bonds, insecure bonds, and broken bonds. Secure bonds involve mutual acceptance, trust, and mental and emotional attunement between persons. Broken bonds involve a decisive ending of relationships: physical, mental, and emotional distance after what was once a close bond.

Insecure bonds are more complex. Bowen (1978; Bowen and Kerr 1988) has called attention to two kinds. A secure bond requires balance between obligation to self and to other. Insecurity can arise because the needs of the other come before one's own. To the extent that one gives up parts of the self to maintain the relationship, one is *engulfed*. But a relationship can also be unbalanced if one's own needs take precedence over those of the other. To the extent that one's own needs dominate, one is *isolated*. Both types of bonds are insecure and unstable; either one's own needs or the others are not honored (either engulfment or isolation).

One further theoretical link is needed to complete the picture—the connection between the state of the bond and emotion. Cooley's (1922) analysis of the "looking-glass self" implies that the state of a relationship is being continuously signaled by emotional expressions. Being able to "hold one's head up in public" is a manifestation of *pride*, the signal of a secure bond. At the other extreme, disgrace—a state of insecure or severed bonds—is signaled by being unable to look others in the eye— a manifestation of a state of *shame*.

Although Cooley's analysis of pride and shame is fundamental, Lewis's (1971) distinction between overt and bypassed shame suggests a qualification of it. Cooley's division of the manifestations of pride and shame into only two states may be incomplete; it ignores the possibility of "false pride."

Looking the other in the eye in a state of pride involves consideration, taking turns looking and being looked at. A stare, an uninterrupted gaze, is rude; it is an attempt to "outface" the other. A stare may be a manifestation not of pride but of false pride, a shame state that is denied or disguised. *False pride* is a vernacular label for bypassed shame, as is the term *shamelessness* (Schneider 1977). A secure bond is marked by normal pride, which leads to a courteous (intermittent) gaze at the other. Insecure bonds are marked by either overt shame (averted gaze) or bypassed shame (a stare).

The concept of the social bond provides a broad context for understanding the role of pride and shame in human experience. When securely bonded with others, pride is the normal state of human beings. Shame arises when bonds are threatened. This a more fundamental definition of the source of shame than the Darwin-McDougall-Lewis definition, which involves only one aspect of threat—negative evaluation of self.

Shame is the signal of alienation at the societal and interpersonal levels, and of internal alienation, the repression of thoughts and emotions. Alienation both causes and is produced by unacknowledged shame. The connection between states of the bond and emotions provides a framework for interpreting the existential positions of Werther and Lotte.

The text suggests alienation in all of Werther's relationships, both those preceding Wahlheim and those he attempted there. The novel begins with Werther's apology to his correspondent (Wilhelm) for leaving, affirming the bond between them: "How glad I am that I got away! Dearest friend, what a thing is the heart of man! To leave you whom I love so much, from whom I was inseparable, and yet be glad! I know you will forgive me." He explains his reason for leaving:

Were not my other attachments deliberately designed by fate to torment a heart like mine? Poor Leonore! And yet I was not to blame. Could I help it that, while her sister's wayward charms provided me with pleasant entertainment, a passion for me grew in her unfortunate heart? And yet, am I wholly without blame? Didn't I encourage her emotions? Didn't I find delight in the wholly sincere expressions of nature which so often made us laugh, however little there was to laugh at?

In a characteristic movement, Werther first disclaims any blame for rejecting Leonore, then questions his disclaimer. Also typical is the first line, in which he blames "fate" for his difficulties. This is a projection or triangle (Bowen 1978) that absolves him of blame. Note how extended is his complaint about his relationships; except for the one with Wilhelm, all others are tormenting. Although he appears to be referring to his romantic relationships, he might be inadvertently expressing the insecurity of all of his social bonds.

In addition to his relation to Wilhelm, Leonore, and her sister, the first letter concerns his mother.

Will you be good enough to tell my mother that I will look after her business as best I can and report to her about it as soon as possible. I spoke to my aunt and found her anything but the disagreeable person we make of her at home. She is a lively, impetuous woman with the best of hearts. I explained to her my mother's complaints about the portion of the inheritance that has been withheld from her; she gave me her grounds, reasons, and the conditions under which she would be prepared to give up everything, even more than we asked.—In short, I don't want to write about the matter now; tell mother that everything will come out all right. And, my dear friend, I have found once again in this little affair that misunderstandings and indolence perhaps cause more error in the world than cunning and malice. (1)

Several features of this passage suggest that there is distance between Werther and his mother, and perhaps enmity on his part. He takes the side of the aunt in the dispute between her and his mother, and he possibly charges his mother not only with misunderstanding but with indolence. He also communicates indirectly with his mother through Wilhelm. Communicating through a third person, forming a triangle, is a key feature of insecure relationships (Bowen 1978).

The text suggests that except for Wilhelm, Werther is adrift. He has broken off his relationship with Leonore, and he seems to be at odds with his mother. There is no mention of Werther's father. Even the bond with Wilhelm seems tenuous. Since there are no letters from Wilhelm, his existence has a hypothetical quality; he is the neutral, silent listener to Werther's outpourings. But there are a few responses by Werther that indicate comments by Wilhelm. These responses suggest that Wilhelm is not always neutral but is occasionally critical of Werther's excesses. From Werther's point of view, Wilhelm may seem to represent cold reason, in contrast to Werther's view of himself as one who represents passion. Not even Werther's bond with Wilhelm seems secure.

In Wahlheim, Werther's two most important relationships are with Lotte and with the Count. He is unable to establish secure bonds with either, however. His response to his own difficulty in balancing his needs against the needs of the other is to renounce his own needs. Apparently he never faces Leonore or his mother directly. He never asks Lotte to leave Albert, nor does he protest the treatment he receives at the hands of the Count during or after the embassy incident. Rather than deal with the issues in the relationship, he breaks off instead; he is *isolated*.

At first glance, Lotte's bonds appear to be secure. In Book 1, she is ensconced in her father's home, acting as mother to her brothers and sisters, engaged to be married. In Book 2, she is happily married. But many of her comments suggest that she is alienated from herself, particularly from her feelings. In an early letter (June 16), Werther reports a comment indicating how she distracts herself from unwanted thoughts and feelings:. "If there is something on my mind, I pound out a quadrille on my out-of-tune piano and everything is immediately right again (15). In the same letter, she indicates that when she is afraid, she pretends to be brave. A later comment shows how she deals with her anger: "When something annoys me and makes me peevish, I jump up, walk up and down the garden, singing a few country tunes, and in next to no times its gone" (22).

These comments indicate a bypassing of emotions. This style of coping with emotions appears inconsequential until the fateful scene with Albert, in which she withholds her thoughts and feelings about Werther's intention to kill himself. Instead of relieving her burden of guilt and fear by sharing it with Albert, she honors his feelings instead. This decision is a manifestation of the inadequacy of her bond with Albert, indicating an imbalance in the relationship; she is engulfed.

Part of the attraction of a person like Lotte for one like Werther, since he is so isolated, would be the appearance she gives of secure bondedness in a community. But if our analysis is correct, that appearance would be mostly an illusion. The discourse in the text suggests that Lotte's bonds might be almost as insecure as Werther's, but unbalanced in the opposite direction: he is isolated in his relationships, while she is engulfed in hers.

We propose that Werther ends his life because he is alienated in all of his relationships. He literally has no one to whom he can turn. Lewis's theory specifies the sequences that lead from alienation to suicide. The intensity of his suffering is caused by a chain reaction of unacknowledged shame.

On his arrival in Wahlheim, he first seeks to dispel the pain through infatuation: the romantic form of infatuation, in his relationship with Lotte, and infatuation in another form—hero-worship of the Count. The delusional quality of his attachments and the collusion of Lotte and the Count in denying shame and anger amplify his pain rather than diminish it.

Werther takes his life not only to end his suffering, but also as revenge. Unable to attack the Count except in fantasy, he kills himself in a way that implicates Lotte. His final actions may be deemed a combination of suicide and attempted homicide. He acts out his humiliated fury toward Lotte, unexpressed in his actual relationship with her, by killing himself in a way that may harm her also.

Goethe's Revenge

A story of unconscious revenge may also be found in the way Goethe wrote and published this novel. Perhaps one of his reasons for writing the book was cathartic; by writing it, he may have felt that he was purging himself of bitter feelings. Another motive, less conscious, may have been vengeance. If one of Goethe's motives in writing the novel was to hurt Charlotte and Johann, he seems to have succeeded; they felt keenly injured by it. Kestner wrote to Goethe, complaining bitterly:

> You have, to be sure, woven into each character something that was foreign to it, or have fused several characters into one. There would be no objection to that. But if you had let your heart have a little to say in the matter during this process of weaving and fusing, you would not have so *prostituted* the actual persons from whom you borrowed certain features. . . . The real Lotte, whose friend, after all, you *pretend* to be, appears in your representation, which contains too much of her not to point strongly in her direction, appears, I say—but no, I will not say it, it pains me too much *even to think of it.* (Rose 1931:140, emphasis added)

Goethe was shocked by Kestner's letter and offered endless apologies. He must have felt that there was some justice to Kestner's complaints, in the revised edition of the novel (1787), he softened the portrayal of Lotte and Albert.

To trace the evidence of vengefulness in Goethe, it is first necessary to note certain key differences between the novel and biographical fact, and as important, elements that are the same. The most important comparison is between Werther's relationship to Lotte and Albert, on the one hand, and Jerusalem's relationship to Elisabeth Herd and her husband Philipp, on the other.

Unlike the way Lotte behaves toward Werther, Frau Herd apparently behaved toward Jerusalem with complete propriety. When she learned of his passion for her, she informed her husband and requested that he forbid Jerusalem any further access. Furthermore, there is no evidence in Kestner's letter of any reaction by Frau Herd to Jerusalem's death.

A second major difference is in the source of the suicide weapons. In Jerusalem's case, he did not borrow them from the husband of the woman he desired—that is, from Philipp Herd. Rather, he borrowed them from Kestner, who had no way of knowing the use to which they were to be put, since his wife, Charlotte, was not involved with Jerusalem.

In the novel, by having the pistols come from Albert, by having Lotte keep secret Werther's declaration of love and self-destruction, and by inventing an extreme reaction to Werther's death, Goethe constructed a complicity for Lotte that was absent in the original model.

We do not argue that these changes are themselves indicative of vengefulness. There are strong artistic grounds for them, since they add an intense dramatic element that is absent in the source. Frau Herd's dutifulness to her husband and the borrowing of the pistols from an uninvolved third party would have made a less dramatic climax in the novel.

Nor are we suggesting that the unattractiveness of Goethe's portrayal of Lotte and Albert is an indication of vengefulness. The portrayal of Werther—Goethe's character—is even harsher than the portrayal of Lotte and Albert. Werther is a picture of madness, albeit madness disguised under the cloak of romance. For all their faults, Lotte and Albert are not possessed with destructive madness like Werther. Although Lotte played a part in the tragedy, she is more Werther's victim than he is hers. Perhaps the best summary would be to say that they are both victims of the system of relationships of which they are part.

The element in the novel that suggests vengefulness on Goethe's part is his failure to protect Charlotte and Johann from being identified with their fictional portrayals. Reiss (1969: 15) has shown that Goethe left virtually all the identifying details about Charlotte and Johann undisguised: their ages, dates, occupations, family relations, and so on. For example, Charlotte Buff, like Lotte, had six brothers and sisters and a father who was an *Amtmann*, an official. Given the wealth of exact details, the one change Goethe made in Lotte—giving her black eyes rather than Charlotte's blue—would appear to be only a token effort to protect Charlotte's identity. Below the level of consciousness,

Goethe may have wanted to cause Charlotte pain, as her "rejection" had caused him pain.

An image that may convey Goethe's vengefulness is one from childhood. The child who feels unfairly treated by its parents can have vengeful fantasies about how sorry his parents would be if he were to die, imagining their anguish over how badly they treated him. In his play *Torquato Tasso* (1789), Goethe had his hero speak for all artists: "Thanks be to God that I can speak my suffering, and not be struck dumb in my agony like other men." Like his hero Tasso, Goethe was speaking his suffering. But in doing so, Goethe failed to protect his sources from the consequences of his fantasies.

This analysis of the dialogue in *Werther* illustrates several aspects of our theory. It suggests a connection between inadequate social bonds, dysfunctional communication, and destructive violence, as specified in chapter 2. Since Werther's style of alienation is isolation, the inadequacy of his bonds is easily seen. Lotte's style, however—engulfment— is more covert. Only a close reading of passages relevant to her bonds reveals that she is also alienated from others and from herself.

A second theme has been the indirection and falseness of the communication tactics used by both Werther and Lotte. Neither of them ever quite says what they mean; frequently, they do not mean what they say. The same indirection that they use with each other is also present in their dialogues with others. Key instances are Werther's dialogue with the Count at the climax of the scene at the embassy party, and Lotte's failure to reveal her fears to Albert when Werther sends for the pistols.

A final theme of this discussion has been the emotional and physical violence that underlies the novel. Although Werther's violence toward himself is made manifest in his suicide, we have suggested that there is a more hidden violence also, that his suicide constitutes an attack on Lotte as well as himself.

The thread that connects these themes is our theory that triple spirals of shame-rage lie at the heart of destructive conflict. The cues that the theory demands for shame sequences are present in the passages that describe Werther's mounting desperation. This congruence between theory and text is not a proof, of course, but it does suggest the theory's plausibility.

We have analyzed text from a novel to show that part/whole inferences about emotion and the social bond can be made even in the absence of a complete recording of all verbal and nonverbal components of discourse. Although part of the context is missing, novels and biographies offer data that compensate, at least in part, by showing the dense sequences of events that occurred before and after the events in any given situation. In everyday life, we can make comparable inferences from letters from our intimates, speeches by our leaders, and so on, because we have a fund of biographical knowledge about these people. Naturally, we make our most confident inferences when both kinds of data are available—in fact-to-face interaction with persons who are well known to us.

In other situations, we make inferences about emotions and relationships from secondhand accounts of discourse. The analysis of emotions and bonds in the next chapter is based on such accounts. A plausible interpretation of relationships and emotions in one patient's family was built up by her therapist, the original researchers (Labov and Fanshel), and ourselves, on the basis of the patient's recounting of discourse with members of her family. In this particular case, unlike everyday life, we have a source of confidence in our interpretations because we can make comparisons between the patient's behavior as she recalled it, and her actual behavior as indicated in the audiotape recording.

7

A New Labeling Theory: Stigma, Emotion, and the Social Bond

This chapter applies our theory of social action to another specific instance of behavior. This case, based on a dialogue between a anorexic woman and her therapist, was the object of an earlier study by Labov and Fanshel (1977). We show how our theory complements earlier work on labeling of mental illness. Unacknowledged shame is seen as a cause of both primary and secondary deviance. In family systems, it causes primary deviance, and in the interaction between the family and the community, it causes secondary deviance.

Labov and Fanshel's case, "Rhoda," provides an extended example. It suggests that the labeling process is subtle and outside of awareness. In the anorexic patient's family, stigmatization is a two-way street; through innuendo, all the family members—including the patient—surreptitiously attack each other. But only the patient's violence is both emotional and overt. Like the family members, she attacks others through innuendo, but she also starves herself. All the others use only emotional violence. Since the violence of the family is hidden, it is the patient who was formally labeled. The labeling appears to be extremely subtle and complex, inadvertently reaffirming the status quo in the family. To the extent that the mental health professions side with the family, they too reaffirm and maintain the status quo.

Labeling Theory

Over the last ten years, we have become critical of Scheff's original formulation of labeling theory (1966, 1984). Like most other theories of human behavior, the original theory was highly specialized, yet insufficiently detailed. It was specialized since it dealt behaviorally with social structure/process. It omitted most inner events, both those concerning mental illness and those concerning the societal reaction.

The original theory was also insufficiently detailed. First, it was formulated in terms of abstract concepts, "black boxes," that were not clearly defined. Second, the causal links between these concepts were not specified. The theory described the societal reaction as a system without defining the major subsystems or the links between them.

Our final criticism is substantive, pointing toward a major deficit at the core of labeling theory: its omission of emotions.[1] Although Goffman (1963) and others discussed stigma, they paid too little attention to emotions, particularly the emotion of shame.

The original labeling theory was also oriented toward the formal labeling process, court hearings, and psychiatric examinations. Labeling (and nonlabeling) in these contexts was crude and overt. But in the family, as we argue here, labeling is covert. It depends upon innuendo, manner, unstated implications, and especially emotion. To detect it, one must interpret words and actions *in context*.

At this stage of theory development, reliable methods may be premature since they strip away context. The next step in developing a theory may be to understand a single case very well. Part/whole analysis allows one to show the relationship between the smallest parts of discourse and the very largest social system (Scheff 1990). When one can demonstrate an understanding of the relation between parts and wholes in a series of cases, the stage is then set for a research mode oriented toward testing hypotheses. Since mental illness at this point is still a mystery and a labyrinth, we need to generate models that are interesting enough to warrant testing—ones that have face validity.

This chapter outlines a theory and method that specify the role of unacknowledged shame in mental illness and in the societal reaction. The theory involves a model of feeling traps, recursive loops of shame and anger. The method involves the systematic interpretation of sequences of events in discourse. Discourse from a psychotherapy session is used to illustrate the theory, to allow us to envision the hypothesized moment-by-moment causal sequence.

Pride, Shame, and the Social Bond

In chapter 2, we developed a theory of the social bond and its accompanying emotions. Cooley (1922) implied that pride and shame serve as

---

[1]Peggy Thoits and John Braithwaite are exceptions. Thoits has published a study (1985) that connects emotions and labeling, and Braithwaite (1989) a theory of stigmatization that explicitly links stigma and shame. Braithwaite's framework links low crime rates with "reintegrative" or what we would call normal shame, and high crime rates with stigmatization (or recursive shame). He also makes a connection between normal shame and community. His work implies the fundamental link between shame and the social bond described in this paper, but it is limited by his omission of the role of pride (see chapter 9).

intense and automatic bodily signs of the state of a system that is otherwise difficult to observe. Pride is the sign of an intact social bond; shame is the sign of a threatened one. The clearest outer marker of pride is holding up one's head in public, looking others in the eye, but indicating respect by alternately looking and looking away. In *overt* shame, one shrinks, averting or lowering one's gaze, casting only furtive glances at the other. In *bypassed* shame, one stares, outfacing the other.

Pride and shame thus serve as instinctive signals, both to the self and to the other, that communicate the state of the bond. We react automatically to affirmations of and threats to bonds. But in early childhood most of us learn to disguise and ignore these signals. The idea of the social bond is repressed in modern societies, masked by the ideology of individualism. The emotions that express the bond—pride and shame—are also deeply repressed (see chapter 1, Scheff 1990; and Lewis 1971).

Lewis's (1971) work is particularly relevant to the conjecture under discussion. She found that in contexts high in potential for shame, (as when a patient appears to suspect that the therapist is critical or judgmental), nonverbal indications of shame are plentiful. These include long or filled pauses ("well," "you know," "uh-uh-uh," and the like), repetition or self-interruption, and particularly, a lowering of the voice, often to the point of inaudibility. These markers are all suggestive of hiding behavior (see chapter 3).

In these contexts, however, the painful affect of overt shame was virtually never acknowledged by name. Instead, other words were used, which Lewis interpreted to be a code language. *Insecure, awkward* and *uncomfortable* are examples of the many code words used in these situations. This language is analogous to the code language for designating other unmentionables, such as sexual or "toilet" terms. Like babytalk about body functions used with children, the denial of shame is institutionalized in the adult language of modern societies. Lewis's findings, like the approaches of Cooley, Goffman, and especially Elias (1978, 1982), suggest that shame is repressed in our civilization.

Although Goffman's, Elias's, and Lewis's treatments of shame are an advance over Cooley's in one way, in another way they are retrograde. Their treatment is much more specialized and detailed than Cooley's, whose discussion of the "self-regarding sentiments" is casual and brief. But Cooley had a vision of the whole system lacking in the more recent discussions. His treatment construes pride and shame to be polar opposites. It therefore lays the basis for our construct of the social bond; pride and shame are continuous signals of the state of the bond, an instant read-out of the "temperature" of the relationship.

The emotion of pride is absent from Goffman's and Lewis's formulations. Goffman's omission of pride is particularly disastrous. Since Lewis dealt only with psychotherapy discourse, we are free to imagine from her work that in normal conversation there is more pride than shame. But Goffman's treatments of "impression management," "face," and embarrassment concerned normal discourse, leaving the reader with the impression that all human activity is awash in a sea of shame. He nowhere envisioned a secure social bond, much less a well-ordered society built upon secure bonds. Goffman's omission of pride and secure bonds is particularly misleading for the study of deviance; it undercuts a crucial distinction between "normal" persons and labeled persons. Social situations usually generate pride for the former and shame for the latter. This difference has extraordinary consequences for the social system.

Goffman's (1963) treatment of stigma, although perceptive and useful, is not complete. Like other labeling theorists, his discussion is specialized, focusing on the behavioral aspects of stigma. He acknowledged the emotional component of the societal reaction only in passing. In particular, he mentioned shame only twice, once early in the essay: "[for the deviant] shame becomes a central possibility," (7), and again at the end: "Once the dynamics of shameful differences are seen as a general feature of social life . . ." (140).

Goffman frequently referred to shame or shame-related affects, but only indirectly ("self-hate and self-derogation", [7]). Without a working concept of the relationship between emotion and behavior, Goffman and the other stigma theorists were unable to show its central role in mental illness and the societal reaction. As a step toward this end, it is first necessary to review once more how emotions may cause protracted conflict.

Shame-Rage Chains in Conflict

An earlier report (Scheff 1987) described emotional bases of interminable conflicts. Like Watzlawick et al. (1967), we argue that some conflicts are unending; any particular quarrel within such conflicts is only a link in a continuing chain. We see both primary and secondary deviance arising out of interminable conflicts. What is the cause of this type of conflict?

As we indicated earlier, Lewis (1971, 1976, 1981, 1983) proposed that when shame is evoked but not acknowledged, an impasse occurs that has both social and psychological components. We sketch a model of impasse, a *triple spiral* of shame and rage *between* and *within* interactants. When a person has emotional reactions to their own emotions and to those of the other party, both become caught in a "feeling trap" (Lewis 1971) from which they cannot extricate themselves. The idea that emotions are contagious *between* individuals is familiar; the concept of spirals subsumes contagion both between and within parties to a conflict.

Our model follows from Lewis's (1971) analysis of therapy transcripts: shame is pervasive in clinical interaction, but it is invisible to interactants (and to researchers), unless Lewis's approach is used. (For methods that parallel Lewis's, see Gottschalk and Gleser's [1969] "shame-anxiety scale.")

Lewis (1971) referred to the internal shame-rage process as a "feeling trap," as "anger bound by shame" or "humiliated fury." Kohut's (1977) concept, "narcissistic rage," appears to be the same affect, since he viewed it as a compound of shame and rage. When one is angry that one is ashamed, or ashamed that one is angry, then one might be ashamed to be so upset over something so "trivial." Such anger and shame are rarely acknowledged and are difficult to detect and to dispel. Shame-rage spirals may be brief, lasting a matter of minutes, or they can last for hours, days, or a lifetime, as bitter hatred or resentment.

Brief sequences of shame-rage may be quite common. Escalation is avoided through withdrawal, conciliation, or some other tactic. In this chapter a less common type of conflict is described. Watzlawick et al. (1967, 107–108) called it "symmetrical escalation." Since such conflicts have no limits, they may be lethal. We describe the cognitive and emotional components of symmetrical escalation, as far as they are evidenced in the transcript.

Labeling in the Family: A Case Study[2]

Labov and Fanshel (1977) conducted an exhaustive microanalysis of a large segment of a psychotherapy session. They analyzed not only *what* was said but also *how* it was said, interpreting both words and manner (the paralanguage). They based their interpretations upon microscopic details of paralanguage, such as pitch and loudness contours. Words and paralanguage are used to infer inner states: intentions, feelings, and meanings.

With such attention to detail, Labov and Fanshel were able to convey unstated *implications*. Their report is evocative; one forms vivid pictures of patient and therapist and of their relationship. One can also infer aspects of the relationship between Rhoda and her family, since Rhoda reports family dialogues.[3] Labov and Fanshel showed that the

---

[2]This section is adapted from Scheff 1989.

[3]Indirect inferences, from a dialogue that is only reported, are made in order to construct a causal model. Obviously, in future research they will need to be validated by observations of actual family dialogue. It is reassuring, however, to find that many aspects of her own behavior that Rhoda reports as occurring in the dialogues with her family are directly observable in her dialogue with the therapist. For example, the absence of greeting, and Rhoda's covert aggression in the dialogue she reports with her aunt can be observed directly in the session itself (not included in this chapter but discussed in Scheff 1989).

dispute style in Rhoda's family is indirect: conflict is generated by nonverbal means and by implication.

The Feud Between Rhoda and Her Family

Rhoda was a nineteen-year-old college student who had a prior diagnosis of anorexia. She had been hospitalized because of her rapid weight loss, from 140 to 70 pounds. When her therapy began, she weighed 90 pounds. At five feet, five inches in height, she was dangerously underweight.

Her therapy sessions took place in New York City in the 1960s. Rhoda lived with her mother and her aunt, Editha; her married sister also figures in the dialogue. The session that was analyzed by Labov and Fanshel was the twenty-fifth in a longer series, which appeared to end successfully. The therapist reported improvement at termination. At a five-year followup, Rhoda was of normal weight, married, and raising her own children.

Labov and Fanshel focused on the web of conflict in Rhoda's life, mainly with her family and to a lesser extent with her therapist. The conflict was not open but hidden. The authors showed that Rhoda's statements (and those she attributed to the members of her family) were packed with innuendo. They inferred that the style of dispute in Rhoda's family was indirect: although the family members were aggressive toward each other and hurt by each other, both their aggression and their hurt were denied.

Labov and Fanshel's method was to state explicitly as verbal propositions what was only implied in the actual dialogue. This method proposed a cognitive structure for the conflict in Rhoda's family: it translated utterances, words, and paralanguage into purely verbal statements. The set of verbal statements served as a compact, clarifying blueprint for a dense tissue of complex maneuvers that were otherwise difficult to detect and understand.

In addition to this type of analysis, Labov and Fanshel also used another. Following the lead of the therapist, they pointed out cues that were indicative of unacknowledged anger. To reveal this emotion, they used verbal and nonverbal signs: words and paralanguage (such as pitch and loudness). Hidden challenges in Rhoda's family were made in anger and resulted in anger. Rhoda's therapist made explicit reference to this matter: "So there's a lot of anger passing back and forth" (5.27[c]). There were also myriad indications of unacknowledged anger and other emotions in the session itself.

Emotions were not central to Labov and Fanshel's study, but they are to ours. Building upon their assessment of cognitive conflict, and their (and the therapist's) analysis of anger, we show shame sequences in the session that were apparently unnoticed by both patient and therapist. Labov and Fanshel frequently noted the presence of embarrassment and of the combined affect they called "hopeless anger," but they made little use of these events.

Our study leads us to conclude that labeling occurs at two different levels—the informal and the formal. At the informal level, labeling is quite symmetrical: Rhoda labeled and blamed Aunt Editha and her mother just as much as they labeled and blamed her. The family members casually insulted each other almost constantly. In some sentences, several different insults were implied at once. As Labov and Fanshel pointed out, conflict seemed to be endemic in this family.

At the formal level of labeling, however, there was no symmetry whatsoever. Although the mother and the aunt were just as violent with their insults, threats, and rejections as Rhoda, it was only Rhoda who was physically violent; she tried to starve herself. In contrast to the constant verbal violence, Rhoda's overt violence was highly visible; her dangerously low body weight bore ostensible witness to her self-assault. Although the verbal violence seemed to be visible to the therapist and was documented by Labov and Fanshel, it was invisible in Rhoda's community. If labeling theory is going to lead to further understanding of mental illness, it will need to take a new direction, to make visible what has hitherto been invisible; violence in the micro-world of moment-to-moment social interaction.

We use two excerpts (Labov and Fanshel 1977: 364, 365). The first involves Rhoda's relationship with her mother; the second, with Aunt Editha.

The first excerpt occurred early in the session—it deals with a telephone conversation that Rhoda reported. The mother was temporarily staying at the house of Rhoda's sister, Phyllis. (Since pauses were significant in their analysis, Labov and Fanshel signified their length: each period equals .3 second.)

Excerpt 1

   1.8 R.: An-nd so—when—I called her t'day, I said, "Well, when do you plan t'come **home?**"

   1.9 R.: So she said, "Oh, why?"

   1.10 R.: An-nd I said, "Well, things are getting just a little too **much!** [laugh] This is—i's jis' getting too hard, and . . . . . . I—"

   1.11 R.: She s'd t'me, "Well, why don't you tell **Phyllis** that?"

   1.12 R.: So I said, "Well, I haven't talked to her lately."

Rhoda, a full-time student, argues that she can't keep house without help. Her mother puts her off by referring her to Phyllis. The implication—that the mother is there at Phyllis's behest—is not explored by the therapist. Rather, she asks Rhoda about getting help from Aunt Editha. Rhoda's response:

Excerpt 2

2.6[a] R.: I said t'her (breath) w—one time—I asked her—I said t'her.
    [b] "Wellyouknow, wdy'mind takin' thedustrag an'justdust around?"

2.7   R.: Sh's's, "Oh-I-I—it looks **clean** to me," . . .

2.8[a] R.: An' then I went like **this**.
    [b]   an' I said to her, "**That** looks **clean** t'you?"

2.9[a] R.: And she sort of . . . . I d'no—sh'sort of gave me a funny look as if I—hurt her in some way,
    [b]   and I mean I didn' **mean** to, I didn' **yell** and **scream**.
    [c]   All I did to her was that "**That** looks **clean** to you?" . . . .

The therapist persists that Rhoda may be able to obtain help from Editha. In a later segment (not shown), Rhoda denies this possibility.

Rhoda's Helpless Anger Toward Her Aunt

We begin with the least complex segment, the dialogue that Rhoda reports between herself and her aunt (2.5–2.9). Labov and Fanshel showed a thread of underlying anger, anger that is denied by both parties.

Rhoda has explained prior to this excerpt that dust "bothers" her—that is, makes her angry. The authors argue that the request that Editha "dust around" (2.6[b]) involves an angry challenge to Editha's authority, a challenge that neither side acknowledges. It assumes that the house is dusty, that Editha knows it, that she has ignored her obligation to do something about it, and that Rhoda has the right to remind her of it.

Although Rhoda uses "mitigating" devices, speaking rapidly and casually, she ignores the etiquette that would have avoided challenge. (Labov and Fanshel wrote, "The making of requests is a delicate business and requires a great deal of supporting ritual to avoid damaging personal relations surrounding it" [96].) To avoid challenge, Rhoda might have begun with an apology and explanation: *4 "You know,

---

4As already indicated, an asterisk (*) is used to denote a counterfactual, a hypothetical statement not made in the actual dialogue.

Aunt Editha, this is a busy time for me, I need your help so I can keep up with my schoolwork." Rhoda's actual request is abrupt.

Editha's response is also abrupt: "Oh-I-I—it looks clean to me . . ." She has refused Rhoda's request, intimating inaccuracy in Rhoda's appraisal. The ritual necessary to refuse a request without challenge is at least as elaborate as that of making one. Editha could have shown Rhoda deference: *"I'm sorry Rhoda, but . . . ," followed by an explanation of why she was not going to honor the request.

Rhoda's response to what she appears to have taken as an insult is brief and emphatic: She contemptuously dismisses Editha's contention. She wipes her finger across a dusty surface and thrusts it close to Editha's face: *"That* looks *clean* to you?" Labov and Fanshel noted the aggressive manner in Rhoda's rebuttal: she stresses the words *that* and *clean*, as if Editha were a child or hard of hearing. They identified the pattern of pitch and loudness as the "Yiddish rise-fall intonation": *"By *you* that's a *monkey* wrench?" implying repudiation of the other's point of view. *"If you think this is clean, you're crazy" (202). Rhoda's response escalates the level of conflict: she has openly challenged Editha's competence.

Finally, Rhoda describes Editha's response, which is not verbal but gestural: she gives Rhoda a "funny look as if I—hurt her in some way." Rhoda denies any intention of hurting Editha, and that Editha has any grounds for being hurt: "I didn't yell and scream," implying that Editha is unreasonable.

Labov and Fanshel noted the presence of anger not only in the original interchange but in Rhoda's retelling of it. The nonverbal signs, they said—choking, hesitation, glottalization, and whine—are indications of *helpless anger*: Rhoda "is so choked with emotion at the unreasonableness of Editha's behavior that she can not begin to describe it accurately" (191). Helpless anger, the authors wrote, characterizes Rhoda's statements *throughout the whole session*: "she finds herself unable to cope with behavior of others that injures her and seems to her unreasonable" (191).

Labov and Fanshel further noted that her expressions of helpless anger were "mitigated":

> All of these expressions of emotion are counterbalanced with mitigating expressions indicating that Rhoda's anger is not extreme and that she is actually taking a moderate, adult position on the question of cleanliness. Thus she is not angered by the situation, it only "bothers" her. Even this is too strong; Rhoda further mitigates the expression to "sort of bothers me."

Mitigation in this instance means denial: Rhoda denies her anger by disguising it with euphemisms.

What is the source of all the anger and denial? Let us start with Rhoda's helpless anger during her report of the dialogue. Helpless anger, according to Lewis (1971), is a variant of shame-anger: we are ashamed of our helplessness. In retelling the story, Rhoda is caught up in a shame-anger sequence: shame that she feels rejected by Editha, anger at Editha, shame at her anger, and so on.

Helpless anger has been noted by others besides Lewis and Kohut. Nietzsche (1887) referred to a similar affect ("impotent rage") as the basis for resentment. Scheler (1912) used Nietzsche's idea in his study of *ressentiment*—pathological resentment. Horowitz (1981), finally, dealt with a facet of helpless anger under the heading "self-righteous anger."

Rhoda and her family are caught in a web of *ressentiment*, to use Scheler's term. Each side attributes the entire blame to the other; neither side sees their own contribution. As Labov and Fanshel showed, one of Rhoda's premises is that *she* is reasonable, and the members of her family are unreasonable. The reported dialogues with her family imply that the family holds the opposite premise: that *they* are reasonable, but she is unreasonable.

Our theory suggests that the dialogue between Rhoda and Editha is only a segment of a continuous quarrel. Since it is ongoing, it may not be possible to locate a particular beginning; any event recovered is only a link in a chain. (Watzlawick et al. 1967; 58). Starting at an arbitrary point, suppose that Rhoda is "hurt" by Editha's failure to help. That is, she feels rejected, shamed by Editha's indifference, and angry at Editha for this reason. She is also ashamed of being angry, however. Her anger is bound by shame. For this reason it cannot be acknowledged, let alone discharged.

Editha may be in a similar trap. Rhoda is irritable and disrespectful, which could cause Editha shame and anger. She could experience Rhoda's hostility as rejecting, arousing her own feelings of helpless anger. Reciprocating chains of shame and anger on both sides cause symmetrical escalation.

The Impasse between Rhoda and Her Mother

Excerpt 1, as reported by Rhoda, may point to the core conflict. It is brief—only three complete exchanges—but as Labov and Fanshel showed, it is packed with innuendo. Our analysis follows theirs, but expands it to include emotion dynamics.

Rhoda's first line, as she reports the conversation, is seemingly innocuous: "Well, when do you plan t'come home?" To reveal the unstated implications, Labov and Fanshel analyzed understandings about role-obligations in Rhoda's family. Rhoda's statement is a demand for action, disguised as a question. They pointed out affective elements: it contains sarcasm (1977: 156), criticism (161), challenge (157, 159), and rudeness (157). The challenge and criticism are inherent in a demand from a child that implies that the mother is neglecting her obligations.

Implicit in their comments is the point we made about Rhoda's approach to her aunt. It was possible for Rhoda to have requested action without insult, by showing deference, reaffirming the mother's status, and providing an explanation and apology. Rhoda's request is rude because it contains none of these elements.

Rhoda's habitual rudeness is also indicated by the absence of two ceremonial forms from all her dialogues, not only with her family, but also with her therapist: any form of greeting, and the use of the other's name and title. Does Rhoda merely forget these elements in her report of the dialogues? Not likely, since they are also missing in the session itself. Labov and Fanshel tell us that the transcript begins "with the very first words spoken in the session; there is no small talk or preliminary settling down. . . . Instead the patient herself immediately begins the discussion." Rhoda neglects to greet the therapist or call her by name. Since Rhoda is junior to the therapist, her aunt, and her mother, the absence of greeting, name, and title is a mark of inadequate deference toward persons of higher status. Rhoda's casual manner is rude.

The mother's response is just as rude and just as indirect. According to Rhoda's report, her mother also neglects greetings and the use of names. Like Rhoda's aunt, she neither honors the request nor employs the forms necessary to avoid giving offense. Rather than answering Rhoda's question, she asks another question—a delay that is the first step in rejecting the request.

Labov and Fanshel stated that the intonation contour of the mother's response ("Oh, *why?*") suggests "heavy implication." They inferred: *"I told you so; many, many, times I have told you so." (When Rhoda gives a second account of this dialogue [4.12–4.15], she reports that the mother actually said, "See, I told you so.") What is it that the mother, and presumably others, has told Rhoda many times? The answer to this question may be at the core of the quarrel between Rhoda and her family.

Whether it is only an implication or an actual statement, the mother's I-told-you-so escalates the conflict from the specific issue at hand—whether she is going to come home—to a more general level: Rhoda's status. Rhoda's offensiveness in her opening question involves her mother's status only at this moment. The mother's response involves a general issue. Is Rhoda a responsible and therefore a worthwhile person, or is she sick, mad, or irresponsible?

Labeling, Shame, and Inadequate Bonds

At a superficial level, the mother's I-told-you-so statement involves only Rhoda's ability to function on her own. As can be seen from Rhoda's complaints at the end of the session, however, this implication is symbolic of a larger set of accusations that Rhoda sees her mother and sister as leveling at her: she is either willfully or crazily not taking care of herself, starving herself, and she doesn't care about the effect of her behavior on her family. Her family's basic accusation, Rhoda feels, is that she is upsetting them, but she doesn't care. Rhoda formulates this accusation at the end of the transcript.

Excerpt 3

    T. What are they feeling?

5.26 R. . . .that I'm doing it on purp—like, I w's— like they . . . well-they s—came out an'tol' me in so many words that they worry and worry an' I seem to take this very lightly.

To Rhoda, the mother's I-told-you-so epitomizes a host of infuriating, shaming charges about her sanity, responsibility, and lack of consideration. Note particularly that the labeling process to which Rhoda refers here is not explicit; it occurs through innuendo.

The labeling of Rhoda by the other family members and its emotional consequences underlie the whole family conflict. Yet it can be detected only by a subtle process of inference, understanding the meaning of words and gestures *in context*, in actual discourse. Both the theory and the method of the original labeling theory were too abstract to detect this basic labeling process.

Rhoda responds (in 1.10) not to the underlying implication of her mother's evasion but to the surface question, *"Why do you want to know?"* Because, she answers, ". . . things are getting just a little too much . . ." The key element in Rhoda's response is the *affect*. Labov and Fanshel stated that the paralanguage (choked laughter, hesitation, glottalization, and long silence [170]) is an indication of embarrassment (171). Rhoda responds to her mother's accusations by becoming *ashamed*. The shame sequence that is described is a marker for stigmatization that is otherwise hidden behind polite words.

Rhoda's shame may indicate that she feels that her family's charges have some basis, or that the implied rejection leads her to feel worthless, or both. Since no anger is visible at this instant, it is either absent or bypassed. The verbal text, however, suggests that Rhoda is feeling shame and guilt. She is acknowledging that she needs her mother—a need she has repeatedly denied in the past. She may feel that she is at fault for this reason.

Labov and Fanshel contrasted the force of the mother's response with the weakness of Rhoda's comment (at 1.10). The mother says, "Why don't you tell Phyllis that?" Labov and Fanshel stated that the hesitation and embarrassment that characterize 1.10 are absent from this response. It is a forceful rejection of Rhoda's claims and, by implication, a criticism of Rhoda for even making the request. The mother's emotional response to Rhoda's embarrassment is not simply unsympathetic; it is aggressively rejecting. From the emotional standpoint, Rhoda's back is to the wall. She is trapped in the helpless role of the blamed, with her mother as the aggressive blamer.

The analysis of shame in this dialogue points to an otherwise hidden issue. At this moment we can see that in her family, Rhoda has literally no one to whom she can turn. She is at odds with her aunt. We know from her reports of her sister's comments that Rhoda and she are also in a tangle. No father is mentioned. Rhoda and her family are in a perpetual war, a war hidden beneath the surface of conventional discourse. All of Rhoda's bonds are threatened, yet she has no way of understanding her complete alienation.

The stage is set for violent emotion and/or violent behavior: for mental illness (Rhoda appears to be delusional about her eating and body weight), murder, or suicide (in this case, self-starvation). (That the potential for suicide arises when individuals have no one to whom they can turn is conjectured by Sacks [1966] on the basis of his analysis of calls to a suicide prevention center.) The repression of shame and the bondlessness that is its cause and effect can give rise to primary deviance in the form of mental illness, murder, or suicide.

In Rhoda's response (1.12), she continues in the role of the one at fault: "Well, I haven't talked to her lately." Her mother has defeated her on all counts. She has refused Rhoda's request without the ritual that would protect Rhoda's "face"; she has implied a victory over Rhoda ("I told you so") that undercuts Rhoda's status, and she has criticized her for making an inappropriate request to the wrong person.

Rhoda appears to feel too baffled, upset, and helpless for an angry counterattack. Her anger at her mother may feel too shameful to countenance. It is reserved for lesser targets: her aunt, her sister, and the therapist. Her mother's rejection, with the implied threat of abandonment, could be the basic source of Rhoda's shame.

Even to the casual reader, the mother's tactics are transparent. Why is Rhoda so baffled by them? Why didn't she use a response like the one suggested by the authors: *"Oh, come off it, Ma! You know it's really up to you when you come home, not Phyllis. Get off my case!"

Rhoda's ineptness may be due to her intense shame, evoked beginning with the first question, asking her mother for help. As indicated, unacknowledged shame is befuddling almost to the point of paralysis.

In its overt form, one is so flustered that speech is disrupted, with inaudibility, repetition, stuttering, and fragmentation. Even though she is only reporting the dialogue, Rhoda's speech shows many of these markers. Bypassed shame, on the other hand, may disrupt one's ability to think clearly, forcing one into a holding pattern, repeating set responses not particularly appropriate to the moment (Scheff 1987). This dialogue suggests that Rhoda is overwhelmed with both kinds of shame.

At the heart of the quarrel is a series of threats between Rhoda and her mother. As in all interminable quarrels, it is not possible to identify the first link. We begin with Rhoda's basic threat, without signifying that it came first: *"If you don't stop shaming me, I will starve myself!" Her mother's basic threat: *"If you don't stop shaming me, I'll abandon you!"

The abandonment threat in this case is literal: the mother has left Rhoda to stay with her other daughter. Normally, the threat of abandonment might be largely symbolic; carrying out a threat of abandonment is probably rare. But whether it is real or symbolic, threats of abandonment may be the key link in the causal chain.

This chain has potentially lethal force because none of it is visible to both participants. There are four links: (1) Rhoda's shame in response to her mother's behavior toward her; (2) her threat to starve; (3) the mother's shame in response to Rhoda's behavior; (4) her threat to abandon Rhoda. Rhoda is aware of none of these links. Nearest to her awareness is the mother's threat to abandon her, and next, the shaming by her mother. Rhoda is unaware that her mother is shamed by Rhoda's aggressive and self-destructive behavior, and she denies that she is starving herself. The mother is aware of only one link: Rhoda's threat to starve herself. Because of this awareness, she talks to and about Rhoda in code, not daring to mention Rhoda's threat. Her shame over Rhoda's behavior, her own shaming of Rhoda, and her threat to abandon Rhoda apparently are not experienced by her.

The driving force in the quarrel is not the anger that was interpreted by the therapist but the shame in the field between Rhoda and her family. The anger in this family is both generated and bound by shame. Rhoda experiences her mother's threat of abandonment and her mother's anger as shaming. The mother experiences Rhoda's threat of self-starvation and Rhoda's anger as shaming. The symmetry is complete: each side is threatened and shamed by the other, and each side can see only the other's threat.

The system of threats and hidden emotions is comparable to that preceding conflict between nations (Scheff 1988). Each side feels its credibility would be diminished by backing down in the face of threat. Each side therefore escalates the level of threat. The resulting emotions have no limit, unless outside mediation occurs or shame is dispelled. Perhaps "war fever" is code language for collective shame-rage spirals.

The theory advanced here attempts to explain the emotional sources of mental illness, and the excessive force of the societal reaction to mental illness, the roots of primary and secondary deviance. Rhoda and her family are caught in an interminable conflict that is driven by triple spirals of shame and anger within and between the disputants. For brevity, we have not included Scheff's (1989) analysis of the trans-action between Rhoda and her therapist, but because of its relevance to our argument, we provide a brief summary.

Although Rhoda attacks the therapist surreptitiously, using the same tactics she uses against the authority figures in her family—her mother and her aunt—the therapist is too wily to become emeshed in them. She gets angry, but she doesn't attack Rhoda back, as Rhoda's mother and aunt do. By avoiding emeshment in the family conflict, the therapist is able to form a secure bond with Rhoda, leading ultimately to a successful course of therapy.

Research in the labeling tradition suggests that therapists like this one are probably rare. Therapists and other agents outside the family often become emeshed in family conflicts, usually siding with the family against the patient. Bowen's (1978) seminal analysis of family systems implies this course. Several of our earlier case studies illustrate the emeshment of the outside agents on the side of the family (Retzinger 1989; Scheff 1967, 1987).

Retzinger's study (1989) of a psychiatric interview goes further; she shows how the psychiatrist is emeshed with the family position, and how this emeshment leads to renewed psychiatric symptoms, as pre-dicted by Lewis's theory (1981). The theory proposed here explains the extraordinary forces underlying mental illness and the reaction to it, chain reactions of shame and anger, feelings traps both in patients and in those reacting to them.

A recent study of mental illness using a strictly biographical method has produced findings parallel to ours. Porter (1990) provides an even-handed assessment of endogenous and environmental contribu-tions to the mental illness of a large number of well-documented cases. His summary of the findings for one case—the nineteenth-century pa-tient John Perceval—can be taken to represent his conclusions for the majority of his cases:

> Perceval believed that religious terror had brought on his insanity, and that the behaviour of his family had exacerbated it. But *the real cause of the appalling severity and prolongation of his condition was the medico-psychiatric treatment* he had received. Perceval unambiguously condemned as intrinsically counter-productive the very philosophy of

placing mad people in lunatic asylums. It set the lunatic amongst "strangers" precisely when he *needed to be with his fellows* in familiar surroundings. It estranged him from his family. It put him in the charge of an unknown doctor, rather than those members of the caring professions he knew well, his regular physician or his clergyman. It set him in the midst of fellow lunatics, who, if truly mad, must surely be those people least capable of sustaining the mind of one who had just been crushed under a terrible blow. Precisely at the moment when a person needed his morale to be boosted, he was thrown into a situation that must *"degrade him in his own estimation."* (180–81, emphasis added)

This statement clearly supports labeling theory and points particularly to the two elements in labeling that are emphasized by our new theory: the weakening of social bonds and the accompanying unacknowledged shame. That the psychiatric treatments of the composer Robert Schumann and the dancer Nijinsky resulted in the complete severing of their social bonds is particularly shocking (Porter 1990: 65–71, 71–75).

The position that Porter, a historian, takes toward his findings seems equivocal. He cites none of the labeling theory literature; he states that he sides neither with the patients nor with the psychiatrists. Yet his closing message acknowledges some strain. The first line of his conclusion reads, "This book has not pleaded a cause" (231). He goes on to say that his aim has been merely to focus attention on a body of forgotten writings, the memoirs of the mad. Yet at the end of the conclusion, he states, "clearly, no reader will have taken the opening statement of this Conclusion at face value" (232). For reasons that are never stated, Porter seems reluctant to acknowledge the implications of his findings. He seems to make the error of equating taking a stand on his own findings with "pleading a cause."

Like the cases in previous chapters, the case in this chapter contains the three elements fundamental to our theory: inadequate bonds, dysfunctional communication, and destructive conflict. Before her contact with the therapist, Rhoda appears to have been alienated from everyone in her family. No father is mentioned, and she seems to have the barest cognitive attunment with her mother and aunt and virtually no understanding at the emotional level.

The dialogues with her mother and aunt that Rhoda reports clearly indicate dysfunctional patterns of communication. She and her mother are extremely indirect, evasive, and withholding with each other, and she and her aunt are violently disrespectful, although in underhanded ways. It is of great interest that although she tries the same tactics she use in her family on the therapist, the therapist is able to sidestep them, giving Rhoda what turns out to be important lessons in how to communicate directly but respectfully.

The theme of violence is present in these dialogues only in the form of Rhoda's attempts at self-starvation. Like virtually all the other important issues in Rhoda's family, these attempts are disguised and denied: Rhoda claims that she is only dieting and that she is not underweight. As in most important issues in social communication, contextual, prospective, and retrospective knowledge beyond the discourse itself is needed to interpret the meaning of statements and events.

Support for the theory is also found in the cues for hidden emotion that both the therapist and Labov and Fanshel point out in their interpretations. Although the therapist only interprets Rhoda's and her family's anger, Labov and Fanshel's careful analysis of microscopic cues in verbal and nonverbal behavior provides support for our theory of shame-rage spirals. Their analysis frequently pointed to instances of "embarrassment" (shame) and "hopeless anger" (shame-rage), suggesting the sequences required by our theory. The theory of shame-rage spirals fills in the wiring diagram of the black boxes in labeling theory: unacknowledged alienation and shame drive the labeling machine.

As in its earlier formulation, our extended labeling theory implies a critique of conventional psychiatry, which is individualistic and affirms the status quo. In focusing exclusively on Rhoda's pathology, it denies the pathology in the family system of which she is a part and, by implication, in the larger social system, our current civilization. In chapter 8, we apply labeling theory at the level of international relations, showing the consequences of the labeling of Germany in the aftermath of World War I. We explain the rise of Hitler in terms of chain reactions of shame-anger (humiliated fury) between and within nations. The unbearably high levels of individual and collective violence in our era may be a consequence of the increasing repression of shame and the associated denial of social bonds.

8

Hitler's Appeal: Alienation, Shame-Rage, and Revenge

Accurate scholarship can
Unearth the whole offense
From Luther until now
That has driven a culture mad,
Find what occurred at Linz,[1]
What huge imago made
A psychopathic god.
—W. H. Auden
"September 1, 1939"

This chapter proposes a solution to the riddle of Hitler's appeal to the German masses. Following Lasswell (1960), we show how Hitler's psychopathology, his paranoia, and his continuous humiliated fury produced a program responsive to the craving of his public for a sense of community and pride rather than alienation and shame. Since neither their alienation nor their pride was acknowledged, both Hitler and his public were trapped in a never-ending cycle of humiliation, rage, and vengeful aggression. We describe the evidence for unacknowledged shame in Hitler's life and in his written statements (mainly *Mein Kampf*).

We propose that the alienation and shame-rage cycle in Germany was (and is) only part of a larger system of alienation and emotional repression within and between nations in the world social system. Hitler's rise to power was produced by the labeling, segregation, and stigmatization of Germany as a consequence of its defeat in World War I. Unless the social and emotional features of the world system change toward more solidarity and less repression, increasingly destructive wars are predicted.

Hitler's appeal to the German people has yet to be explained. In his person, he was singularly unprepossessing, to say the least. From a logical point of view, his speeches were disasters; he rambled incoherently, with little order and less substance. His political program was no better; it was disorganized, vague, and silent on key issues.

Beneath the surface, matters were still worse. From the testimony

---

[1]Linz was Hitler's birthplace.

of his intimates, Hitler's personality was bizarre to the point of madness. His delusions, phobias, sadism, sexual aberrations, and utter isolation are well documented. All the biographies clearly show manifold symptoms of severe mental illness.

The puzzle is that this extraordinarily unattractive madman had charismatic appeal not only to the masses but also to a large coterie of devoted followers. These latter individuals knew most or all of the unsavory details, yet they were fanatically loyal. In this chapter we first review earlier attempts to resolve this problem. Then, building on these explanations, we outline a new approach, focusing on the emotional bases of charisma. We propose a new theory of the dynamics of shame, which suggests that unconscious vengefulness motivated Hitler and connected him to his followers.

Earlier Explanations of Hitler's Appeal

A conjecture by Lasswell (1960) provides the foundation for most discussions of Hitler's appeal. Lasswell proposed that successful leaders make assets out of their psychological difficulties by rationalization; they externalize their internal conflicts in political programs. Those whose personal needs exactly correspond to those of their countrymen have charismatic—that is, emotional—appeal.

Lasswell's proposal implies that if we are to understand Hitler's appeal during the years he came to power, we need to understand during that period (1) the personal needs of Germans in the mass; (2) Hitler's personality; and (3) the linkage between (1) and (2). This is a problem of culture and personality, the link between the one and the many. Such problems were much discussed several decades ago but are now neglected. The central difficulty was the lack of a theory and method for conceptualizing the link between individual and collective behavior. We use recent developments in theory and method for the study of emotions to outline a model that might provide such a link.

There are many studies of the first two issues listed above, but the third—the link between Hitler and his public—is treated only briefly and casually. As a framework for our discussion, we first summarize several approaches to this problem.

Of the many discussions of the social bases of Hitler's rise to power, we review three representative ones: Mitchell (1983), Dahrendorf (1967), and Waite (1977). Like most of the other studies, Mitchell's (1983) explanation of Hitler's appeal is quite brief (259–66) and very late in the text—the last eight pages. He proposed that a sequence of disasters lead to a state of anomie, the breakdown of an entire society (Germany's defeat in World War I, the humiliation of the

Treaty of Versailles, the Great Inflation, and finally, the Great Depression in 1929). These events created an economic, intellectual, political, and emotional crisis in Germany.

In this crisis, Hitler offered what seemed to many Germans attractive solutions. Of the several concepts which Mitchell and others propose, we emphasize two, anomie and shame. Instead of anomie, Hitler offered community (*Volksgemeinschaft*, "a community of the folk"), and instead of humiliation, he offered pride and self-confidence. The idea of the folk-community intimated a restoration of what had been lost, the traditional rural community from which many Germans had recently been deprived. The community Hitler offered, "race and blood," seemed easily attainable by the mass; it was heedless of most of the usual distinctions (such as region, class, income, and education). It excluded only a small proportion of the population—mainly the Communists and the Jews.

Most commentators have linked anomie, the breakdown of community and societal bonds, to the rise of Hitler. Dahrendorf (1967) treated this issue in greatest detail. He suggested that anomie was prevalent in German society even before World War I, because industrialization had come late, rapidly, and more completely than in England, the United States, and France. These countries had several hundred years to develop new forms of community during industrialization. But rapid and thorough industrialization led to a more extensive state of anomie in Germany than in the older industrial countries. Dahrendorf proposed that this condition provided the basis for the appeal of a totalitarian leader.

The other concept proposed by Mitchell and others was that Hitler offered pride instead of shame, the restoration of what Mitchell called self-confidence, and "an escape route from the deep pits of humiliation to nearly unlimited adventure" (262). This same solution is implied in Mitchell's discussion of Hitler's ability to "direct popular emotions" (262), although pride and shame are not named explicitly.

These two dimensions of Hitler's appeal—restoring a lost sense of community and pride—are also mentioned in virtually all the other discussions, with about the same amount of detail as Mitchell, or less. Waite's (1977) discussion, however, treated the issue of restoring lost pride at greater length. He noted several times that Germans referred to the Treaty of Versailles as the "Treaty of Shame," and the particular ways in which it triggered the crisis in the Weimar Republic. After coming to power, Hitler usually referred to the Weimar Republic only as "fourteen years of shame and opprobrium."

The Germans felt betrayed; because of Wilson's fourteen points, they had expected a treaty of reconciliation. Instead, the treaty transferred large parts of German territory to other nations, seized all German colonies, and excluded Germany from membership in the League of Nations as unworthy. The treaty spoke in general terms about disarmament, but in actuality, only Germany was forced to disarm. Apparently the most disturbing part of the treaty was one that involved a symbolic rather than a material issue.

In Article 231, Germany was required to confess sole responsibility for causing World War I—a patent absurdity. (We will return to the issue of blame in our discussion of conflict in family and social systems.) Furthermore, the Germans were compelled to sign the treaty since they were threatened with continued blockade until it was signed. The blockade was in fact extended ten months beyond the end of the war, causing starvation and a further sense of injustice and betrayal.

As it turned out, the Allied treatment of Germany in the Treaty of Versailles was neither fish nor fowl: it visited suffering and humiliation on Germans without destroying their capacity to make war. An earlier victor over the German tribes, Julius Caesar, had a different policy: after defeating them he either killed every member of a tribe or treated them generously, fearing revenge. Although the French feared revenge, the Allies neither scorched the German earth nor restored Germany to the community of nations.

After recounting the realistic bases for the German sense of betrayal and humiliation, Waite went on to describe the irrational ones: the legend of the *Dolschstoss* ("stab-in-the-back") and the anti-Semitism to which it was closely tied. The stab-in-the-back legend was that the "November criminals"—traitorous Jews and revolutionaries at home—surrendered, rather than the victorious armed forces. This legend was pure fiction (307). The military command compelled surrender well before the revolution; General Ludendorff forced an unwilling civilian government to sue for peace. Although both legends were false, Hitler always took them to be factual: they played an important role in his appeal. (We return to the emotional appeal of these legends later.)

Hitler's Personality

The need of Germans for solidarity and for pride are prominent in a reverse way in the many studies of Hitler's psychopathology. They all stress Hitler's complete isolation from other people and the prominence of shame (and anger) in his makeup. The descriptions of Hitler's isolation will be summarized first.

The biographies and psychological studies emphasize Hitler's isolation as a child and adult (Bromberg and Småll 1983; Bullock 1964; Davidson 1977; Miller 1983; Stierlin 1976; Toland 1976). As an infant and youth, he was pampered by his mother. But even as young as three, his relationship with his father was charged with violence, ridicule, and contempt. By the age of six, he apparently was walled off from everyone, including his mother (Bromberg and Small 1983; Miller 1983; Stierlin 1976).

The three most likely candidates with whom he had a close relationship are August Kubizek, Eva Braun, and Albert Speer. Hitler and Kubizek were companions for three years, beginning when they were both sixteen. Kubizek's memoir of Hitler (1955) shows that his relationship to Hitler was not that of friend but that of an adoring admirer. Kubizek described Hitler as a compulsive talker, brooking no interruptions, let alone any disagreement. Lacking any other listeners at this age, Hitler used Kubizek as an audience.

Speer, an architect-engineer, was closest to Hitler among his officials during the last years of World War II. In an interview after the war, Speer revealed that although he spent countless hours with Hitler, there was no personal relationship between them (Bromberg and Small 1983: 112): "If Hitler had friends, I would have been his friend."

Eva Braun's diary (Bromberg and Small 1983: 107–108) shows that she, as Hitler's mistress, came no closer to him than Kubizek and Speer. For most of their fifteen-year relationship, he attempted to keep it hidden, confining her to her rooms during meetings with others. A few entries suggest the tone of the whole diary. In 1935, when she was twenty-three and Hitler forty-six, she complained that she felt imprisoned, that she got nothing from their sexual relationship, and that she felt desperately insecure: "He is only using me for definite purposes" (March 11). Most of the women with whom Hitler had sexual relations either attempted or committed suicide. (Small and Bromberg count seven such relationships, with three of them attempting, and three completing suicide [1983: 125].) Eva Braun herself made two such attempts.

In 1942, Hitler inadvertently suggested the extent of his isolation from Eva. Hearing of the death of one of his officials, Fritz Todt, chief of armaments, he said that he was now deprived of "the only two human beings among all those around me to whom I have been truly and inwardly attached: Dr. Todt is dead and Hess has flown away from me!" (Toland 1976: 666). As Bromberg and Small (1983) note, this statement leaves out Eva entirely, mentioning instead "a remote man who could rarely be induced to sit at Hitler's table and a man he could not bear to converse with, denounced as crazy, and wished dead" (150).

Neither as a soldier nor as a politician did Hitler have close attachments. His experience as an enlisted man in the army during and after World War I is illustrative. Although he was a dedicated soldier who demonstrated courage in battle, he was a "loner"; he had no intimates.

This may be one of the reasons that although he was decorated for bravery, he was little promoted; after four years, he left the army at the rank of lance corporal—the equivalent of private first class. In his evaluations, he was described as lacking in leadership.

After becoming the leader of the Nazi party, he moved no closer to human relationships. A description of his campaign the year before he gained power is representative:

> Hitler used superhuman energy to storm every German state by train, car, and still-novel airplane. Yet he had almost no real contact with people, not even with his associates, who felt they were touring with a performer. He did not permit them to be colleagues on a team and kept them away from any important people, storing information only in his own memory. He remained a lone wolf, now even harsher, often jealous, more distant from his senior associates, and contemptuous of them. (Small and Bromberg 1983: 108)

Although he was the adored leader of millions of people, Hitler apparently had no secure bond with anyone.

The other characteristic of Hitler's personality noted by most of the studies is the prevalence of shame and anger. Diagnostic studies (Bromberg and Small 1983; Miller 1983; Stierlin 1976) point to shame and humiliation as prominent features in Hitler's makeup, both as a child and as an adult. Hitler's father, Alois, was a brutal and tyrannical ruler of his family, but his most intense wrath was turned on Adolf, whom he repeatedly beat and humiliated. Hitler's mother, Klara, pampered him, but she did nothing to protect him from his father since she too was brutalized by Alois. The studies mentioned above interpret Hitler's early childhood experiences as the source of his later aberrations, his temper tantrums, his sadomasochism, and his fanatical anti-Semitism. (We will return to this issue after discussing the shame dynamics.)

Although the earlier studies are useful, they do not solve the puzzle. The discussions of the first issue, Hitler's psychopathology, are compelling enough. The argument about the needs of the German masses is merely plausible, however, since it is quite abstract in the main and is supported only in part by actual evidence. With respect to the third question—the basis of the overwhelming response to Hitler—the arguments are thin; they might be described as barely plausible.

The existing literature on this question is unconvincing because it lacks not only evidence but even the most rudimentary form of theory and method. The arguments lack a conceptual framework. For this reason, and because they are post hoc, it is unclear how one might choose between the different versions. None of the explanations propose directions for future research.

Our purpose here is to outline a theory linking the charismatic leader's personality and the response of his followers, and a method for the analysis of his discourse. As background, two steps are necessary. In chapters 1 and 2, we have shown the connection between social structure and the emotions of pride and shame. In this chapter, we go on to develop a model of the dynamics of these two emotions within and between leader and followers.

Pride and Shame

The psychoanalytic idea of repression may be helpful in understanding defenses against inadequate bonding. If the ideology of the self-sufficient individual is a defense against the pain of threatened bonds, what is being repressed is the *idea* of the social bond. Freud, however, argued that repression concerns not only ideas but also the *feelings* that accompany them. He thought that repression could be lifted only if both the idea and the emotions were expressed. If modern societies repress the idea of the social bond, what are the associated feelings that are also repressed?

As we have seen, Cooley (1922) implied that pride and shame are the primary social emotions. These two emotions have a signal function with respect to the social bond. In this framework, pride and shame serve as intense and automatic bodily signs of the state of a system that is otherwise difficult to observe. Pride is the sign of an intact bond; shame is the sign of a threatened bond. The clearest outer marker of pride is holding up one's head in public, looking others in the eye, and indicating respect by taking turns looking and looking away. In *overt* shame, one shrinks, averts or lowers one's gaze, and casts only furtive glances at the other. In *bypassed* shame, one stares, outfacing the other.

The two forms of shame are polar opposites in terms of thought and feeling. Overt shame involves painful feeling with little ideation, bypassed shame, the opposite pattern: rapid thought, speech, or behavior, but little feeling. Overt shame is marked by furtiveness, confusion, and bodily reactions such as blushing, sweating and/or rapid heartbeat. One may be at a loss for words, with flustered or disorganized thoughts or behavior, as in states of embarrassment. Many of the common terms for painful feelings appear to refer to this type of shame, or to its combinations with anger: feeling peculiar, shy, bashful, awkward, funny, bothered, or miserable; in adolescent vernacular, it is being freaked, bummed, or weirded out. The phrases "I feel like a fool" or "a perfect idiot" may be prototypical of overt shame.

Bypassed shame is manifested as a brief painful feeling, usually lasting less than a second, followed by obsessive and rapid thought or speech. A common example is feeling insulted or criticized. At that moment (or later, in recalling it), one may experience a jab of painful feeling (producing a groan or wince), followed immediately by imaginary but compulsive and repetitive *replays* of the offending scene. The replays are variations on a theme: how one might have behaved differently and thereby avoided the incident, or responded with better effect. One becomes *obsessed*.

In our theory, unacknowledged shame is the cause of revenge-based cycles of conflict. (This formulation was anticipated in the work of Geen [1968] and Feshbach [1971].) We argue that shame-rage may escalate continually to the point that a person or a group can be in a permanent fit of shame-rage, a kind of madness.

Studies of Shame and Aggression

The theory we outline is supported by several exploratory studies. Katz (1988) analyzed descriptions of several hundred criminal acts: vandalism, theft, robbery, and murder. In many of these cases, Katz found that the perpetrator felt humiliated, and had committed the crime as an act of revenge. In some of the cases the perpetrator's sense of humiliation was based on actual insults:.

> [A] . . . typical technique [leading to a spouse being murdered] is for the victim to attack the spouse's deviations from the culturally approved sex role. . . . For example, a wife may accuse her husband of being a poor breadwinner or an incompetent lover . . . or the husband may accuse his wife of being "bitchy," "frigid," or promiscuous. (1988: chap. 2, page 8)

In other cases it was difficult to assess the degree to which the humiliations were real and/or imagined. Whatever the realities, Katz's findings support the model of the shame-rage feeling trap. In his analysis of the murder of intimates, he says, "The would-be-killer must undergo a particular emotional process. He must transform what he initially senses as an eternally humiliating situation into a blinding rage" (11). Rather than acknowledge his or her shame, the killer masks it with anger, which is the first step into the abyss of the shame-rage feeling trap, which ends in murder. Katz reported similar though less dramatic findings with respect to the other kinds of crimes he investigated.

One issue that Katz's study did not address is the conditions under which humiliation is transformed into blind rage. Since not all humiliations lead to blind rage, there must be some ingredient that is not indicated in Katz's cases. The studies of family violence by Lansky strongly suggest what this extra ingredient is. In order to lead to blind rage, the shame component in the emotions that are aroused must be *unacknowledged*.

Lansky has published three papers on family violence. The first paper (1984) describes six cases; the second (1987) describes four; and the third (1989), one. The third paper analyzes a session with a single couple. In most of the cases, Lansky reports similar emotional dynamics: in the cases he studied, violence resulted from the insulting manner that both husbands and wives took toward each other. Although some of their insults were overt, in the form of cursing, open contempt, and disgust, most of them were covert, taking the form of innuendo or double messages.

Underhanded disrespect gives rise to unacknowledged shame, which leads in turn to anger and violence, in the way predicted by Lewis. It is difficult for the participants to respond to innuendo and to double messages; these forms of communication confuse them. But instead of admitting their upset and puzzlement, they answer in kind. The cycle involves disrespect, humiliation, revenge, counter-revenge, and so on, ending in violence.

That both spouses seem to be unaware of the intense shame that their behavior generates can be seen in Lansky's description of one of the cases:

> A 32-year-old man and his 46-year-old wife were seen in emergency conjoint consultation after he struck her. Both spouses were horrified, and the husband agreed that hospitalization might be the best way to start the lengthy treatment that he wanted. As he attempted to explain his view of his difficult marriage, his wife disorganized him with repeated humiliating comments about his inability to hold a job. These comments came at a time when he was talking about matters other than the job. When he did talk about work, she interrupted to say how immature he was compared to her previous husbands, then how strong and manly he was. The combination of building up and undercutting his sense of manliness was brought into focus. As the *therapist* commented on the process, the husband became more and more calm. . . . After the fourth session, he left his marriage and the hospital for another state, and phoned the therapist for an appropriate referral for individual therapy. On followup some months later, he had followed through with treatment. (1984: 34–35, emphasis added)

The wife humiliates the husband in this case not through innuendo, since her disparagement is overt. Her shaming tactics seem to be disguised by her technique of alternately praising her husband, by stating how "strong and manly" he is, then cutting him down. (Perhaps she confused *herself* with this tactic as much as she did her husband.)

A lack of awareness of shaming and shame can be seen in Lansky's 1989 article, which reports a conjoint session with a violent man and his wife. In this session, Lansky reports, the wife was dressed in a sexually provocative way, and her bearing and manner were overtly seductive toward the interviewer. Yet neither spouse acknowledged her activity, even when the interviewer asked them whether the wife was ever seductive toward other men. Both answered affirmatively, but their answers concerned only past events. The lack of comment on what was occurring at that very moment in the interview is astounding. It would seem that blind rage requires not only shaming and shame, but blindness toward these two elements.

The relationship between collective violence and unacknowledged shame has been suggested in a recent analysis of the Attica riots (Scheff, Retzinger, and Ryan 1989). Violence of the guards toward the inmates began with a series of events that the guards perceived as humiliating: without consulting the guards, a new warden intent on reform increased the rights of the prisoners, which resulted in a series of incidents with prisoners that the guards experienced as humiliating. Since the guards did not acknowledge their humiliation, their assault on the prisoners followed the sequence predicted by the Lewis theory: insult, unacknowledged shame, rage, and aggression.

The conjecture that unacknowledged humiliation is the source of lethal aggression would seem to solve the problem both of Hitler's motivation and of his appeal to his public. Hitler himself continuously expressed the dominant affect among the Germans—bypassed shame-rage, humiliated fury—and he encouraged them to express it. Denying his own overwhelming shame and rage, he projected it onto the outside world, particularly upon the Jews. Unacknowledged shame was prevalent in Hitler's life and in his discourse.

Humiliated Fury as the Key Affect in Hitler's Life

The Swiss psychoanalyst Alice Miller (1983) has called attention to what may be the origin of Hitler's psychopathology—the conjunction of his father's physical and emotional violence and his mother's complicity in it. Miller argues that the rage and shame caused by his father's treatment may have been completely repressed because of his mother's complicity. Although she pampered Hitler and professed to love him, she didn't protect him from his father's wrath or allow Adolf *to express his feelings about it.* Klara, as much as Adolf, was tyrannized by her husband, but she offered obedience and respect in return. Because of his mother's "love" for him, as a young child Adolf was required not only to suffer humiliation by his father in silence but to respect him for it—a basic context for repression.

In *Mein Kampf,* Hitler glossed over his treatment by his parents, behavior that is congruent with repression. He described his father as stern but respected and his childhood as that of a "mother's darling living in a soft downy bed" (Bromberg and Small 1983: 40). But Alois's other son, Alois, Jr., left home at fourteen because of his father's harshness. His own son, William Patrick, reported that Alois, Sr., beat Alois, Jr., with a hippopotamus whip. Alois, Jr.'s, first wife, Brigid, reported that Alois, Sr., frequently beat the children, and on occasion, his wife Klara, Hitler's mother (Bromberg and Small 1983: 32–33).

It would appear that Hitler's early childhood constituted an external feeling trap from which he had no escape. This external trap is the exact analogue to the internal trap proposed by Lewis (1971): when shame is evoked but goes unacknowledged, it generates intense symptoms of mental illness and/or violence toward self or others. Under the conditions of complete repression that seem to have obtained, Hitler's personality might have been severely damaged. His biographies suggest that he was constantly in a state of anger bound by shame.

One indication of Hitler's continual shame-rage was his temper tantrums. Although in later life some of them may have been staged, there is no question that in most of his tantrums he was actually out of control. His older stepbrother reported that even before he was seven,

> He was imperious and quick to anger from childhood onward and would not listen to anyone. My stepmother always took his part. He would get the craziest notions and get away with it. If he didn't have his way he got very angry. . . . [H]e had no friends, took to no one and could be very heartless. He could fly into a rage over any triviality. (Gilbert 1950: 18).

In his teens, Hitler's rages were frequent and intense, evoking such expressions as "red with rage," "exceedingly violent and high-strung," and "like a volcano erupting" (Kubizek 1955).

Hitler's early shame-proneness is suggested by the slightness of the provocations that triggered his rage. Kubizek's memoir provides two examples: an occasion when Hitler learned that he had failed to win a lottery, and another when he saw Stephanie, a girl whom Hitler longed to meet but never did, with other men. He was infatuated with her but never introduced himself (Bromberg and Small 1983: 55–56).

The most obvious manifestations of Hitler's shame-proneness occurred after he became chancellor. Although he was easily the most powerful and admired man in Germany, he was constantly fearful that he would appear ridiculous.

> Before he ventured on a political appearance in a new suit or headgear, he had himself photographed to study its effect. In addition to

asking his valet whether he looked the part of the Fuehrer, he would
check with Hess the manner of speech he should use on different
occasions. His anxieties lest he appear ridiculous, weak, vulnerable,
incompetent, or in any way inferior are indications of this endless
battle with shame. (Bromberg and Small 1983: 183)

Further manifestations of chronic shame states occurred in his relationships with women and in his sexual relationships. In attempting to
interest a woman in himself,

even the presence of other persons would not prevent him from repul-
sive groveling. [He would] tell a lady that he was unworthy to sit near
her or kiss her hand but hoped she would look on him with
favor. . . . One woman reported that after all kinds of self-accusations
he said that he was unworthy of being in the same room with her.
(Bromberg and Small 1983: 183)

Bromberg and Small (1983: 243–47) establish that Hitler was
never able to have a normal sexual relationship with a woman. Instead,
he practiced a type of perversion in which both he and his partner were
humiliated. Although the humiliation of the partner is not explicitly
described, Hitler's part is: he first required that the partner squat over
his face. After a lengthy inspection of her genitals, he demanded that
his partner urinate on his face. Apparently this was the only way he
could achieve satisfaction.

To this point, the descriptions of Hitler's shame states suggest
overt, undifferentiated shame, emotionally painful states involving feelings of inadequacy and inferiority. How, then, is one to understand the
other side of Hitler's personality—his arrogance, boldness, and extreme
self-confidence? How could a man so shame-prone also be so shameless?

Lewis's concept of the bimodal nature of shame states—overt and
bypassed—may provide the answer to this puzzle. In addition to the
overt shame states already discussed, Hitler also had a long history of
bypassed shame. Many aspects of his behavior suggest bypassed shame,
but here we will review only three: his temper tantrums, his "piercing
stare" (Bromberg and Small 1983: 309), and his obsessiveness.

Shame theory suggests that protracted and destructive anger is always generated by unacknowledged shame. Normal anger, when it is
not intermixed with shame, is usually brief, moderate, and constructive,
serving to call notice to adjustments that are needed in a relationship
(Retzinger 1988). Long chains of alternating shame and anger, however, are experienced as blind rage, hatred, or resentment if the shame
component is completely repressed. In this case, the expression of anger
serves as a disguise for the hidden shame, projecting onto the outside

world the feelings of shame that are unacknowledged within. According to Lewis, many "would rather turn the world upside down than turn themselves inside out." This idea exactly captures the psychology of Hitler's lifelong history of intense rage states and his projection of his inner conflict onto scapegoats.

The second indicator of bypassed shame is Hitler's demeanor, especially his gaze. As early as sixteen, it was described as "blank" or "cruel" (Bromberg and Small 1983: 51). On the other hand, at a later time (21) he was described as having "an evasive manner," as being "shy" and "never looking a person in the eye," except when he was talking politics (70). These descriptions suggest that Hitler may have been in a virtually permanent state of shame, manifested as either bypassed shame (the stare) or overt shame (avoiding eye contact). As his power increased, the bypassed shame was more and more in evidence, in the form of arrogance, extreme self-confidence, isolation, and obsession.

According to Lewis, the rapidity of speech and behavior that is the prime outer indicator of bypassed shame is usually accompanied by a primary inner manifestation—obsessiveness. Persons who are in a state of chronic shame may avoid and deny their emotional pain by obsessive preoccupation. Hitler's principal obsession, "the Jewish problem," is particularly indicative of unacknowledged shame. At the center of Hitler's belief system was the concept of racial superiority—that the "Aryan race" was the superior race and that the Jewish "race" was inferior. His many obsessions with superiority-inferiority, racial purity, pollution, and contamination can be interpreted as operations for bypassing shame. Textual evidence supports the conjecture that Hitler was motivated by unconscious shame.

Shame-Anger Sequences in *Mein Kampf*

Hitler's book, "My Struggle," was written during his imprisonment after a failed attempt to overthrow the government of Bavaria in 1923. The first half of the book is part autobiography, part a history of the Nazi party. The second half describes the program of the party. Although indications of shame and anger are scattered throughout the book, they are the most prevalent in the latter half.

The most frequent sequence is the progression from shame to pride. One example is his discussion of "scientific education":

> There is ground for *pride* in our people only if we no longer need to be *ashamed* of any class. But a people, half of which is wretched and careworn, or even depraved, offers so sorry a picture that no one

should feel any *pride* in it. Only when a nation is healthy in all its members, in body and soul, can every man's joy in belonging to it rightfully be magnified to that high sentiment which we designate as national *pride*. And this highest *pride* will only be felt by the man who knows the greatness of his nation. (427, emphasis added)

There is a reference to pride in each of the four sentences in this passage, but only one reference to shame (the word *ashamed* in the first sentence). This pattern is characteristic: an initial reference to shame is followed by repeated references to pride. One intimation seems to be that although now ashamed, the future will be proud, but only if the Nazi program is carried out. This pattern also suggests the denial of shame, which is mentioned only once, compared with the repeated references to pride—a more "respectable"—that is, less shameful—emotion.

The meaning of the passage is also of interest because it may imply proneness to shame. The phrase *any pride* at the end of the second sentence suggests that if a group has *any* reason for shame, then *all* pride is lost. A more normal response would be that we always have reason for both pride and shame; that is the human condition.

In the passage just quoted, the references to pride and shame are explicit. In the following passage, which has the same structure, the references are indirect:

Particularly our German people which today lies broken and defenseless, *exposed to the kicks of all the world,* needs that suggestive force that lies in *self-confidence*. This *self-confidence* must be inculcated in the young national comrade from childhood on. His whole education and training must be so ordered as to give him the conviction that he is absolutely *superior* to others. Through his physical strength and dexterity, he must recover his faith in the *invincibility* of his whole people. For what formerly led the German army to victory was the sum of the *confidence* which each individual had in himself and all together in their leadership. What will raise the German people up again is *confidence*. (411, emphasis added)

Once again there is a progression from shame to pride, and once again a single reference to shame is followed by repeated references to pride. But this time both feelings are evoked obliquely. In the middle of the first sentence is an image of the German people "exposed to the kicks of all the world." Although the word *shame* is not used, the image is clearly one of gross humiliation, of being subjected to a humiliating assault by anyone and everyone.

This passage too, moves very quickly from shame to many references to pride. But like the reference to shame, the references to pride are indirect, using the cognates *self-confidence* and *confidence* rather than the word *pride* itself. This passage contains three more references to confidence as well as two additional *pride* cognates—a conviction of "superiority to others" and a "faith in invincibility." This pattern, like that in the first passage, suggests the denial of shame, since references to it are quickly negated by many references to pride. The entire passage, like many others, is suggestive of the denial of emotions since shame and pride are referred to only indirectly.

Although direct references to pride are found throughout *Mein Kampf*, there are many more indirect references. In addition to *self-confidence, honor, superiority,* and *faith* in one's invincibility, Hitler frequently invokes "dignity" (and being "worthy") as valued characteristics. The task of the "folk-state" "is not to preserve the decisive influence of an existing social class, but to pick the most capable kinds from the sum of all the national comrades and bring them to office and *dignity*" (431; emphasis added). This passage contains both key elements in Hitler's appeal, community and pride; it negates social class in the interest of community, and it promises prideful office to the most capable, regardless of background.

Most of the manifestations of pride and shame are disguised, requiring reading between the lines. The emotional content of the following passage is invisible unless one realizes that the basic shame context is seeing oneself negatively in the eyes of the other (see Sartre 1956; Lewis 1971):

> How terrible is the damage indirectly done to our Germanism today by the fact that, due to the ignorance of many Americans, the German-jabbering Jews, when they set foot on American soil, are booked to our German account. Surely no one will call the purely external fact that most of this lice-ridden migration from the East speaks German a proof of their German origin and nationality. (390)

In this passage, Hitler seems to be seeing himself (and the German people) negatively in the eyes of the other, the American people. Because the shameful ("lice-ridden") Jewish migrants speak German, the Americans denigrate Germans and Germany. In the second sentence, he goes on to protest the injustice of this situation produced by his imagination. There is a gratuitous element to this passage that is difficult to define explicitly, but it captures the kind of emotional aura characteristic of Hitler's prose; it is shame-haunted.

In *Mein Kampf*, the many manifestations of shame are virtually always hidden in encoded terms. Hitler repeatedly refers to disgrace, lack of self-confidence, inferiority, and "bowing and scraping" (625) in describing the German people or their representatives. Frequently shame manifestations are even more indirect, as in the passage quoted above about the "German-jabbering Jews." One of Hitler's frequent themes is other nation's lack of respect for Germany:

> Will any [nation ally itself with] a state . . . whose characteristic way of life consists only in *cringing* submissiveness without and *disgraceful* oppression of national virtues within; . . . with governments which can boast of *no respect* whatsoever on the part of their citizens, so that foreign countries cannot possibly harbor any greater admiration for them? No, a power which itself wants to be *respected* . . . will not ally itself to present-day Germany. (621; emphasis added)

Like Hitler's statements, his actions were also haunted by the specter of shame. Bromberg and Small (1983: 119) note in passing Hitler's obsession with giantism, of building bigger than anyone. He explained to the workers on one of his building projects, "Why always the biggest? I do this to restore to each individual German his *self-respect*. . . . I want to say to the individual: We are not *inferior*; on the contrary, we are the complete equals of every other nation" (Speer 1970: 69, 107; emphasis added). Because the references to pride and shame are in code language, Bromberg and Small miss their significance. A huge part of Germany's resources, even during wartime, were devoted to the attempt to make Hitler and his followers feel large (proud) rather than small (ashamed).

The primary manifestation of shame in Hitler's behavior was not in construction, however, but in destruction. As Lewis's theory predicts, an individual in a state of chronic shame is very likely to perceive the source of this feeling as an attack by another, generating rage toward that other. Lewis's theory suggests that *protracted* rage *always* has its source in unacknowledged shame, without exception. In her theory, unacknowledged shame is *the* cause of destructive aggression because it generates blind rage.

The sequence "unacknowledged shame, followed by rage, followed by aggression" can be traced in particular passages in *Mein Kampf*, as well as in the book as a whole. The following passage is representative. In one of his many attacks on the Treaty of Versailles, after describing it as an instrument of "abject humiliation," Hitler states:

> How could every single one of these points have been burned into the brain and emotion of this people, until finally in sixty million heads, in men and women, a common sense of *shame* and a common hatred would have become a single fiery sea of flame, from whose heat a will as hard as steel would have risen and a cry burst forth:
> *Give us arms again!* (632, emphasis added)

In this excerpt, the text moves from humiliation to fury to aggression, the last in the form of rearmament for the battle that Hitler prescribes as the destiny of Germany.

What is the battle for which Hitler wants Germany to prepare? It is a battle against both external and internal enemies. At first glance it appears that France is the external enemy, since Hitler refers many times to the "eternal conflict" between the two countries (674, for example). He also repeatedly refers to the French motive for destroying Germany, its "thirst for vengeance" (624, for example), with great indignation, quite oblivious to his own vengefulness. Hitler does not aver that revenge is his own motive, but he is quick to detect it in others; for example, he ascribes to another "hereditary enemy," Negroes, "the perverted sadistic thirst for vengeance" (624).

It becomes apparent quite quickly, however, that the ultimate enemy that Hitler sees everywhere is the Jewish people—or as he puts it, the "International Jew." Hitler had a classical idée fixe, a fanatical and unswerving belief, that behind every enemy nation, race, occupation, or class, the source of every disaster was the Jewish conspiracy, whose aim was world conquest. Hitler's rage is directed against Jews, whom he confabulates with all other enemies. In Hitler's discourse, all capitalists, traitors, revolutionaries, and Marxists are either Jews or are in the pay of Jews.

In *Mein Kampf*, Hitler's solution to what he calls the Jewish problem is only slightly disguised. Hitler repeatedly alludes to "the settling of accounts" and a "day of reckoning." In the middle of the last chapter, which has the ominous title "The Right of Emergency Defense," Hitler gives a foretaste of what he has in mind:

> If at the beginning of the War and during the War twelve or fifteen thousand of these Hebrew corrupters of the people had been held under poison gas, as happened to hundreds of thousands of our very best German workers in the field, the sacrifice of millions at the front would not have been in vain. On the contrary: twelve thousand scoundrels eliminated in time might have saved the lives of a million real Germans, valuable for the future. (679)

The cycle of shame and rage is focused on a mythical enemy, the Jewish conspiracy and those Hitler believed to be in its pay, but his destructive aggression killed millions of real people.

The evidence we have reviewed suggests, first, that from very early childhood, Hitler's actions were determined by unacknowledged shame, alternating between overt and bypassed states. This conjecture is congruent both with his lack of personal relationships and with his most frequent emotional states—abject humiliation, arrogant dominance (what Adler called the "drive for power"), and protracted rage.

Second, the evidence suggests that the combination of insecure social bonds and humiliated fury was endemic among the German masses. Although the particular family in which Hitler's personality was formed was an extreme instance, many Germans, perhaps a majority, were probably raised in similar families, dominated by a harsh, tyrannical father and a "loving" mother who yielded completely to the father. This family system, as Miller (1983) has argued, sets the stage for extreme repression. In the societywide crisis in Germany, beginning with its defeat in World War I and culminating in the Great Depression, both outer and inner conditions were ripe for an explosion of humiliated fury. (To complete our argument, it is necessary to gather evidence of humiliated fury from statements by ordinary Germans during the period under study.)

Third, the evidence suggests that repressed shame and rage were the link between Hitler and the masses. Hitler's statements and manner sanctioned the intense emotional states that existed unexpressed in his public. Although they lack a theoretical framework, Bromberg and Small's analysis comes near to this formulation:

> The abundant, almost unheard-of expression of hate and rageful anger . . . fired [Hitler's] successful orations. . . . [He spoke] the unspeakable for them. His practice of touching off hostile emotions rather than conveying mere critical ideas was wildly successful. (1983: 313)

This summary formulation by Bromberg and Small focuses on rage, ignoring what we consider to be the causal emotion, unacknowledged shame. But an earlier statement concerning the basic source of Hitler's motives include shame:

> Hitler's efforts to *deny his shame* and to avoid situations that would make him feel ashamed pervade much of what he said, wrote, and did. . . .
>
> He inveighed against anything he considered indicative of weakness, inferiority, or defeat. Himself far from his tall, blonde, trim, lithe, tough, ideal German male, he allied himself with the tough image. He who feared to swim or sit in a boat or on a horse boasted of racial, political, and military superiority, superlative courage, and physical excellence. In writing and speeches he denied his awareness of *humiliating weakness* with boasts of his "granite hardness," brutality, mercilessness, and unchangeability, all of which he equated with masculinity. Hardness, brutality, mercilessness, and stubborn perseveration also marked his acts. (184; emphasis added)

In order to explain Hitler's appeal, all that is missing from this statement is that his public was also in a state of chronic shame. Lewis's theory of the shame-rage feeling trap provides a conceptual model for explaining Hitler's behavior, that of the German masses, and the connection between the two. The model is not an abstract one that leaves out the causal chain, the moment-to-moment links between leader and followers, as in the psychoanalytic formulations.

The theory proposed here suggests that Hitler and his public were united by their individual and joint states of emotion, a triple spiral of shame-rage. They were ashamed, angry that they were ashamed, ashamed that they were angry, and so on, without limit. Hitler's hold on the masses: instead of ignoring or condemning their humiliated fury (the mistake that Carter made in the Iran hostage crisis, for example), he displayed it himself. In this way, as Bromberg and Small suggest, he sanctioned their fury.

Our explanation of Hitler's appeal thus goes further than that of psychoanalytic formulations; it explains how Hitler, in justifying the fury of the Germans, would have seemed to them to mitigate it. His rage and his projection of German shame onto the Jews would have temporarily lessened the level of pain of the average German, by interrupting the chain reaction of overt shame and rage: his own behavior and beliefs implied, "You needn't be ashamed of being humiliated and enraged: it's not your fault." The secret of charisma may be that it is not the cognitive content of the message, but the emotional one, that is important. *The leader who is able to decrease the shame level of a group, interrupting the contagion of overt shame, no matter how briefly or at what cost, will be perceived as charismatic.*

For comparative purposes, this conjecture can be used in other, less extreme circumstances, such as to explain Ronald Reagan's charisma in dealing with the Iran hostage crisis, and Jimmy Carter's lack of it. Reagan's response to the crisis was to get angry: he expressed insult and outrage, much like the average voter. Carter, however, refrained from expressing emotion, counseling patience and rationality. To people in the grip of humiliated fury, counsels of this type fail to mitigate pain and may even increase it; they may feel more ashamed of their shame and anger in the face of advice that seems to deny or condemn it.

In his public statements, Carter seemed not only to lack emotion himself but to deny it in others. Early in the hostage crisis, a reporter asked, "How can you satisfy the public demand to end such embarrassment?" (November 28, 1979) In the main, Carter did not respond to the implication that the nation had been embarrassed. Instead, he discussed legal and ethical issues in a detached manner. But toward the end of his statement, he responded to the emotional content of the question in an oblique way, saying that "acts of terrorism may cause *discomfiture* of a people or a government." This distanced response virtually denies all emotion. *Discomfiture* is a genteelism for *shame,* but the hypothetical and abstract nature of the phrasing disguises it out of existence.

The most striking aspect of Carter's stance during the crisis is the absence of anger on his part toward Iran. At no point did he express anger; at most he expressed disappointment and frustration. Like *discomfiture,* these words concern feeling but also disguise and diminish it. Carter seldom expressed emotion, and when he did, it was almost entirely disguised.

Not so his successor. Reagan treated hostile acts by foreign powers as insults not only to the national honor but to his own. He often responded with anger. His tone was set early in his first term. At the press conference of January 29, 1981, he was asked, "Will your policy toward Iran be one of revenge or reconciliation?" Reagan's initial response was not emotional: sounding somewhat like his predecessor, he discussed only legal considerations. By doing so, he first established his moderation and rationality in the face of the temptation toward an emotional response.

His answer to the next question, however, concerning the possibility of U.S. retribution to future terrorism, struck a different note. After first saying that he would not give a specific answer, he went on:

> People have gone to bed in some of these countries that have done these things to us in the past confident that they can go to sleep, wake up in the morning, and the United States wouldn't take any action. What I mean by that phrase is that anyone who does these things, violates our rights in the future, is not going to go to bed with that confidence.

The emotional style in this passage is quite different from Carter's. Although he made no direct threat, he intimated that he might use fire to fight fire. The references to sleeping and waking seem to threaten night-fears to potential terrorists. This passage also suggests self-righteous anger at enemies, an emotion that Carter always avoided.

Reagan referred explicitly to this emotion—and expressed it—in his statement of September 5, 1983, on the downing of the Korean jetliner by a Russian fighter: "With our horror and our sorrow, there is a righteous and terrible anger. It would be easy to think in terms of vengeance, but that is not a proper answer." This statement shows a pattern similar to that of statements about the hostage crisis; they express righteous anger, but they deny the propriety of acting on the basis of that emotion. With this maneuver, Reagan managed to suggest both that he was forceful (angry) and that he was moral, since he at least gave the appearance of ruling out vengefulness. It is important to note, however, that he did not give the impression of ignoring or condemning the temptation to take revenge.

Carter's response to insult was to express only the second component—moral righteousness. When asked late in his term (November 2, 1980) about the hostages, he spoke of honor: "[O]ur policy is based on two fundamental objectives, protecting the honor and the vital interests of the United States, and working to insure the earliest possible release of the hostages." Carter indicated later in this statement that he would use only those means that would uphold the "national honor . . . and integrity." Carter's idea of honor was quite different from Reagan's. Honor for Reagan meant removing dishonor by meeting force with force, but for Carter it meant prudence and moral virtue.

In this instance, Carter urged restraint rather than yielding to the demands for force and retaliation. His counsel of restraint gave him anticharisma, alienating the majority of the voters. Even though his tactics ultimately proved successful, he got little credit for them. His management of the crisis left an image of weakness and a residue of angry feeling directed toward him. By contrast, when faced with public outcry against Libyan terrorism several years later, Reagan bombed Tripoli. Where Carter had ignored and by implication condemned the feeling trap of the majority of voters (humiliation-rage-aggression), Reagan capitulated to it.

In alienated societies, leaders face the dilemma illustrated by Carter's and Reagan's approaches to the management of emotions. If they resist the shame-anger spiral of the public, they run the danger of losing power, as Carter did. But if they give in to it, they endanger world peace and further the process of self and social alienation, as Reagan did in his actions toward Libya and Iran, and as Hitler did in his whole career. Perhaps the wisest course would be to acknowledge public emotion, as Reagan did, but to avoid acting on it, as Carter did.

The cartoon by Garry Trudeau in figure 2–1 suggests how shame-rage dynamics may propel leader-public relations. To avoid acknowledging shame—both his own and that of the group—the leader may disguise it with anger and aggression.

This chapter outlined the connection between Hitler and the mass of Germans. Both Hitler and his public were in a state of chronic emotional arousal, a chain reaction of shame and anger that gave rise to humiliated fury. The shame component took the bypassed form, which resulted in a cycle generating rage and destructive aggression, since the shame component was not acknowledged.

In seeking to solve the problem of Hitler's appeal to the German masses, this chapter has focused considerable attention on Hitler's personality. We want to emphasize, however, that our analysis does not imply that destructive conflict is solely the product of a unique individual like Hitler or Stalin, a reduction of historical causation to psychological individualism. On the contrary, Hitler seems to have been only a part in a larger system of causation, one that transcended particular individuals, no matter how depraved. To underscore this point, we briefly review the larger historical setting in which Hitler rose to power.

The foundation for Hitler's rise to power was laid by the treatment Germany received at the end of World War I at the hands of the victors. The terms that the Treaty of Versailles imposed on Germany were not conciliatory but punitive. The punishment took not only a material form but a symbolic one. The blame placed on Germany as the sole originator of the war was a case in point; the exclusion of Germany from the League of Nations as unworthy was another. These two actions served to formally label and stigmatize Germany, isolating it from the world community. If, as Simmel suggested, conflict has its roots in separation, material and symbolic exclusion may generate violence.

Although controversy remains about the details, there is now evidence that France played a considerable role in the instigation of the World War I. Goodspeed (1977), among others, has traced a chain of secret diplomacy before the assassination of Archduke Ferdinand at Sarajevo—the event that triggered the war—that implicates France and Russia. According to Goodspeed, the French president, Poincaré, seems to have told the Russian czar to encourage the Serbian terrorists to an act of violence. He backed up this incitement with the assurance that France would support the Russians "whatever the consequence"—that is, that France would go to war if Germany sought to punish Russia for instigating the assassination.

Goodspeed, like other historians, has argued that France had the most to lose by delaying a war that all the Great Powers thought inevitable. The Poincaré government was particularly concerned about the Germanization of Alsace-Lorraine, the part of France that had been ceded to Germany as a result of the loss of the Franco-German war in 1871. France wished to reclaim the lost provinces before its youth were converted to the German language and culture. In 1913, after forty-two years of German hegemony, time was running out.

To most of the French, the loss of Alsace-Lorraine represented a stain on the national honor—that is to say, it was felt to be shaming. Goodspeed's assessment is widely held among historians: "The French, humiliated and vengeful, could not reconcile themselves to the loss of past glories and were continually reminded of their shame by the "living wound" of the two lost provinces. (1977: 6).

This judgment brings us back to the core of our argument. For much of the period 1871–1914, *revanche* (revenge) was a watchword in French politics, helping to bring about World War I. French aggression and vindictiveness toward Germany, which prevailed over Wilson's advocacy of a conciliatory peace, was an emotional response to their feeling of humiliation in their earlier defeat by Germany. World War II was a result of the Treaty of Versailles, as World War I was a result of the treaty that ended the Franco-German War in 1871. France and Germany were entangled in an interminable conflict driven by unacknowledged shame on both sides.

To the extent that our argument is true, the German aggression that led to World War II was a product not of Hitler's unique personality but of the alienation among nations in the civilization of that time, and the chain reactions of unacknowledged shame and rage that that alienation produced and reflected. The lack of attunement among nations is exemplified by the gross miscalculations of all the contenders in World War I concerning the cost and duration of the war. Both sides were convinced that they would win quickly and easily in less than three months, with little loss of life. The Allies thought they would win because they had more armaments and many more troops; the Central Powers, because they had better armaments and vastly better planning and organization. Each side demonstrated an utter lack of understanding and misunderstanding of the other.

The lack of attunement both among and within nations can be exemplified by the role that England played in the maneuvering that lead to World War I. The leaders of England were apparently uncertain as to whether they would fight in a war between France and Germany until the very moment that mobilization began on the Continent. Although the English and French general staff had been cooperating in planning a war against Germany, this cooperation was kept a secret not only from Germany and the world at large but from the English themselves; not even the English cabinet was informed. Uncertainty as to whether England would fight seems to have been one factor in the German willingness to fight. Had English determination been clear, the German government might have been less aggressive in its demands after Sarajevo.

The European nations in the period 1870–1945 bear a strong resemblance to the dysfunctional families so clearly described by theorists of family systems (like Bowen 1978). Conflicts in such families are interminable because of alienation between and within family members. Each is deceptive toward the other not only out of malice, but more significant, out of self-deception: each family member has disguised or denied his or her own core feelings and needs (see chapter 7). The family of nations in our civilization was, and apparently still is, dysfunctional; lack of attunement between and within nations sets the stage for the humiliation-rage-aggression cycle described in this essay.

The analysis in this chapter points to the need for further studies of charisma within a micro-macro, part/whole framework like the one used here. Many studies of World War I are still focused on the single issue of war guilt; a continuing debate on this issue is being waged, particularly in Germany, United States, and France. Although understanding the role of the various powers in the instigation of the war is a legitimate problem, it is also a very narrow one and ignores many important issues.

A viewpoint that relates parts to wholes in the national-international *system* particularly suggests two large and crucial issues. First, to what extent are studies of war guilt a part of the problem rather than a part of the solution? The blaming that goes on in dysfunctional families is virtually always one of the causes of interminable conflict: each side blames, often in a way that insults (humiliates and angers) the other, continuing the cycle of unconscious vengeance. To what extent are studies of war guilt a continuation, by scholarly means, of the war itself?

This first question raises a broader second question. To what extent do studies which focus on only one party to a conflict (on an individual like Hitler or Poincaré, or on a nation like Germany or France) divert attention from the whole system of which the individual or nation is only a part? It is possible that a narrow focus on individuals or single nations is an unconscious means of protecting the reigning status quo, the overall relationships within and between nations, little changed in the last hundred years.

The present world system is based on carefully regulated relationships within nations and virtual anarchy among them. The framework developed in this chapter, based both on family systems and on Durkheim's theory, suggests that both sets of bonds may be inadequate. The relationships *within* nations seem to be engulfing, involving too much mutual dependency; those *among* nations seem to be too little (isolation). If Simmel and other theorists were right, this system inevitably leads to perpetual conflict. Until we see the system clearly and as a whole, we may continue to repeat the mistakes of the past.

The next chapter reviews our discussion and introduces a final case analysis—that of Albert Speer, Hitler's architect and minister of armaments. His case illustrates what we consider to be a supremely important issue—conscience and conscience-building.

Part III
Conclusion

9

Shame and Conscience: Society as a Moral Order

This chapter reviews and summarizes our findings and applies them to several theoretical and practical issues. In particular, we develop a model of *conscience* that shows how this mysterious entity is related to cognition and emotion and its place in individual and collective experience. In the last section, we compare our explanation of violence with several others, noting the strengths and weaknesses of each.

The case-study chapters of this book illustrate the crucial role of social separation in conflict. Although it has often been implied, Simmel's formulation may be the most succinct: conflict is produced by separation more than the other way around. But Simmel and theorists with similar ideas are abstract and diffuse. In analyzing concrete conflicts, we have attempted to flesh out this general idea, showing precisely how it fits actual behavior.

Our treatment of conflict rests on three postulates that differ radically from prevailing opinion. The first two are theoretical, the third is methodological. The first postulates that conflict is a social phenomenon and has social roots. To understand destructive conflict, it is necessary to understand the social structure and process not only of the conflict itself but also of the civilization in which it occurs. The type and amount of conflict are determined by the nature of the dispute, the character of the disputants, and the civilization of which they are part.

Our second postulate is that alienation and emotion play a central role in destructive conflict. Two emotions in particular are singled out—pride and shame, which may be the keys to cooperation and conflict. Pride and shame provide highly visible cues to the state of a relationship, which otherwise would be largely invisible. They signal the "temperature" of a relationship; moreover, these signals are constantly available, an instant "read-out," as suggested in chapters 2 and 3. Pride signals and generates solidarity and attunement among persons and groups; shame signals alienation and lack of attunement. When shame is acknowledged, it can be used to repair damaged bonds.

When shame is not acknowledged, it can lead to rage, which in turn can lead to disrespectful communication tactics. These tactics, in turn, can lead to further shame and rage, ad infinitum. Denying and disguising shame walls off persons from each other, since explicit shame cues signal the state of the bond, allowing repair when the bond is damaged. For this reason, open acknowledgment and expression of shame draws people together (Lynd, 1958). Unacknowledged shame is the critical element that turns disagreement into interminable conflict.

We are assuming that in the absence of unacknowledged shame, in the absence of what Goffman called "character contests" (1967), a compromise can always be found that is most rewarding or perhaps least damaging to both parties. In functional families and societies, attitudes toward a particular conflict are oriented toward the good of the whole system and toward the long run. In athletic contests, as we have noted, the intelligent coach seeks to win games but knows better than to humiliate the other team. The coach sees matters in terms of the whole picture and knows that sooner or later, retribution will follow humiliation. In the violence of conflict at the family and international levels, this knowledge is often lost upon the participants. In his policy toward the Gallic and Germanic tribes, Julius Caesar either treated the defeated tribe magnanimously or killed them all, fearing their revenge. Following the end of World War II, the Allies were magnanimous toward the defeated Germans and Japanese, but this was a historical accident; they feared a Communist takeover, so they helped the defeated enemy rebuild its shattered societies. Even if unintentional, this move may have helped to break the cycle of violence described in chapter 8.

Our third postulate suggests a method of investigating the exact nature of destructive conflict: the use of verbatim texts. When these texts are dialogue, they allow an analysis of *sequences* of events. Sequential analysis leads to an explanation of causes of conflict. Given the plethora of details in texts, the application of a general theory to actual instances provides a sense of agency, of how the acts of the participants lead to conflict and resolution. In human affairs, we understand causation to the extent that we can form a full picture of the identity of the persons involved and the context in which their actions occur.

Applying these three postulates to concrete instances has led to a framework for understanding the roots of destructive conflict. The framework concerns three elements: the state of the social bond, emotion sequences, and communication tactics. To understand dysfunctional communication tactics, which are observables, we make inferences on the basis of words and gestures about the microworld of social relationships and emotions, which are not directly observable. These three elements occur in a reciprocating feedback system, as shown by the figures in chapters 2 and 4.

The state of a social bond and emotion are reciprocally related. Shame and alienation are aspects of the same reality: shame is the emotional aspect of alienation, just as alienation is the relational aspect shame. Being connected to others of their kind is instinctive in humans and all other social creatures.

In each of the case studies, examination of the dialogue provides a clear picture of the first element in the system, *dysfunctional communication*. Werther and Rhoda both can be seen as caught in a fixed and repetitive system, in which the patterns of communication reciprocate. Each party to a dispute blames the other and denies their own responsibility. The more each blames and denies, the more the other does the same thing. This kind of mirror conflict is characteristic of dysfunctional social systems.

The pattern of blaming and denial found in Werther's and Rhoda's cases can be seen even more clearly in the case of Hitler and the Germans. Hitler's denial and blaming were preemptive to the point of being delusional. He and his fellow Germans were completely idealized, and enemies were constructed who were completely vilified. It should be clear that this analysis does not blame Germany alone but sees it as caught up in a rigidly dysfunctional international system. Labeling theory is appropriate to all three cases: Werther, Rhoda, and Germany *act out* and make visible the hidden pathology of the larger social systems of which they are a part. To isolate one person or country as the sole cause is to ignore and deny the larger system of which they are only a part.

The investigation of the minute details of actual texts provides a direct way to assess social structure, the mixture of solidarity and alienation among individuals and groups. Both social structure and emotion ride on gestures and implicature. Verbal statements are usually conventional. Even Hitler's verbal statements are usually clothed in morality. But by closely examining the manner of an utterance in its particular context, it is possible to make inferences about unstated suppositions and feelings and the quality of the social bond among the participants.

In everyday life, we all learn to make inferences about unseen elements that vitally affect us; the thoughts, feeling, intentions, and character of other people, and the strength and reliability of their bonds with us. This process of inference has been described in theoretical terms, such as in the social psychology of G. H. Mead, but it has never been made explicit, moment to moment, in actual dialogue. The cases in this book were used for this purpose.

Alienation and the Social Bond

As Durkheim's study of suicide and Bowen's later work on family systems both suggest, alienation between persons and between groups takes two distinct forms—*engulfment* and *isolation*. In engulfing relationships, the individual gives up parts of the self in order to be accepted by others. Behavior is dominated by loyalty and conformity at the expense of individuality. In isolation, one cuts oneself off from others. Behavior is dominated by individuality at the expense of loyalty. Both types of alienation give rise to pathologies of self and of communication.

The two types of alienation usually occur in tandem within social systems. One manifestation of engulfment, *infatuation*, can be seen in Werther's relationship with Lotte and in Rhoda's relationship with her mother. Infatuation is often mistaken for love. But in love, one knows and understands the other and accepts what one knows, which leads to attunement—a secure bond. Infatuation, by contrast, is not about the real other but about a fantasy of the other. Werther is "in love" with a fantasy, the idealized version of Lotte to which he refers as his "angel." Infatuation is just as disruptive of relationships as hatred and isolation, but its action is more hidden and insidious.

As long as engulfment is disguised as infatuation, conflict is avoided and denied, giving rise to a format in which conflict is hidden, the *"silent impasse."* Werther wants Lotte for himself, but he never discusses the matter with her openly. The form of alienation between them dramatically shifts when she forbids him to see her. He cuts off from her; the relationship switches to the isolation mode of alienation. It is in this mode that violence occurs: suicide in this instance, and duels, vendettas, and wars in other instances. Isolation is characteristic of the mode of open dispute, or *"quarrels."*

Large social systems are often characterized by isolation *among* groups and engulfment *within* them. This seems to be the case in the situation that led to the rise of Hitler, as outlined in chapter 8. Idealization and blind obedience to leaders who are willing to go to war suggest an extreme form of engulfment within nations and isolation among them. This particular combination of the two forms of alienation may be the lethal mixture causing the acceleration of violence in our civilization.

What can be done? If our thesis is correct—that interminable conflict is caused not by alienation and shame but by *unacknowledged* alienation and shame—then acknowledging our condition would be a first step toward de-escalating violence. This formulation is so general and abstract, however, that it gives little concrete guidance. To illustrate some of the implications of this conjecture, we will focus on one particular idea—the meaning of conscience. To begin our analysis, we first draw upon an important study by Braithwaite, in which conscience and conscience-building play an important role.

Crime, Shame, and Reintegration[1]

Braithwaite's (1989) study proposes and tests a new theory of crime causation, in what may be the most effective application of sociological theory to statistical data since Durkheim's *Suicide*. Braithwaite's approach enlarges and expands Durkheim; it corrects what now seems to be an error in the *Division of Labor*, confirming the idea of *Moral Education*. The new study supports and elaborates the relationship we have proposed between alienation and shame, on the one hand, and destructive behavior, on the other.

Braithwaite begins with the basic facts that a theory of crime needs to explain, facts that represent the strongest and most consistent findings in criminology. He first establishes that there are thirteen such facts. To give the flavor, we condense five of them into a single sentence: Crime is committed disproportionately by (1) young, (2) unmarried (3) males at the (4) bottom of the social structure, (5) living in large cities. Another example is the finding that crime rates have been increasing in most countries since the end of World War II , except for Japan and possibly Switzerland.

How well do existing theories explain these basic facts? Braithwaite argues that not even the most effective theory, learning theory (Wilson and Herrnstein, 1985), explains all of them, and that most of the theories (control, opportunity, subculture, and labeling) explain only a few at best. Some are not sufficiently explicit to apply (differential association and labeling), while others too limited in their parameters.

Braithwaite proposes that a theory of shaming explains all thirteen of his propositions. Shaming theory postulates that crime is punished in two quite different ways—either by reintegrative shaming or by stigmatization. The former results in low crime rates, while the latter results in high crime rates.

Reintegrative shaming is defined as responses to crime in which "expressions of community disapproval . . . are followed by gestures of reacceptance into the community of law-abiding citizens" (55). Public shaming is a painful punishment, but it is temporary, followed very rapidly by reacceptance. The initial image of this type of shaming comes from the "family model," a loving family in which punishment

---

[1]This section is based, in part, on Scheff's review of Braithwaite's book, (1991).

for wrongdoing is administered within the framework of reconcilable, mutually supportive interests among family members.

Stigmatizing shame, by contrast, involves assigning a master status to a person based on their lawbreaking; the person, rather than the behavior, is rejected. This type of shaming is likely to create a class of outcasts. In shaming theory, shaming is analyzed in a two-phase sequence: shaming followed by rituals of reacceptance is reintegrative, while shaming that is not followed by such rituals is stigmatizing.

Although the idea of reintegrative shaming originates in the family setting, Braithwaite argues that it also applies to larger groups. He suggests that in Japan and other countries that have relatively low crime rates, there is strong emphasis on reintegrative shaming. Many examples are provided. A typical example, taken from a study of nations with low crimes rates, is Bulgaria: "Particularly effective appears to be the public reprimand, expressed before a social group to which the offender belongs" (85).

Japan offers the strongest possible contrast to shaming practices in the West. Although Japan is a modern, highly industrialized society, reintegrative shaming seems to be the norm there. Public shaming, repentance, and acknowledgment of responsibility are found up and down the social ladder. The following excerpt from a news story is one of many that Braithwaite offers:

> The president of Japan Air Lines faced the relatives of victims of the world's worst single-plane disaster and bowed low and long. . . . In a voice that sometimes quavered, [he] asked for forgiveness and accepted responsibility . . . The service marked the culmination of a two-month exercise in accountability. . . . The airline mobilized its staff, from the president on down, to offer gestures of apology and regret. . . . dispatching executives to every victim's funeral. . . . JAL set up a scholarship fund to pay for the education of children whose parents died in the crash. . . . [The president] has pledged to resign as a gesture of responsibility. (quoted 164)

As Braithwaite suggests, the contrast between this behavior and the actions of American corporations in comparable situations is dramatic: the Americans deny responsibility, make no immediate or direct contact with the relatives, cover up the lack of public involvement through hidden legal maneuvers, and so on.

Braithwaite argues that punishment for wrongdoing in Japan and other countries with low crime rates involves public shaming and acknowledgment of responsibility and reacceptance of wrongdoers afterward. As required by the theory of reintegrative shaming, these same countries also use much less stigmatization (that is, prison sentences) than the United States and the other countries that have high crime rates.

Braithwaite shows that his theory of shaming explains all thirteen of the statistical findings better than any other theory. In a tour de force, he goes on to show that by adding only a single dimension—type of shaming—he is able to synthesize all the previous theories into a new, more powerful one. He does this graphically (Braithwaite, 1989, 99), which shows that with the addition of the shaming variable, all five of the existing theories become subcomponents in a single flow chart. Braithwaite has brought the parable of the elephant and the blind men to vivid life and breath.

This study has an important implication for current sociological theory. Although Braithwaite does not refer to it directly, it is one of the underlying themes of his discussion. In the *Division of Labor*, Durkheim classified responses to deviance as punitive and retributive, and he seems to have implied that the latter is more effective and just than the former. In his later work, *Moral Education*, Durkheim changed his mind: "Since punishment is reproaching, the best punishment is that which puts the blame—which is the essence of punishment—in the most expressive but least expensive way possible" (quoted in Braithwaite 1989:178). At first glance, this passage seems to reiterate Durkheim's earlier advocacy of retributive justice. But it actually acknowledges the need for punishment, even as it advocates using the least amount but the most expressive punishment possible. The need for an expressive punishment—that is, one that is highly visible—is part of Durkheim's emphasis in this later book on society as a moral order, built on individual and collective conscience. We agree with Braithwaite's interpretation that this passage—indeed, that all of *Moral Education*—adumbrates the theory of reintegrative shaming.

Braithwaite raises this issue because modern social science has a tendency to ignore the moral-emotional aspects of order, as evidenced by models such as "rational choice" and "economic rationalism." Braithwaite gives examples of these models, criticizing each as inadequate. In these schemes, lawbreakers are not to be punished but only fined to the extent of the damage they cause, as suggested in early Durkheim. Braithwaite points out that social control works to the extent that it has a moral, denunciatory component. Without such a component, various forms of evasion and outright cheating are rife (141–45) and the community demoralized. His study is a contribution to sociological theory as well as to criminology and the sociology of emotions.

Like any groundbreaking work, this study is not the last word. We see two directions for further developing an already powerful framework. In the first place, his approach focuses almost entirely on shaming *behavior*, rather than on the emotion of shame; on the stimulus, rather than on the response. This focus is both a strength and a limitation. It is a strength, first, because it compensates for an omission in an adjacent field of study. Overwhelmingly, sociology of emotion studies of shame—including our own—have focused on the emotion itself rather than on shaming behavior. For this reason, Braithwaite's study is not only a contribution to criminology but serves to complement and correct work in the sociology of emotion.

The second strength of Braithwaite's focus on shaming behavior is subtle. Shame is expressed and discussed openly in traditional societies, but it is disguised and denied in modern civilization, both by individuals and by institutions. Our institution of language itself conspires to hide shame. For example, we may say "It was an awkward moment for me," rather than "I was embarrassed." In a complex maneuver, this statement *denies* inner shame, *disguises* it with a code word ("awkward"), and *projects* it onto an external object, the "moment." In our civilization, shame is shameful; except under extreme circumstances, we deny its existence.

The denial of shame may be the cause of many problems in our society; not the least of these problems is that it has served to impede the scientific study of shame. Most emotion researchers do not recognize shame as a major emotion for adults in modern societies. Braithwaite's focus on shaming behavior can help breach the denial of shame in social and behavioral science. Although the emotion of shame is disguised in our society to the point of virtual invisibility, shaming behavior is more visible. We are much more aware of behaviors that ridicule, reject, or degrade than we are of their effects—that is, the states of shame caused by these behaviors—because the shame is usually hidden. To the extent that Braithwaite's theory of shaming behavior is accepted, it may demand the study of shame itself.

This demand can be turned back on the Braithwaite study. It is partly anecdotal but largely correlational; he shows the statistical association between types of shaming behavior and rates of crime. To demonstrate a causal connection between shaming behavior and crime, the sequence of steps that lead from the societal reaction (shaming) to emotion (shame) to behavior (crime) needs to be stated explicitly. Sequential data will be needed to demonstrate causation.

To show the linkage between shaming behavior and the causation and control of crime, it will be necessary to develop a working concept of shame to uncover what is almost always disguised. A working concept would draw attention to the sources, correlates, and consequences of shame, acknowledging what goes largely unacknowledged.

It is important to note that Braithwaite's method partitions shame into a dichotomous variable: shaming is either reintegrative or stigmatizing. Because he applies this method only to dichotomized statistical data, he is able to show an association between the form of shame and the rates of crime in nations. But as we look at sequences of events in single cases, we have found that shaming may be a mixture of normal and unacknowledged shame. Accurate rating of shaming sequences mav require further development of the concepts of shame and shaming. The same is true of future studies that investigate conscience and conscience-building.

Needless to say, the demand for causal analysis is an exacting one; it goes beyond most current studies. But Braithwaite's study is so stimulating that it could start a new trend—we think it deserves both replication and extension.

A second possible limitation of Braithwaite's approach may be an imbalance between his treatment of the positive and negative aspects of social control. His framework underemphasizes the positive side—the way acceptance and reacceptance lead to pride, solidarity, and law-abiding behavior. That is, a complete theory of social control would give equal emphasis to pride and shame, solidarity and alienation.

Braithwaite gives much more attention to acceptance and solidarity than earlier shame theorists did; by implication, they are components of his theory. Goffman (1967), Elias (1978, 1982), and Lewis (1971) had little to say about the role of pride and solidarity in their analysis of social action. The exception is Cooley (1922), who gave pride and shame central and equal status in his approach (Scheff 1988). Although Braithwaite's framework shows a better balance than those of Goffman, Elias, and Lewis, it is mainly focused on the way stigmatization leads to alienation.

The underlying problem is that Braithwaite's theory of crime implies a larger theory of society-building and disruption. This theory is not spelled out, however. Braithwaite's analysis of crime and crime control implies a general theory of the building, maintenance, and disruption of social order without actually explicating it.

We will briefly outline the bare contours of the larger framework that Braithwaite's study implies and show how it applies to the problem of international order. The building of a stable, just, and effective social order requires a certain type of social control. In such a society, efficacious, ethical, and law-abiding behavior is quickly and copiously encouraged by highly visible rewards. In this way, crime and other forms of socially deleterious behavior may be avoided before they occur. Such practices build and maintain moral conscience and social cohesion when employed by parents and teachers in the socialization of children, and by economic, legal, and other institutions in reactions to behavior of individuals and groups.

It goes without saying that in human groups, as is particularly the case today in the actions of nations, there will always be behavior that is not ethical, efficacious, or law-abiding. In a just social order, deviant behavior, according the general framework outlined here, would be

punished by highly visible public shaming, followed by public reacceptance, as suggested in Braithwaite's theory of reintegrative shaming.

This general formulation equalizes the positive and negative sides of
social control and socialization. The new theory suggests that there are
three roads to the deterioration of social order and anarchy. To the
extent that a society (or a civilization) fails to offer rapid and highly
public rewards for desirable acts, offer highly visible shaming of undesirable acts, and offer rapid and complete reacceptance after shaming, it
invites division, conflict, and anarchy. One implication of this theory is
that a stable, just, and efficacious social order requires not only a
government to enforce laws but a social infrastructure to generate the
three kinds of sanctions listed above.

The implications of this framework can be seen when it is applied
to the problem of the relations among the nations of the world. Today's absence of a just and efficacious order among nations, a situation
bordering on international anarchy, is due not only to the lack of an
international government but also to the lack of an infrastructure that
builds and maintains community by material and moral means. There
are few organizations that reward desirable acts of individuals and
nations, and even fewer that shame undesirable acts. The Nobel Prize
award and the international Olympics are examples on the positive
side. On the negative side, only one organization is well known—
Amnesty International, whose publication of the names of persons un-
justly punished performs the function of public shaming of the
governments responsible.

The rewards and punishments offered by these organizations presumably generate pride and shame within nations and so fulfill in part
some of the functions that the theory suggests are required for a social
order. But the areas they cover are narrow and, in the case of the
positive awards, infrequent. Conscience and community-building within
and among nations would require rewards and punishments in all areas
of human activity, and the sanctions would need to be virtually continuous. It seems unlikely that the United Nations in its present form
would ever fulfill such a role, since it is organized in such a way that
the member governments seek to preserve the present national and
international orders rather than develop new ones.

The theory implied in Braithwaite's study suggests the need for new
organizations whose work would complement that of the Nobel Prize
committee and Amnesty International. Achievements in broad areas not
now recognized could be brought to world attention. Perhaps awards
like the Nobel could be organized across the board, recognizing not
only accomplishments in science but in all other fields—the arts, language, economics, education, ecology, gender relations, race relations,
class relations, and the like. Contests similar to the Olympics might

also be developed in some of these areas, such as mathematics, teaching, and graphic design. Unlike existing organizations and programs, the new ones would also censure, but as Braithwaite's theory suggests, they would be quick to remove censure when socially undesirable behavior stops. If these practices received only a small part of the attention the world gives to the Olympics, they might build conscience and community among nations, and the beginnings of worldwide culture.

Conscience, Cognition, and Emotion: The Case of Albert Speer

The idea of conscience plays a prominent role in Braithwaite's theory, but it is left undefined. Braithwaite's treatment is no different in this respect from anyone else's. Even in psychoanalytic theory, in which guilt plays a large role, conscience is not defined; it is treated as a primitive term. Early in the development of his theory, Freud sidestepped the problem of definition by using another term, *superego*. Like the word for which it is a substitute, it goes undefined.

In this section, we propose a cognitive-emotional model of conscience. Conscience implies both a cognitive process (part/whole analysis) and an emotional process (experiencing normal pride and shame). To illustrate the new model, we apply it to a single text, the memoirs of Albert Speer (1970).

Our analysis of Speer's writings proposes that his adult conscience went through two stages. During the time of his service to Hitler, he was without conscience; neither the cognitive nor the emotional component was functioning. During the course of his twenty-year imprisonment, he was able to develop, to some extent, the cognitive side of conscience. The 1970 text suggests, however, that the emotional side was still not functioning: that is, even after twenty years of self-analysis, his conscience was still impaired. Before discussing Speer, we will first formulate an abstract model of conscience, beginning with the cognitive component.

As indicated in chapter 2, adaptive problem-solving requires *part/whole analysis*, understanding the relations between parts and wholes. This is largely a cognitive capacity, although emotions also play a part. Moral behavior requires understanding the consequences of one's actions, of the part they may play in the whole system of relationships in which one is involved. Although part/whole analysis can be undertaken intentionally, slowly, and systematically, as in careful linguistic work on the structure and meaning of dialogue, and in the ethnography of cultural artifacts, it is usually involuntary, rapid, and covert.

The expression and understanding of utterances in natural language is the most frequent occurrence of this kind of processing. By noting context and drawing upon one's "mastery of practice," to use Wittgenstein's phrase, incomplete and ambiguous statements can be correctly understood in the context in which they occur. This is not to say that such statements are always understood correctly, but that we have the cognitive equipment to do so. The faculty that is referred to as "intuition" seems to be grounded in the type of instinctive part/whole analysis we have in mind.

At first glance, part/whole analysis may seem to be completely devoid of emotion, to be entirely the lightning-fast following of branching networks of associations between words and ideas. But it may be that emotions also play a part in understanding the relationship between parts and wholes. Languages and cultures are so complex that one would often be completely stymied if emotions were neglected. Champion problem-solvers such as chess masters or great physicists almost always mention their emotions when they try to explain how they think.

Freud's idea that emotions have a signal function, although developed in a difference context, may be relevant. Pascal said that the heart has its reasons, which reason may not know. Emotional reactions often follow a logic that is independent of reasoning, yet they call our attention to features of a problem that we might otherwise overlook. Since these reactions are virtually instantaneous, it is plausible that they could be an important element in rapid part/whole analysis. Moral behavior requires rapid responses to complex situations. It seems likely that any impairment of the ability to experience emotions would interfere with the functioning of conscience.

The emotions most central to conscience are probably pride and shame. Lewis refers to these emotions as the "moral emotions" (1976). Normal shaming is conscience-building. The caretaker's approval of the child results in pride; disapproval, in shame. In terms of their overt behavior, conscience in children is built up by experiencing pride in moral and conforming conduct, and by experiencing shame in immoral or nonconforming conduct.

But there is another aspect of conscience-building that is in some ways prior to and more important than rewards and punishments for behavior. The basis for conscience seems to be laid down less by approval of what the child *does* than by approval of what the child *is*. A secure bond involves what Stern (1985) calls *attunement*: the parent and child are intellectually and emotionally connected in a way such that each ratifies and legitimates the other's existence. Goffman implied a similar idea in his description of "state of talk" (1967; see chapter 2 of this book).

The desire for ratification of oneself, of both being and doing, seems an instinctive feature of all humans and other social creatures. Hearne (1986) makes this case even for domesticated animals such as dogs, horses, and cats in their relations with humans. Without a secure bond, the person (or animal) becomes "crazy," incapable of moral behavior.

Braithwaite's discussion of reintegrative shaming elaborates on this basic idea in a most crucial way. To develop conscience in a child, the child's undesirable behavior must be shamed in a way that is painful but transitory, and be quickly followed by reacceptance. This type of shaming discriminates between being and doing; the behavior was unacceptable but the person is acceptable. Reintegrative shaming builds both conscience and self-esteem.

Not all types of shaming are conscience-building. Intense humiliation that is not immediately followed by loving reacceptance has the opposite effect, as suggested by Hitler's childhood. What Braithwaite calls stigmatization destroys conscience and lowers self-esteem.

The theory of social control through pride and shame augments Braithwaite's theory, since it emphasizes the building of pride through acceptance and the building of what is usually called self-esteem, just as much as it emphasizes reintegrative shaming. Since desirable actions by children occur much more frequently than undesirable ones, it is important for caretakers to emphasize the necessity of accepting behavior more than shaming behavior.

Conscience-building is as necessary for adults as it is for children, since moral codes must be confirmed if they are to be preserved. Braithwaite's approach to public punishment for crime applies equally well to an entire moral code: use it or lose it.

As we have seen, in modern societies adults deny and disguise their pride and shame. Because shame is especially repressed, the nature of conscience in adults is more complex than it is in children. Lewis's formulation concerning the two routes of repression of shame is crucial for a concept of conscience.

In what Lewis called the overt, undifferentiated form of shame, conscience takes the direction of neurotic self-blame—the excessively responsible, paralyzingly cautious individual. Even though such persons are ineffectual, one might argue that at least some conscience remains intact. The link between their behavior and their painful feelings has not been destroyed.

To avoid paralysis of self-blame by cutting off from others and from one's own feelings is the route of bypassed shame. Isolation and resentment is a path that people often take to avoid engulfment in families and in organizations. Schools are usually engulfing for young children, for the most part, since they have nowhere else to turn. There are exceptions, of course, such as Montessori schools, which do not depend on indoctrination or obedience. But practices in most schools exact loyalty, obedience, and conformity.

Most students go one of two ways: either they become intellectually rigid, or they become isolated and bitter about the very possibility of education. Others alternate between overt and bypassed shame, being alternately intellectually paralyzed and embittered.

To the extent that one takes the route of bypassed shame, the link between immorality and suffering is broken. No matter how immoral one's behavior, little or no painful feeling occurs as a consequence. Feelings of shame serve as a moral gyroscope. Even though they are instinctive, they can be repressed by an upbringing that is physically and/or emotionally abusive, just as the instinctive traits of thoroughbred animals can be destroyed by abusive training.

The idea that there can be a universal, specieswide morality among humans is not in fashion, even though Cooley had suggested it with his concept of "primary group values" (1922). In current social and behavioral science, cultural relativism is taken for granted. Recent findings, however, suggest that there is considerable evidence for human universals that cross-cut culture and historical era (Brown 1990). Both Lewis (1976) and Brown cite evidence for a universal morality like that described by Cooley.

As we have seen in chapter 1, the poet Ovid suggested that there was a connection between shamelessness and wickedness. In his last stage of the world, "every species of crime burst forth, . . . and shame, truth and honor took flight." In bypassed shame, one becomes shameless. This progression, already suggested for the case of Hitler in chapter 5, takes a more complex form in the impairment of conscience in the case of Albert Speer.

Conscience and Albert Speer

Speer entered Hitler's service in 1933, when Hitler came to power, as one of his personal architects. Apparently, Speer was prepared to dedicate himself to Hitler's commands for two reasons. First, before he ever met Hitler, he had been convinced by one of his speeches that he was the man to lead a new Germany. Speer explains in his memoirs, however, that when he joined the Nazi party at that time, his attachment was not ideological but personal. Second, service to Hitler would secure his career, a career that up until his meeting with Hitler had been languishing.

Speer is somewhat contradictory about how important self-advancement was to him in this stage of his life. On the one hand, he states: "Had Hitler announced, before 1933, that a few years later he would burn down Jewish synagogues, involve Germany in a war, and kill Jews and his political opponents, he would at one blow have lost me and probably most of the adherents he won after 1930" (23). But only a few pages later, he states the contrary:

> During the twenty years I spent in Spandau prison I often asked myself what I would have done if I had recognized Hitler's real face and the true nature of the regime he had established. The answer was banal and dispiriting: My position as Hitler's architect had soon become indispensable to me. Not yet thirty, I saw before me the most exciting prospects an architect can dream of. (38)

This latter statement seems to have much more energy in it than the first one. It is immediately followed by a declaration that seems to go to the heart of the matter, the way in which the Speer of this period allowed himself to be totally absorbed into his role as architect

> Moreover, the intensity with which I went at my work repressed problems that I ought to have faced. A good many perplexities were smothered by the daily rush. In writing these memoirs I became increasingly astonished to realize that before 1944 I so rarely—in fact almost never—found the time to reflect about myself or my own activities. (38–39)

Speer's statement illustrates the impairment of the cognitive side of his conscience during this period of his life. He ignored the consequences of his actions by avoiding analysis of the part he played in the whole of Hitler's program. He adopted the narrow point of view of the specialist, allowing himself to see only the technical part of his role as problematic.

This theme is repeated in many variations in his memoirs. He explains that his closed view was not unique to him but existed throughout Germany:

> Everyone kept to his own group—of architects, physicians, jurists, technicians, soldiers, or farmers. The professional organizations to which everyone had to belong were called chambers (Physicians' Chamber, Art Chamber), and this term aptly described the way people were immured in isolated, closed-off areas of life. (39)

He repeatedly shows how he himself adopted this narrow view: "I felt myself to be Hitler's architect. Political events did not concern me" (134). "The habit of thinking within the limits of my own field provided me, both as an architect and as Armaments Minister, with many opportunities for evasion" (135). This kind of narrowness is of course not limited to Nazi Germany but continues to characterize life in all modern societies.

In the division of labor, specialization of *function* may be quite unavoidable in advanced industrial societies. Such specialization does not require specialized *thinking*, however. Scheff (1990) has argued that the health of societies requires that the mind of the average member remain at least partially free of encumbrance by role or creed.

This idea has been very well expressed by the polymath Elias Canetti in his *Comedy of Human Vanity* (1983). Although not explicit, his work implies a critique of modern society, in which not only members' roles become specialized, but also their souls: each has "a completely personal view of things" and moves in a linear mode, in a fixed direction. They "can no longer cast about promiscuously, but can only feel and think along certain channels." The idea of promiscuity is crucial here, since linearity, system, and narrowness are so valued in modern civilization that deviations may be seen as flaws. Actually, the opposite is true; specialization has its uses, but a general problem-solving ability—that is, basic human intelligence—requires exactly the playful, spontaneous kind of thinking and feeling that Canetti implies.

Speer's memoirs contain many variations on the theme of how he ignored the larger picture in favor of the smaller one. In the course of writing the memoirs, however, he apparently developed the cognitive side of his conscience. He acknowledges his responsibility, by explaining how he deceived himself about mass murder: "But in the final analysis I myself determined the degree of my isolation, the extremity of my evasions, and the extent of my ignorance" (135). Despite such indications of an awakening conscience, however, not even the cognitive component is fully developed. Often Speer seems to be denying responsibility by blaming his environment.

> The ordinary party member was being taught that grand policy was much too complex for him to judge it. Consequently, one felt one was being represented, never called upon to take personal responsibility. The whole structure of the system was aimed at preventing conflicts of conscience from even arising. (39)

Blaming his environment for his actions is a recurring theme. In this passage, Speer explains how casually he joined the Nazi party:

> As an intellectual I might have been expected to collect documentation with the same thoroughness and to examine various points of view with the same lack of bias that I had learned to apply to my preliminary architectural studies. This failure was rooted in my inadequate political schooling. As a result, I remained uncritical, unable to deal with the arguments of my student friends, who were predominantly indoctrinated with the National Socialist ideology.(22)

In this passage, Speer blames not himself for joining but his "inadequate political schooling."

Most notable in Speer's memoirs is the absence of strong feelings. There is virtually no indication that he himself ever felt grief, fear, anger, love, or hatred. Often, when feelings are mentioned, they are linked not to what we would consider his moral lapses but to lesser matters. For example, this passage concerns his reaction to the first open attack by the Nazis on the German Jews:

> On November 10, driving to the office, I passed by the still smoldering ruins of the Berlin synagogues. That was the fourth momentous event that established the character of this last of the prewar years. Today, this memory is one of the most doleful of my life, chiefly because what really disturbed me at the time was the aspect of disorder that I saw on Fasanenstrasse: charred beams, collapsed façades, burned-out walls—anticipations of a scene that during the war would dominate much of Europe. Most of all I was troubled by the political revival of the "gutter." The smashed panes of shop windows offended my sense of middle-class order. (133)

The feeling behind the scene of destruction, its "dolefulness," is linked not to its moral meaning—the attack on the Jews—but to the violation of middle-class order.

Speer is so cut off from his emotions that when he does describe feelings, the result is often unintentionally comedic. One instance occurred during a moment of triumph for Hitler. In June 1940, he and his entourage were awaiting news that France had signed the armistice acknowledging its defeat:

> Shortly before the agreed time Hitler gave orders to turn out the light and open the windows. Silently, we sat in the darkness, swept by the sense of experiencing a historic moment so close to the author of it. Outside, a bugler blew the traditional signal for the end of fighting. A thunderstorm must have been brewing in the distance, for as in a bad novel occasional flashes of heat lightning shimmered through the dark room. Someone, overcome by emotion, blew his nose. (204)

Speer, cut off from his feelings, fails to see the humor in his own writing.

The only genuine shows of emotion in the memoirs belong to others, such as the many descriptions of Hitler's anger and rage. Perhaps the most intense moment of emotion described in the memoirs is that of Speer's father, an architect himself and a conservative who never accepted the Nazi regime. Speer and his father chanced to meet Hitler during intermission at a theater during the war.

> When my father—still erect and self-controlled in spite of his seventy-
> five years—was introduced to Hitler, he was overcome by a violent
> quivering such as I had never seen him exhibit before, nor ever did
> again. He turned pale, did not respond to Hitler's lavish praise of his
> son, and then took his leave in silence. Later, my father never men-
> tioned this meeting, and I too avoided asking him about the fit of
> nerves that the sight of Hitler had produced in him. (160)

It may be significant for our understanding of Speer's emotional
style that father and son never discussed this incident. We learn that
Speer's mother joined the Nazi party at about the same time as Speer
did, but neither even told the other, let alone the father. Perhaps Speer
was raised in a way that he was isolated from his parents, as they seem
to have been isolated from each other.

Just as the overt style of shame is associated with engulfing families, the bypassed style is associated with isolating families. The absence
of emotion in Speer's memoirs and the hints of isolation in his family
of origin are suggestive of the impairment of the emotional side of his
conscience—that is, of bypassed shame. The story of Hitler's upbringing suggests that physical violence from his father and emotional betrayal by his mother could have led to his shamelessness. Speer's
memoirs hint that the emotional foundations for his conscience were
destroyed not by his parent's violence and betrayal but by their silence.

The idea that the cognitive but not the emotional side of Speer's
conscience was functioning during the writing of his memoirs might
explain some of its features. We have already referred to his tendency
to blame his environment for his lapses rather than himself. Another
feature, more difficult to describe, is a failure of tone, a failure that
runs throughout the entire document. One instance occurs in his account of joining, at the age of twenty-six, the Nazi party:

> By entering Hitler's party I had already, in essence, assumed a respon-
> sibility that led directly to the brutalities of forced labor, to the de-
> struction of war, and to the deaths of those millions of so-called
> undesireable stock—to the crushing of justice and the elevation of
> every evil. In 1931 I had no idea that fourteen years later I would
> have to answer for a host of crimes to which I subscribed beforehand
> by entering the party. I did not yet know that I would atone with
> twenty-one years of my life for frivolity and thoughtlessness and
> breaking with tradition. (24)

In a way that is difficult to convey, the characterizations in the last
sentence—"frivolity," "thoughtlessness," and "breaking with tradition"—somehow do not match the scope and vileness of the crimes

recited in the earlier part of the paragraph. The passage faintly suggests self-justification and a lack of feeling of responsibility, tone, and scale.

In his very perceptive review of Speer's memoirs, Steiner (1971) notes what seems to be a similar quality. He refers to Speer's attempts to make apologetic statements as "motions, presumably sincere in their own hollow, cerebral way, of retrospective horror." Our ordinary, everyday moral framework is dreadfully inadequate to the nightmare of Nazidom, so Steiner resorts to Milton's verse descriptions of the relationship between Satan and his lieutenant, the architect Mulciber, to convey the dimensions of Nazism's immorality. Steiner notes that Speer was an early convert to the Nazi party, a part of a mass movement, one of many fallen angels:

> Nor did they not percieve the evil plight
> In which they were, or the fierce pains not feel;
> Yet to their General's voice they soon obeyed.

Steiner's conclusion also evokes Milton's poetry:

> a certain degree of appalled humanity does emerge from these doctored remembrances, and a quite formidable resilience. Even before his close confinement at Nuremberg, Speer had found himself "not lost in loss itself." His sheer survival and the strength of this book are no mean feat. But the last word is Milton's. Whatever his architectural talents and personal graces, Mulciber was of the damned:
> > nor did he scape
> > By all his engines, but was head-long sent
> > With his industrious crew to build in hell.

Our explanation of the failure of tone of the memoirs goes back to the model of conscience proposed here. Moral decisions are so complex that they require that the machinery of understanding be intact, not only the cognitive side but also the emotional side. We assume that Speer's shame was bypassed during his period of service to Hitler as well as afterward; he made some progress toward developing a conscience, but his progress was incomplete. Moral discourse requires uncovering repressed shame, which seems to have eluded Speer.

It appears that during the period of Speer's service to Hitler, although he was brilliant in other ways, he had no conscience; he was a moral imbecile. During the course of his imprisonment, he developed the cognitive side of his conscience, but insufficiently. The memoirs reveal a man of high intelligence who was still morally crippled.

Failure of both components of conscience—part/whole understanding and acknowledging shame—can be inferred from Hughes's analysis (1983) of the emotional style of Germany's leaders just prior to World War I. One aspect of the leaders' style, which she calls "the fatalistic temper," is to deny one's own responsibility for decisions by projecting it onto the environment. The best-known example of this maneuver is the reaction of the German leadership to the beginnings of military mobilization that ultimately led to the war: "Events take control." Rather than acknowledging the part that they themselves contributed to these events and their ability to intervene in them, they projected responsibility onto the outside events. This theme is a strand of Hughes's precise interpretation of the character of the two male protagonists in the novel *Effie Brest* (215–18). This strand is a route to the breakdown of part/whole understanding, realizing the consequences of the part that one is playing in a quarrel.

The other strand in her analysis of the fatalistic temper is closely related to the bypassing of shame. One of the male characters in the novel receives what he considers to be a insult. Even though he realizes the futility of dueling, he feels compelled to it because he has revealed his experience of insult to the other character, his closest male friend. Although Hughes does not make the shame component explicit, it is clear from her description that the man who feels insulted is compelled to remove the stain to his honor because he fears seeing himself in a negative way in the eyes of the other man, the generic shame context. He acts out the code of honor to bypass shame. The model of conscience proposed here seems to apply as well to the characters in the Hughes study as it does to Speer.

Our analysis of Speer's moral state does not bode well for modern civilization. Speer's family life and his education may be quite representative of that of the average middle-class person in our society today. There is still an emphasis on the suppression of emotion and specialization in raising children, especially those who are being prepared for careers. As recently as twenty years ago, the bypassing of shame and the narrowing of outlook was usually reserved for males, but increasingly it is practiced on both genders today. We may be producing an entire generation of Speers, waiting for their Hitler.

In this chapter we have reviewed our ideas and findings and outlined a model of conscience. We propose that conscience has two components. The first is the capacity for part/whole analysis, so that one can understand the consequences of one's actions, how they fit into the larger world of which one is a part. The second is the ability to experience normal pride and shame, so that the morality of one's actions is immediately and involuntarily signaled: one feels pride for moral actions, and shame for immoral ones. To the extent that the bypassing of shame becomes a part of one's character, it would seem to interfere with the functioning of conscience.

In summary, we will discuss possible objections to our approach to violence by comparing it with explanations alternative to ours. We argue that the *social system* creates destructive violence to the extent that *alienation and shame go unacknowledged*. We propose that this formulation is a general theory, applicable to all cultures and historical eras.

One objection to our approach might be that it is overly ambitious, that the quest for a general theory of any kind of human behavior is futile. The best kind of social science, according to this view, is content with middle-range theory and small-scale studies devoted to highly specific types or instances of behavior.

One supposition that seems to underlie this objection is the notion that theory is virtually useless in empirical research; rather, one should rely only on inductive methods—pure observation undistorted by conceptual presuppositions. Although it is true that induction sometimes results in scientific discoveries, too much emphasis on induction more often impedes research. A strong theory helps direct the researcher through the labyrinth of choices that must be made. Without a theoretical framework, research may be distorted by unexaminined presuppositions, particularly those that are currently in fashion.

A second supposition that may underlie such an objection is the notion that the specialization of viewpoint and method has unlimited benefits and no penalties. Although it is true that specialization allows closer focus and more precise techniques, specialized research may be extremely limited by its inability to relate parts and wholes. Typically, empirical research focuses on the small, while theory focuses on the big picture. What may be needed in human studies is a constant shuttling back and forth between large and small. If the subjects of research are vastly more complex than the approach that is being used to study them, as Scheff has argued elsewhere (1990), then the results may be simplistic or irrelevant.

An example is the field of quantitative studies of self-esteem. Scheff, Retzinger, and Ryan (1989) describe an immense body of such studies—some eleven-thousand—that use two-hundred different scales. Although the methodology is sophisticated and reliable within each study, the field seems to be deadlocked. Findings are virtually nil; no progress is being made. We think that the absence of a theory is an important cause of the impasse. Without a theory, scales have been constructed that are either overly simple or based on contradictory suppositions, or both.

A second objection, which could be raised even by those who accept the usefulness of theory in guiding research, is that our theory is too imperial; instead of proposing a general causal theory of violence, we should admit multiple causes and be content with specifying the conditions under which unacknowledged alienation and shame lead to violence. This is a more difficult objection to meet, since it suggests a clash of philosophies of science. Our response is that the first obligation of a theory is clarity. If propositions are stated clearly enough, they are easily refuted by negative instances. The more ambiguous the statement, the more difficult it is to refute.

The cases we have presented all seem to support our theory. Using cases such as we have gathered, we do not claim to have *proved* anything, we only claim that we have shown the theory to be *plausible*, even when the data are examined in microscopic detail. Our purpose has not been to verify a theory but to construct one. Verification is yet to come, since our concepts and hypotheses are incompletely operationalized. We point to new directions for research on violence, directions that emphasize alienation and emotion as concepts, and discourse and part/whole analysis as methods. If pushed to the wall, we would admit that we do not advocate that all research on violence should go in this direction, since it is new, counterintuitive, and unproven. We welcome research that would refute the theory, or at least specify the conditions under which it is true, since we ourselves have not yet gotten that far.

What about explanations alternative to ours? We will begin at the level of individual emotions other than shame, since we focus so intensely on this one emotion. The most common lay explanation for violence is in terms of anger or *rage*. People often explain destructive behavior in this way: "I'm sorry that I flew off the handle" or "He knocked her down in a fit of rage." Even among professionals, this kind of explanation was current as late as the 1960's. For example, Rhoda's therapist (chapter 6) seems to have assumed that hidden anger is the cause of the interminable conflict in Rhoda's family.

It may be significant that in more recent lore among psychotherapists, this explanation is no longer accepted at face value. Most psychotherapists would maintain that rage typically is not the cause of violence, but rather a mask for what they might call "the underlying *hurt*." To use the language that Masters and Johnson use in their advice for marriage counselors, anger is not a primary emotion but a secondary one; it disguises other, less respectable emotions.

If one equates "hurt" with unacknowledged shame, as we do in chapters 4 and 5, then our cases support this position. In all the cases in this book, unacknowledged shame precedes anger. This sequence is particularly well documented in chapters 4 and 5. If one looks closely enough at moment-by-moment sequences and include both verbal and nonverbal indicators, we predict that unacknowledged shame will always precede destructive anger. In theory, of course, destructive anger could exist in pure form, untriggered by shame; pure frustration could give rise to such a state. We have been watching for such instances in videotaped and audiotaped sequences for the past ten years without success.

In psychoanalytic theory, violence is usually explained not in terms of shame but in terms of anxiety, fear, or guilt. (As indicated in earlier chapters, Adler and Horney are admirable exceptions.) Gaylin's (1984) book on violence is an example. His analysis is unusual in that he seems to recognize unacknowledged shame as a causal agent in violence. But he does not use this phrase; rather, he uses what we have called code words, such as "damage to self-esteem" and "insults to pride." This part of his analysis is parallel to and supportive of ours.

Gaylin makes fear an equally important cause of violence, however. We agree that fear (as well as other emotions, such as grief) may be found in sequences that lead to destructive violence. Our rejoinder, however, is that in the absence of shame, these other emotions, like anger, would be harmlessly discharged without resort to violence. Unless shame is present to serve as inhibitor, our cultures and our bodies provide us with harmless ways of discharging anger, fear, and grief. For example, ceremonies of mourning may provide opportunities for discharging grief through its appropropriate biological process, weeping (Scheff 1979). When shame is present and unacknowledged, however, the social and biological discharge processes are blocked, leading to limitless spirals.

It is significant that in cases where we have a mechanical recording of sequences, there are no threats of physical violence; nor is there evidence of fear or anxiety. Yet all these cases involve interminable conflicts, which suggests that protracted quarrels and silent impasses need not be based on fear. In other words, fear seems not to be a *necessary* condition for implacable conflict. We cannot rule out the possiblity, however, that it may be a *sufficient* condition, since none of our tapes contain threats of physical danger. A close study of such tapes would be one direction that we suggest for future research.

Guilt is another primary explanatory concept used in psychoanalysis. We could have coded manifestations of this affect using the Gottschalk-Gleser scales, but we did not do so. Manifestations of guilt are obvious in two of our cases. Our analysis of Lotte's reaction to Werther's death suggests that she had feeling of guilt about his suicide that might lead to her own. And in Rhoda's conversation with her mother, the role of guilt in inhibiting Rhoda's anger toward her mother seems quite prominent. Why have we failed to use guilt as an explanation of violence?

The answer is that in our theory, guilt is not in itself a primary emotion, like shame and anger, but is a code word for a shame-anger sequence. Psychoanalytic theory treats guilt as an elemental cause, but we treat it as a compound affect: guilt is a shame-anger sequence in which anger is directed at the self, just as resentment and hatred are shame-anger sequences in which anger is directed out. Our analysis of shame/anger dynamics in violence subsumes and undercuts psychoanalytic explanations in terms of guilt.

Finally, we turn to psychological and sociological explanations alternative to ours. We will use Tomkin's theory of emotion and Kemper's theory of power and status to make a general point about all other explanations alternative to ours. Most theories do not attempt to include the major causal links in the chain of events that lead to violence but are content to focus on a *single* link. Even if such theories are true, they may fall far short of providing a useful explanation.

Tomkins's theory of emotions provides a case in point. Besides Lewis, Tomkins has given more attention to shame than any other writer; the second volume of his major work (1963) deals almost entirely with shame (he calls it humiliation)—about four hundred pages of discussion. But most of his discussion is descriptive, not conceptual; it describes situations that give rise to shame and the effects of shame, with little attempt to use general concepts and hypotheses.

Tomkins's actual theory of emotion deals only with changes in levels of bodily arousal, making it a pure theory of individual behavior. His formulation for the causation of shame concerns its relation to changes in two other emotions: "The innate activator of shame is the incomplete reduction of interest or joy" (1963: II, 123).

This formulation seems a bit circular. If shame is caused by the incomplete reduction of interest or joy, what causes this change, and what activates the interest or joy? Tomkins provides no conceptual answer to either question. His explanation of the causes of interest and joy is neurological; the former is caused by "optimal rates of increase of stimulation density" (341), and the second by "steep reduction of the intensity of stimulation or neural firing" (371).

Tomkins's explanation avoids dealing with the context in which emotion arises. Interest, joy, and shame are explained in physical rather than social or psychological terms. Even if his propositions were completely and exactly true, they would still comprehend only a few simple links in what appears to be a long and complex causal chain. Unlike his descriptions of shame contexts and effects, which are rich and evocative, his theory is virtually useless for explaining violence.

Although Kemper's theory of power and status includes the social and psychological components that Tomkin's omits, it shares with Tomkin's the fault of focusing only on a few links in a long causal chain. Because of Kemper's social-psychological emphasis, his analysis at times runs parallel to ours. Like our analysis and unlike most others, he calls attention to pride as an important emotion in its own right. (He refers to it as "justified pride" [280].) Similarly, he recognizes that shame may be an ingredient of punishment (255–57). He calls attention to shame-anger sequences, acknowledging the possiblity that shame rather than anger may be the causal agent in aggression (261–262)—a crucial element in our own analysis.

In the main, however, Kemper avoids using emotions as causal agents. He treats pride virtually in passing, mentioning it as only one on a list of emotions. He similarly reduces the importance of shame as a component of punishment by making it only one of a group of emotions—depression, guilt, and anxiety. His treatment of shame-anger sequences is brief, even incidental to his main argument about the effect of social-structural variables on emotions.

Tomkins and Kemper both attempt to construct formal theories, but their formulations are so abtract and specialized that they do not specify full causal chains. Both resort to reified explanations. Tomkins reifies physical processes, stimulation, and neural firing, while Kemper reifies social structure. Each theorist has decided a priori that one element in the individual-environment relationship is causal, instead of granting them parity, as we do.

We have harped on the weakness of Tomkins's and Kemper's theories because we think the same failings are found in virtually all theories of violence. These theories do not provide both conceptual and operational definitions of their major concepts, specify the causal linkage between the concepts, or attempt to give a comprehensive explanation of all causal components. What is missing is a sense of the relationships between parts and wholes; not just some parts and some whole, but *all* parts and *all* wholes.

Most theories of violence are highly specialized. They reify biological, psychological, or social commponents, but they do not integrate them. Since our theory attempts to integrate, specify, and use explicit concepts and measures, it looks like no other. Of course only further research can determine its most crucial characteristic—whether it is true—or whether it is at least useful in moving toward understanding the causation of violence.

Our theory proposes that interminable conflict arises from hidden alienation (inadequate social bonds) and the emotion that generates and signals alienation, unacknowledged shame. Although almost invisible to the untutored eye, the state of the bond and shame are signaled by dysfunctional communication tactics, on the one hand, and the code words and gestures that indicate separation and shame, on the other. Given these tools, it is possible to detect not only the more obvious form of alienation—isolation—but also the more hidden form, engulfment, the development of intense attachment that masks an inadequate bond. Both types of alienation impair conscience at the individual and the group levels, and the ability to resolve conflict.

The structure of our civilization seems to be increasingly characterized by the failure of conscience, by relationships that are either engulfing or isolating. The rise of cults and sectarian and single-interest groups is seen everywhere. These groups reproduce within nations the bimodal alienation that has proven so lethal among nations: engulfment within groups, and isolation between them. Unless some renewal occurs, the spiral of increasing alienation and violence will probably continue apace. A first step toward renewal might be to pay attention to the nature of our social bonds and to the moral emotions of pride and shame that underlie them. If we can understand and acknowledge our true condition, perhaps we can change it.

References

Adamson, L., H. Als, E. Tronick, and T.B. Brazelton. 1977. "The Development of Social Reciprocity between a Sighted Infant and Her Blind Parents." *Journal of the American Academy of Child Psychiatry* 16: 194–207.

Adler, A. (1907–37). *The Individual Psychology of Alfred Adler*. New York: Basic Books, 1956.

Amrine, F., F. Zucker, and H. Wheeler. 1987. *Goethe and the Sciences: A Reappraisal*. Boston: D. Riedel.

Benedict, Ruth. 1946. *The Chrysanthemum and the Sword*. New York: Houghton Mifflin.

Bok, S. 1979. *Lying: Moral Choice in Public and Private Life*. New York: Vintage.

Bowen, M., and M. Kerr. 1988. *Family Evaluation*. New York: Norton.

Bowen, M. 1978. *Family Therapy in Clinical Practice*. New York: J. Aronson.

Bowlby, J. 1969. *Attachment and Loss. Vol. 1. Attachment*. New York: Basic Books.

Bowlby, J. 1973. *Attachment and Loss. Vol. 2. Separation: Anxiety and Anger*. New York: Basic Books.

Bowlby, J. 1980. *Attachment and Loss. Vol. 3. Loss*. New York: Basic Books.

Braithwaite, J. 1989. *Crime, Shame, and Reintegration*. Cambridge: Cambridge University Press.

Brazelton, T. B. 1982. "Joint Regulation of Neonate-Parent Interaction." In E. Tronick, ed. *Social Exchange in Infancy*. Baltimore: University Park Press.

Brazelton, T. B., B. V. Koslowski, and M. Main. 1974. "The Origins of Reciprocity: Early Mother-Infant Interaction." In M. Lewis and L. Rosenblum, eds., *The Effect of the Infant on Its Caregiver*. New York: Wiley and Sons.

Bromberg, N., and V. Small. 1983. *Hitler's Psychopathology*. New York: International Universities Press.

Brown, D. 1990. *Human Universals*. New York: McGraw Hill.

Brown, P., and S. Levinson. 1987. *Politeness: Some Universals in Language Usage*. Cambridge: Cambridge University Press.

Bruner, J. 1983. *Child's Talk*. New York: Norton.

Bullock, A. 1964. *Hitler: A Study in Tyranny*. New York: Harper and Row.

Burlingham, D., and A. Freud. 1942. *Young Children in Wartime London*. London: Allen and Unwin.

Canetti, Elias. 1983. *The Comedy of Human Vanity*. New York: Performing Arts Journal Publications.

Coleman, J. 1957. *Community Conflict*. New York: The Free Press.

Cooley, C. H. 1902. *Human Nature and the Social Order*. New York: Scribner's.

Coser, L. A. 1956. *The Functions of Social Conflict*. Glencoe, Ill.: Free Press.

Dahrendorf, R. 1967. *Society and Democracy in Germany*. Garden City: Doubleday.

Darwin, C. 1872. *The Expression of Emotion in Man and Animals*. London: John Murray.

Davidson, E. 1977. *The Making of Adolf Hitler*. New York: Macmillan.

de Waal, F. 1982. *Chimpanzee Politics*. New York: Harper.

Dodds, E. R. 1951. *The Greeks and the Irrational*. Berkeley: University of California Press.

Durkheim, E. 1893. *The Division of Labor in Society*. New York: Free Press (1933).

———. 1905. *Suicide*. New York: Free Press (1951).

———. 1961. *Moral Education*. New York: Free Press.

Edelman, R. 1989. "Self-Reported Experiences of Embarrassment in Five European Cultures." *Journal of Cross-cultural Psychology* 20: 357–371.

———. 1987. *The Psychology of Embarrassment*. New York: Wiley.

Eibl-Eibesfeldt, I. 1975. *Ethology*, 2d ed. New York: Holt, Rinehart and Winston.

Ekman, P., and W. Friesen. 1978. *Facial Action Coding System*. Palo Alto: Consulting Psychologists Press.

Ekman, P., and W. Friesen. 1975. *Unmasking the Face*. New Jersey: Prentice-Hall.

Ekman, P., P., Ellsworth, and W. Friesen. 1972. *Emotion in the Human Face*. New York: Pergamon.

Ekman, P., and W. Friesen. 1982. "Felt, False and Miserable Smiles." *Journal of Non-verbal Behavior* 6: 238–52.

Elias, Norbert. 1978, 1982, 1983. *The Civilizing Process, Vols. 1–3*. New York: Vintage.

Feshbach, S. 1971. "The Dynamics and Morality of Violence and Aggression." *American Psychologist* 26: 281–92.

Freud, S. 1905. "Jokes and Their Relation to the Unconscious." *Standard Edition*, Vol. 7. London: Hogarth.

Freud, S. 1911. "Psychoanalytic Notes on an Autobiographical Case of Paranoia." *Standard Edition*, Vol. 12. London: Hogarth.

Friedman, H., M. Harris, and J. Hall. 1984. "Nonverbal Expression of Emotion: Healthy Charisma or Coronary-prone Behavior?" in C. Van Dyke, L. Temoshok, and L. Zegans, eds. *Emotions in Health and Illness*. New York: Grune and Stratton.

Gaylin, W. 1984. *The Rage Within*. New York: Simon and Schuster.

Geen, R. G. 1968. "Effects of Frustration, Attack, and Prior Training in Aggressiveness upon Aggressive Behavior." *Journal of Personality and Social Psychology* 9: 316–21.

Giddens, A. 1984. *The Constitution of Society*. Berkeley: University of California Press.

Gilbert, G. 1950. *The Psychology of Dictatorship*. New York: Ronald.

Goethe, J. W. 1774. "Die Leiden des Jungen Werthers." In *Gedenkausgabe der Werke, Briefe und Gespräche*. Zurich: Emil Beuteler, 1949.

———. 1785. *Philosophical Studies*, quoted in B. Fairley, *A Study of Goethe*. Oxford: Clarendon Press, 1947.

———. 1787. *The Sufferings of Young Werther*. New York: Norton, 2d ed., 1963.

———. 1789. *Torquato Tasso*. London: Doves Press. 1913.

Goffman, E. 1959. *The Presentation of Self in Everyday Life*. New York: Anchor.

———. 1963. *Stigma*. Englewood Cliffs, N.J.: Prentice-Hall.

———. 1967. *Interaction Ritual*. New York: Anchor.

Goldberger, A., et al. 1990. "Fractals." *Scientific American*, 262 (February) 43–49.

Goodspeed, D. 1977. *The German Wars: 1914–1945*. Boston:. Houghton Mifflin.

Gordon, S. 1981. "The Sociology of Sentiments and Emotion." In M. Rosenberg and R. H. Turner, *Social Psycholoqy*. New York: Basic Books.

Gottman, J. 1979. *Marital Interaction*. New York: Academic Press.

Gottschalk, L., C. Wingert, and G. Gleser. 1969. *Manual of Instruction for Using the Gottschalk-Gleser Content Analysis Scales*. Berkeley: University of California Press.

Harlow, H. 1962. "The Heterosexual Affectional System in Monkeys." *American Psychologist* 17:1–9.

Hearne, Vicki. 1986. *Adam's Task*. New York: Vintage.

Heller, E. 1984. "Man Ashamed." In *In the Age of Prose*. Cambridge: Cambridge University Press.

Heritage, J. 1985. Recent developments in conversational analysis. *Sociolinguistics*, 15, 1–19.

Hitler, A. 1927. *Mein Kampf*. Boston: Houghton Mifflin. 1943.

Hochschild, A. 1983. *The Managed Heart*. Berkeley: University of California Press.

Horney, K. 1950. *Neurosis and Human Growth*. New York: Norton.

Horowitz, M. 1981. "Self-Righteous Rage." *Archives of General Psychiatry*, 38 (November) 1233–38.

Hughes, Judith. 1983. *Emotion and High Politics*. Berkeley: University of California Press.

Hume, D. 1739. *Treatise on Human Nature. Vol. 2: The Passions*. Oxford: Clarendon Press, 1968.

Izard, C. 1971. *The Face of Emotion*. New York: Appleton-Century-Crofts.

Izard, C. 1977. *Human Emotions*. New York: Plenum.

James, W. 1910. *Psychology*. New York: Henry Holt.

Johnston, J., and L. Campbell. 1988. *Impasses in Divorce*. New York: The Free Press.

Katz, J. 1988. *The Seductions of Crime*. New York: Basic Books.

Kemper, T. 1978. *A Social Interactional Theory of Emotions*. New York: Wiley.

Kohut, H. 1979. *The Search for Self, vol. 2.* New York: International Universities Press.

Kohut, H. E. 1971. "Thoughts on Narcissism and Narcissistic Rage." *The Search for the Self.* New York: International University Press.

Komarovsky, M. 1967. *Blue Collar Marriage.* New York: Vintage.

Kreisberg, L. 1973. *The Sociology of Social Conflicts.* New Jersey: Prentice-Hall.

Kubizek, A. 1955. *The Young Hitler I Knew.* Boston: Houghton Mifflin.

Labov, W., and D. Fanshel. 1977. *Therapeutic Discourse.* New York: Academic Press.

Lansky, M. 1984. "Violence, Shame, and the Family." *International Journal of Family Psychiatry* 5: 21–40.

———. 1989. Murder of A Spouse: A Family Systems Viewpoint. *International Journal of Family Psychiatry* 10, 159–178.

———. 1987. "Shame and Domestic Violence." In D. Nathanson, ed. *The Many Faces of Shame.* New York: Guilford.

Lasswell, H. 1960. *Psychopathology and Politics.* New York: Viking.

Lerner, D., ed. 1963. *Parts and Wholes.* Cambridge: Harvard University Press.

Levenson, R. 1986. Personal communication.

Levine, D. 1985. *The Flight from Ambiguity.* Chicago: University of Chicago Press.

Lewis, H. 1971. *Shame and Guilt in Neurosis.* New York: International Universities Press.

———. 1976. *Psychic War in Men and Women.* New York: New York University Press.

———. 1979. "Using Content Analysis to Explore Shame and Guilt in Neurosis." In Gottschalk, ed. *The Content Analysis of Verbal Behavior.* New York: Halstead Press.

———. 1981. *Freud and Modern Psychology. vol. 1. The Emotional Basis of Mental Illness.* New York: Plenum.

———. 1983. *Freud and Modern Psychology. vol. 2. The Emotional Basis of Human Behavior.* New York: Plenum.

Lynd, H. 1958. *On Shame and the Search for Identity.* New York: Harcourt.

MacDougall, W. 1908. *An Introduction to Social Psychology.* London: Methuen.

Mannheim, Karl. 1936. *Ideology and Utopia.* London: Routledge.

Marx, K. 1964. *Economic and Philosophic Manuscripts of 1844.* New York: International Publishers. 1844.

Massie, H. 1982. "Affective Development and the Organization of Mother-Infant Behavior from the Perspective of Psychopathology." In E. Tronick, ed. *Social Interchange in Infancy.* Baltimore: University Park Press.

McDougall, W. 1908. *An Introduction to Social Psychology.* New York: University Paperbacks.

Mead, G. H. 1934. *Mind, Self, and Society.* Chicago: University of Chicago Press.

Miller, A. 1983. *For Your Own Good.* New York: Farrar, Straus, Giroux.

Mills, C. Wright. 1959. *The Socialogical Imagination.* 1959: London: Oxford University Press.

Mitchell, O. 1983. *Hitler Over Germany*. Philadelphia: Institute for the Study of Human Issues.

Neuhauser, P. 1988. *Tribal Warfare in Organizations*. Cambridge, Mass.: Ballinger.

Nietzsche, F. 1887. *On the Geneology of Morals*. New York: Vintage, 1967.

Ovid. A. D. 7. *Metamorphoses*. Bloomington, Ind.: University of Indiana Press, 1955.

Parsons, T. 1951. *The Social System*. Glencoe, Ill.: The Free Press.

Payne, R. 1951. *Hubris: A Study of Pride*. New York: Harper.

Piers, G., and M. Singer. 1953. *Shame and Guilt: A Psychoanalytic and Cultural Study*. New York: Norton.

Pittenger, R., C. Hockett, and J. Danehy. 1960. *The First Five Minutes*. Ithaca, N.Y.: Paul Martineau.

Porter, R. 1990. *A Social History of Madness*. New York: E. P. Dutton.

Reiss, H. 1971. *Goethe's Novels*. Coral Gables: University of Miami Press.

Retzinger, S. M. 1985. "The Resentment Process: Videotape Studies." *Psychoanalytic Psychology* 2: 129–53.

———. 1987. "Resentment and Laughter: Video Studies of the Shame-Rage Spiral." In H. B. Lewis, ed. *The Role of Shame in Symptom Formation*. Hillsdale, N.J.: Erlbaum.

———. 1988. *Marital Conflict: the Role of Emotion*. Unpublished Ph.D. diss., University of California, Santa Barbara.

———. 1989. "A Theory of Mental Illness: Integrating Social and Emotional Aspects." *Psychiatry* 52: 325–35.

———. 1991. *Violent Emotions: Shame and Rage in Marital Quarrels*. Newbury Park: Sage Publications.

Ritzer, George. 1991. "Agency-Structure and Micro-Macro Linkages: Crossroads in Contemporary Theorizing." In Bjorn Wittrock, ed. *Social Theory and Human Agency*. London: Sage.

Rose, W. 1931. *Men, Myths, and Movements in German Literature*. London: Allen and Unwin.

Sacks, H. 1966. *The Search for Help: No One to Turn To*. Unpublished Ph.D. diss. University of California, Berkeley.

Sartre, J. 1948. *The Emotions: Outline of a Theory*. New York: Philosophical Library.

Sartre, J. 1956. *Being and Nothingness*. New York: Philosophical Library.

Satir, Virginia. 1972. *Peoplemaking*. Palo Alto: Science and Behavior.

Scheff, Thomas J. 1966. *Being Mentally Ill*. Chicago: Aldine.

———. 1968. "Negotiation of Reality: Notes on Power in the Assessment of Responsibility." *Social Problems* 76: 3–17.

———. 1984. "The Taboo on Coarse Emotions." *Review of Personality and Social Psychology* 5: 146–69.

———. 1985. "The Primacy of Affect." *American Psychologist* 40: 849–50.

———. 1987. "The Shame-Rage Spiral: Case Study of an Interminable Quarrel." In H. Lewis, ed. *The Role of Shame in Symptom Formation*. Hillsdale, N.J.: Erlbaum.

———. 1987a. "Creativity and Repetition: A Theory of the Coarse Emotions." In *Psychoanalytic Sociology*, J. Rabow, G. Platt, and M. Goldman, eds. New York: Krieger.

———. 1988. "Shame and Conformity: The Deference-Emotion System." *American Sociological Review* 53: 395–406.

———. 1989. "Cognitive and Emotional Components in Anorexia: Re-analysis of a Classic Case." *Psychiatry* 52: 148–60.

———. 1990. *Microsociology: Discourse, Emotion and Social Structure*. Chicago: University of Chicago Press.

———. 1990. Review of John Braithwaite, "Crime, Shame and Reintegration." *American Journal of Sociology*, 96, 741–46.

Scheff, T., and U. Mahlendorf. 1987. "Emotion and False Consciousness: Analysis of an Incident from *Werther*." *Theory, Culture and Society* 5: 57–88.

Scheff, T., S. Retzinger, and M. Ryan. 1989. "Crime, Violence and Self-Esteem: Review and Proposals." In A. Mecca, N. Smelser, and J. Vasconcellos, eds. *The Social Importance of Self-Esteem*. Berkeley: University of California Press.

Scheler, M. 1912. *Ressentiment*. Glencoe, N.Y.: Free Press, 1961.

Schneider, C. 1977. *Shame, Exposure, and Privacy*. Boston: Beacon Press.

Simmel, G. 1955. *Conflict and the Web of Group-Affiliations*. Glencoe, N.Y.: The Free Press.

———. 1960. *The Sociology of Georg Simmel*. Chicago: University of Chicago Press.

Speer, A. 1970. *Inside the Third Reich*. New York: Macmillan.

Spitz, R. A. 1946. "Anaclitic Depression: An Inquiry into the Genesis of Psychiatric Conditions in Early Childhood II." *Psychoanalytic Study of the Child* 2:313–32.

———. 1965. *The first years of life*. New York: International Universities Press.

Stearns, C., and P. Stearns. 1986. *Anger: The Struggle for Control in America's History*. Chicago: University of Chicago Press.

Steiner, G. 1971. Review of *Inside the Third Reich*. *New Yorker* 47 (July 24): 70–73.

———. 1975. *After Babel*. London: Oxford University Press.

Stern, D. 1985. *The Interpersonal World of the Child*. New York: Basic.

———. 1971. "A Micro-analysis of Mother-Infant Interaction." *Journal of American Academy of Child Psychiatry* 10: 501–17.

Stierlin, H. 1976. *Adolf Hitler: A Family Perspective*. New York: Psychohistory Press.

Taylor, G. 1985. *Pride, Shame, and Guilt*. Oxford: Clarendon.

Thoits, P. 1989. "The Sociology of Emotions." In W. R. Scott and J. Blake, eds. *Annual Review of Sociology*, vol. 15, Palo Alto, Calif.: Annual Reviews.

———. 1985. "Self-Labeling Processes in Mental Illness: The Role of Emotional Deviance." *American Journal of Sociology* 91: 221–48.

Toland, J. 1976. *Adolf Hitler*. Garden City, N.Y.: Doubleday.

Tomkins, S. 1963. *Affect/Imagery/Conciousness*, vol. 1. New York: Springer

———. 1963. *Affect/Imagery/Consciousness, vol. 2: The Negative Affects*. New York: Springer.

Tronick, E. 1980. "The Primacy of Social Skills." *Exceptional Infant* 4.

———. 1982. *Social Interchange in Infancy*. Baltimore: University Park.

Tucker, R. C. 1978. *The Marx-Engels Reader*. New York: W.W. Norton.

Turner, Frederick. 1990. *Reconstructive Postmodernism*. Albany: State University of New York Press.

Vico, G. 1744. *The New Science*. Ithaca, N.Y.: Cornell University Press, 1968.

von Raumer, W. 1857. *The Education of Girls* (Cited in Elias 1978).

Waite, R. 1977. *The Psychopathic God: Adolf Hitler*. New York: Basic Books

Watzlawick, P., J.H. Beavin, and D. Jackson. 1967. *The Pragmatics of Human Communication*. New York: Norton.

Weber, M. 1946. *From Max Weber*. New York: Oxford University Press.

————. 1947. *Theory of Social and Economic Organization*. Oxford: Oxford University Press.

Wilson, John, and Herrnstein, Richard. 1985. *Crime and Human Nature*. New York: Simon and Schuster.

Wittgenstein, L. 1953. *Philosophical Investigations*. New York, Macmillan.

Wurmser, L. 1981. *The Mask of Shame*. Baltimore: Johns Hopkins University Press.

Index

Abandonment, threat of, 65, 86, 136
Abduction process, ix–x
Adam and Eve (*Expulsion of Adam and Eve*, Masaccio painting), 4, 52
Adler, A., 12, 29, 104, 105, 158
Aggression, x, xiii, 12, 64, 128, 148–150. *See also* Violence
Alienation, 59, 60, 65, 85; bimodal, xiv–xv, 192; defined, 21, 36, 39; repression and, 8, 14; of self, 103, 114, 115; shame and, 3, 15, 36, 39, 86, 103, 115, 167, 169, 171; social bonds and, 64, 103, 170–171, 192; solidarity and, 22, 169; in *Sorrows of Young Werther*, 106, 114–118, 120; stigmatization and, 175; suicide and, 117–118, 170; unacknowledged, 36, 191; violence and, xviii–xix, 188, 192
Amnesty International, 176
Anger and rage, 19, 44, 66; denial of, 118; escalation of, 79–81; helpless/blind, 88, 89, 129, 130–132, 135, 139, 148–149, 150; of Hitler, 146, 151, 152; in marital conflicts, 87–88; protracted, 152, 156, 158; repression of, 19–20; at self, xiii, 13, 105; separation and, 64; shame and, 65, 69, 148, 152–153, 156, 168; unacknowledged, 128, 132; unacknowledged shame and, 168, 188–189; violence and, 188; visual cues for, 72

Animals, 52, 64
Anomie, 22, 142, 143
Anorexia, 128, 129, 135, 136, 139
Aristotle, 6
Attica prison riots, 150
Attunement, xi, 21, 163, 167, 178; communication and, 22, 31–36, 39, 60; cooperation and, 59–60; emotions and, 21–22, 26–31, 43–53, 60; social bonds and, 21, 24–26, 35, 38; victory and, 55, 57

Behavior: biological basis of, 64; destructive/deviant, 171, 175–176; escalation of conflict and, 86–87; hiding, 44–53, 57, 59, 87, 125; moral, 179; passive-aggressive, 88; real vs. remembered, 121; shame as determinant of, 10, 104; shaming, 27, 173–174, 179; social control and, 175–176. *See also* Violence
Bible, 4–7, 15
Blame, 144, 169
Blushing, 7
Bonding. *See* Social bonds
Bowen, M., 15–16, 170
Braithwaite, J., 124n; shaming theory and crime causation, 27, 31, 171, 172, 173, 174–175, 176–177, 179
Braun, Eva, 145
Bromberg, N., 152, 156, 158, 159
Bruner, J., 24
Buff, Charlotte, 106, 119–120
Bulgaria, 172

About the Authors

Thomas J. Scheff is a professor of sociology at the University of California, Santa Barbara. He received his Ph.D. at Berkeley and taught at the University of Wisconsin, Madison. He is the author of *Being Mentally Ill, Catharsis in Healing, Ritual, and Drama*, and many articles on social psychology, emotions, and social theory. His most recent book is *Microsociology: Emotion, Discourse, and Social Structure* (University of Chicago Press, 1990). He has served as a consultant to the Task Force on Self-Esteem for the State of California and as an associate of the Task Force for the Seriously Mentally Ill. He is the current chair of the Sociology of Emotion section of the American Sociological Association.

Suzanne M. Retzinger received her Ph.D. from the University of California, Santa Barbara, in 1988. She is currently assistant research sociologist at the Community and Organization Research Institute at UCSB, and family relations mediator for the Superior Court of Ventura County. She is presently conducting a study of protracted child-custody disputes in high-conflict families, using case history methods in combination with videotape. Dr. Retzinger is the author of *Violent Emotions: Shame and Rage in Marital Quarrels* (Sage Publications, 1991), and articles on conflict, emotions, self-esteem, mental illness, and mediation.

26 BONDLESSNESS → VIOLENCE/MENTAL ILLNESS
27 SHAME IS THE EMOTIONAL ASPECT OF
      ' OF DISCONNECTION BETWEEN PERSONS.
28 'SHAME CONTEXT' = VIEWING ONESELF FROM A NEGATIVE OTHER
      SHAME AS MOST PREVALENT EMOTION
            " MOSTLY UNACKNOWLEDGED
            "   "   DISGUISED/DENIED < OVERT
                                        < BYPASSED → LOSS OF
                                                      CONSCIENCE
            " UNACKNOWLEDGED → RECURSIVE   → VIOLENCE
                                 SELF-PERPETUATING SHAME WHICH J
30 'REINTEGRATIVE' VS. 'STIGMATIZING' SHAMING

34 FOUR BASIC DIMENSIONS OF RELATIONSHIPS
36 UNACKNOWLEDGED ALIENATION/EMOTION ALWAYS → DYSFUNCTIONAL
                                                COMMUNICATION & CONFLICT